THE PENGUIN BOOK OF AUSTRALIAN SPORTING ANECDOTES

After a 35-year book publishing career with, to name a few, ACP (Frederick Muller), Ure Smith, Angus & Robertson and the ABC, **Richard Smart** has entered the calmer though fairly impecunious waters of publishing consultancy, in Sydney. Sport rates fairly highly on his list of music, reading, walking (or, more accurately strolling), film and current affairs (particularly politics) interests. He retains a belief in writer Cyril Connolly's description of a publisher: 'As repressed sadists are supposed to become butchers or policemen so those with an irrational fear of life become publishers'. Which is probably why he is now a consultant.

THE PENGUIN BOOK OF AUSTRALIAN SPORTING ANECDOTES

Edited by
Richard Smart

PENGUIN BOOKS

Penguin Books Australia Ltd
487 Maroondah Highway, PO box 257
Ringwood, Victoria 3134, Australia
Penguin Books Ltd
Harmondworth, Middlesex, England
Viking Penguin, A Division of Penguin Books USA Inc
375 Hudson Street, New York, New York 10014, USA
Penguin Books Canada Limited
10 Alcorn Avenue, Toronto, Ontario, Canada M4V 3B2
Penguin Books (NZ) Ltd
182–190 Wairau Road, Auckland 10, New Zealand

First published by Penguin Books Australia 1996

10 9 8 7 6 5 4 3 2

Typeset by Midland Typesetters, Maryborough, Victoria.
Printed in Australia by Australian Print Group, Maryborough, Victoria

National Library of Australia
Cataloguing-in-Publication data:

The Penguin book of Australian sporting anecdotes.

ISBN 0 14 025795 0.

1. Sports - Australia - Anecdotes. 2. Athletes -
Australia - Anecdotes. I. Smart, Richard, 1943- .
II. Title: Book of
Australian sporting anecdotes.

796.0994

CONTENTS

INTRODUCTION

'A sports writer is entombed in a prolonged childhood.'

Jimmy Cannon

The oldest written reference to sport in Australia appears to have been a brief item in the *Sydney Gazette* in January 1804, referring to the fact that hot weather over the previous few weeks had encouraged more and more of the colony's cricketers to take to the field. This was a mere sixteen years after the colony was established, although the modern sports fan, far from being impressed by this, might well wonder why it took so long for sport to get a mention, given that cricket and other games had probably been played at Sydney Cove since the First Fleet dropped anchor. Sport may be an essentially unimportant subject, but most of us take it very seriously indeed. After we play it or watch it we expect to be able to read about it.

Of course, historians will tell you that people did

Introduction

not always follow sport with as much interest as they do today. Indeed, until the mid-nineteenth century sport was basically just a pastime. It wasn't a form of mass entertainment and certainly not a focus of national aspirations. An intriguing question arises: what on earth did ordinary people find to cheer about before they had sports champions and sporting teams to follow? We do know they took a sporting-type interest in the fortunes of their armies and navies. In England, the home of many of the sports we play, people followed military campaigns against the French with the same kind of passion that soccer fans today might follow their World Cup team. When the British won, as invariably they did, there were boozy celebrations around the country, even in the smallest villages. The diary of a village shopkeeper named Thomas Turner in eighteenth-century Sussex gives us an insight into this. While celebrating a certain win by the British navy over the French, Turner drank so much that he could not stay on his feet, 'the liquor,' as he describes it, 'opperating so much in the head that it rendered my leggs useless.' Master Turner would have felt quite at home 200 years later, you feel, at a post-match party in Melbourne.

One of the most remarkable features of nineteenth-century sports writing is the speed with which jargon came to be established. My own research has turned up many examples of this in cricket, and no doubt the same is true of all sports. The *Sydney Mail* in February 1879 said the visiting English batsmen had 'collared' the bowling of Fred Spofforth and Ted Evans. The same newspaper in 1885 reported that the batsman George Bonnor had 'opened his shoulders'. Five years earlier, in 1880, Bonnor was described as willing to 'have a go' – an expression appearing in quotes then, as if it were already well-established. In March 1883 the *Sydney Mail* said a certain batsman had 'broken his duck' and in August that year reported allegations that Dave Gregory had been 'chucking'. There is a press reference to a 'bump ball' in 1882 and to the appeal 'How's that?' at least as far back as 1890. An even older example of cricketing jargon may be found in the *Victorian Cricketers' Guide* of 1860. It said a player had 'opened his account', an expression which remarkably, after all these years, has survived both in business and cricket.

A great many words about Australian sport have been written since that first item appeared in the *Sydney Gazette*. What began as a trickle long ago became a flood. From one newspaper alone, the *Sydney Morning Herald*, which I happen to work for, roughly 10 000 words about sport, not counting results, are delivered to readers every day on average, and these are but a tiny fraction of the total being pumped out on the subject by the media. It may sound like mass-production, but the truth is that the quality of the words being written about sport is markedly higher today than it used to be. It was Norman Gunston, I think, who once wondered why the IQ of newspaper readers should automatically fall by thirty per cent the moment they turned from the front page to the back. He was alluding to the fact that even broadsheets tended to serve up their sport in tabloid style. Happily, this is no longer so.

Writers like to write on sport at least as much as readers like reading about it. The subject inspires them. It gives them scope to exercise their literary skills. In sport you find colour, conflict, heroism, tragedy and triumph, sometimes all at once. The challenge of capturing it all in print attracts not only full-time sports writers. Over the years there have been plenty of political writers, feature writers, even finance writers who have felt an urge from time to time to stray into the sporting arena. Peter Bowers is one example. A Canberra-based political correspondent, he began writing about tennis for light relief in the early 1980s and soon came to be recognised as the most readable of all Australian tennis writers. Evan Whitton is another example. Royal commissions, political corruption and organised crime are his stock in trade, but he also happens to be Australia's most incisive writer on rugby.

Similarly, people outside sport have liked using sporting metaphors. In 1943, after Mussolini had been beaten but Hitler remained defiant, a British MP declared, 'We have got Ponsford out cheaply, but Bradman is still batting.' When the New South Wales Premier Neville Wran resigned, one of his ministers, Rodney Cavalier, said, 'Following Neville Wran is like going in to bat after Bradman.' During the 1996 federal election, sporting metaphors flew like missiles in every direction. Michael Duffy, the former Labor minister, was quoted by Alan Ramsey as likening John Howard to 'a batsman who pushes and prods and bores everyone to sobs because he's so careful'. He went on, 'Give him a rank full toss outside the off stump and instead of hitting it for four he pushes it past point for a single . . . He's hard to get out because he doesn't make mistakes. Some time in this election campaign the new ball will have to be taken to try and blast him out.' To which John Howard replied, 'The opposition tried Carmen Lawrence for an over, but she had to be taken off for tampering with the ball. Ralph Willis . . . had a few very sloppy overs with the new ball and he's now been confined to fine leg.'

Of the millions of words that have been written about Australian sport this book is but a tiny distillation. The book's editor, Richard Smart, asked a number of sports writers to provide stories, quotes or anecdotes about their favourite sports. The choice was entirely theirs, although it was clear that some sports did not have the literature base from which to extract the required number of quotes. Smart's stipulation that each item ought to have an Australian connection might not have bothered Jim Main, who has supplied the excellent section on Australian Rules football, but for the other contributors it did mean the exclusion of countless gems. Personally, I would like to have included Robin Williams's description of cricket as 'baseball on valium'. Or the observation by the British soccer coach Tommy Docherty that 'cricket is organised loafing – it's the only sport you can put on weight playing.' Or the opinion of the British playwright Harold Pinter, 'that cricket is the greatest thing that God ever created – certainly better than sex, although sex isn't too bad, either.' Or Lord Monckton's assertion that 'cricket is a game which the British, not being a spiritual people, had to invent in order to have some concept of eternity.'

Still, as the following pages demonstrate, Australian sport provided more than enough material for all six contributors, whom at this point I should introduce. Jim Main, who has already been mentioned, is a leading authority on the Australian code and one who is especially renowned in his home town, Melbourne. To paraphrase Evan Whitton, without Jim Main's knowledge not a sparrow falls in the world of AFL. Alan Clarkson of Sydney provided not one but two sections – on rugby league and tennis. They are hardly kindred sports, but Clarkson became an expert on both in his newspaper days, switching nimbly from one to another as the seasons, winter and summer, came and went. Our horse racing contributor is Bill Whittaker, whose expertise in his field has stood the test of time and whose reputation as one of the country's best-informed racing scribes (who also happens to be a skilled writer) has spread beyond his home base, Sydney.

Jim Webster is the most versatile of all. He contributed the golf, swimming and athletics sections, but given the depth of his knowledge of all sports, gained during a long and distinguished newspaper career, he might easily have put this whole book together on his own. The rugby union section comes from Greg Growden, already a seasoned campaigner on the rugby circuit which, happily for the journalists who travel it, takes in Britain, France, Canada, South Africa, Italy and other agreeable destinations. Rugby abounds with stories, and Growden, as readers of this book will discover, knows most of them.

Finally, there is Ray Connelly, our boxing

contributor. Although not strictly a journalist, Connelly has spent a lifetime working in and around newspapers. More importantly, he is Australian boxing's most enduringly familiar face, having introduced bouts in Sydney for more than forty years. His material did not come to him second-hand. He saw and heard it all with his own eyes and ears.

Thus ends this brief curtain-raiser. Readers should now take their seats in the grandstand and have their binoculars ready. The game is about to begin.

Philip Derriman

CRICKET

Philip Derriman has written regularly on cricket for the *Sydney Morning Herald* for many years and is the author of a number of cricket books. They include *The Grand Old Ground, Bodyline, True To The Blue, The Top 100 & the 1st XI and Eighty Not Out – A Celebration of Test Cricket At The Sydney Cricket Ground*. He also compiled the anthology *Our Don Bradman – Sixty Years of Writings About Sir Donald Bradman* and with Pat Mullins co-compiled the anthology *Bat & Pad – Writings On Australian Cricket 1804–1984*.

Philip is grateful to a number of people for permission to reproduce various items. They include Arthur Morris for an extract from a tribute to Bill O'Reilly, Peter Philpott for his memory of fielding with Keith Miller, Neil Marks for his story about his father and Don Bradman, Keith Miller for his account of the origin of the eighty-seven superstition, Peter O'Reilly for writings and for extracts from a speech by his father Bill, Alan McGilvray for two anecdotes, Jack McHarg for several items from his cricket biographies, Brian Booth for his explanation of why he always called heads, Arthur Mailey Junior for writings by his father Arthur Mailey, Warwick Hadfield for his account of Kim Hughes's resignation as Australian captain, Melvyn Bragg and Leo McKern for extracts from essays, Malcolm Gemmell for two extracts by Jack Fingleton and Richard Stilgoe for his verse 'Lilian Thomson'. Special thanks is also owed to Pat Mullins, not only for the extract from his family history but for permission to use a number of other items which he had collected.

CRICKET'S A FUNNY GAME

Anon.

The game's eternal truth. Of unknown origin, this quotation is repeated incessantly, season after season, by cricketers and cricket followers everywhere, in all kinds of situations. It owes its popularity to the fact that it has been shown, season after season, to be true.

I hate it here. I couldn't live here. I want to live in a place where you can play cricket out in the street and get twenty overs in before the first car comes.

Steve Merrick, Australian rugby union halfback and resident of Singleton, speaking of living in Sydney. Quoted by Peter FitzSimons in the *Sydney Morning Herald*, 29 July 1995.

Cricket

Ramadhidn't.

Jim Macdougall. A one-word comment in the Sydney *Sun* on the failure of the West Indian 'mystery' spin bowler Sonny Ramadhin in the Sydney Test, 1951–52.

Can you please do something to get out, so these bastards will stop bowling bumpers?

Mark Waugh in a mid-pitch conversation with his batting partner, Craig McDermott, during the Antigua Test in 1991. McDermott's arrival at the crease had provoked a barrage of bumpers at both batsmen. From *McDermott – Strike Bowler,* ABC Books, 1992.

It looks to me like they're going to bowl an underarm off the last ball ... this is possibly a little disappointing.

Bill Lawry on Channel 9 when Trevor Chappell prepared to bowl his infamous underarm delivery against New Zealand in 1981. Adrian McGregor, *Greg Chappell*, Collins, 1985.

But then it was within the rules
 Of our ancient and noble pastime

To roll it down, along the ground
Though no bugger could remember the last time.

Jeff Hewitt, *The Underarm Incident*, 1995.

At a minimum Greg Chappell should apologise.

Malcolm Fraser, Australian Prime Minister, after the underarm incident.

It was the most disgusting effort I can recall in the history of cricket, a game which used to be played by gentlemen.

New Zealand's Prime Minister Muldoon after the underarm incident.

New Zealand cricket should thank Greg Chappell for what he did because it created such a huge interest within the game in New Zealand. The crowds kept coming, we became a more and more successful unit, and it was a boon to New Zealand cricket, and the catalyst was the underarm incident, so in the long term we should be thankful to Greg Chappell and Trevor Chappell.

Cricket

Geoff Howarth, New Zealand captain at the time of the underarm incident, in a recorded message broadcast at a 15th anniversary lunch in Sydney, 1996.

I just shuffle in and go whang.

Jeff Thomson when asked by Philip Derriman to discuss his bowling technique in an interview for the *Sydney Morning Herald*.

This bunch didn't have a chance. Poor selection, inexperienced captaincy, senseless batting, weak bowling ... no doubt about it, we're down and out.

Keith Miller in the Sydney *Sun* after Australia lost to Pakistan in the 1979 World Cup.

Cricket has often looked in need of the men in white coats. The problem is they are already running things.

Stephen Moss in the *Guardian* after England beat South Africa in a farcial, contrived end to a rain-shortened World Cup semi-final at Sydney, March 1992.

He hates Australians. The mere sight of one upsets him.

Pelham Warner, writing in a letter about Douglas Jardine. Quoted by Jack Fingleton.

Lindwall was perhaps the only bowler whom Jardine would have found acceptable as substitute for the Larwood of 1932–33.

J. M. Kilburn, *Cricket Decade – England v Australia 1946 to 1956*, William Heinemann, 1959.

We may be a small and callow race but there is a divinity to our cricket.

Thomas Keneally. From an essay in *Summer Days – Writers On Cricket*, edited by Michael Myer, Oxford University Press, 1983.

'I don't know about you Acka, but I'm having trouble picking him up,' said Don Bradman to my father at the Gabba one summer day.

They were batting for NSW against Queensland and both were having difficulty coping with the sheer pace of Queensland's Aboriginal fast bowler, Eddie Gilbert. After a couple of overs of ducking, snicking and missing, the two had come together for a mid-wicket conference.

'I'm having the same trouble, Braddles,' my father replied. 'But I'm going to take to him! Eddie doesn't like it when the batsman gets on top.' Alec Marks walked back to his crease with aggression on his mind and a prayer in his heart.

The first ball of the next over from Gilbert was well up. Marks placed his foot down the pitch and thrashed the ball between mid-off and cover for four. The next ball was a blistering bumper which my father hooked from in front of his face, over square leg for four. The third ball was a replica of the second but this time it clipped the top edge of the bat and crashed into his head, just above the left eyebrow.

The ball dropped at the batsman's feet and he nonchalantly pushed it back to the bowler. 'Well bowled Eddie,' he smilingly commented. Marks did not compliment the bowler to show the world that he was a good sport; he was only obeying the time-honoured maxim: 'When they hit you, never show 'em you're hurt!'

The contest continued until the end of the over and, if judges had been awarding points, they would probably have declared it a draw.

Drinks came onto the field and my relieved father, with blood on his shirt, walked up to his friend, thankful for at least a couple of minutes' reprieve.

'How are you feeling, Acka?' asked Bradman.

'A bit shaky but I'm okay.'

'You know you were very lucky,' said Bradman.

'I'll say I was,' replied Dad. 'An inch lower and the ball would have hit me in the eye.'

'No, I mean you were lucky it hit you in the head, otherwise you'd have been caught behind.'

This is just one example of why 'the Don' was a better batsman than Dad – and every other batsman who ever lived, for that matter.

Neil Marks, *Tales From The Locker Room*, Ironbark Press, 1993.

She [Sydney] is, as the wits point out, three hours ahead of anything else that matters in the whole of Australia, in spite of all that the clocks can say – Our Harbour, Our Bridge, and Our Bradman.

Thomas Wood, *Cobbers,* Oxford University Press, 1934.

Dear Mr Yardley, I have no interest whatever in cricket and do not care who wins. But the other day,

Cricket

quite by accident, I listened for a few moments to a Test match broadcaster. He said that something or someone called Lindwall was bowling. It sounded a peculiar name to me, but when the commentator proceeded to say that this bowler had two long legs, one fine short leg and a square leg, I was shocked. Tell me, Mr Yardley, what kind of creatures are these Australian cricketers? No wonder we can't win.

A letter received by the England captain, Norman Yardley, during the final Test of the 1948 series against Australia at the Oval. Quoted by Lionel Lord Tennyson in *Sticky Wickets*, Christopher Johnson Publishers, 1950.

When tempers were frayed Maurice Leyland had the happy knack of introducing humour. Fielding on the boundary on one occasion during the 'bodyline' tour of Australia somebody threw a cushion at him. This was followed by a dust bomb and then an empty beer bottle. Maurice took no notice until a full bottle of beer came sailing over his shoulder. He picked it up, turned to the crowd and said, 'Now then, can anybody lend me an opener?' There was a laugh. Openers were proffered. He whipped off the top, wished 'em 'Good health,' and put the bottle down on the boundary edge with the injunction, 'Look after it for me.' They did. Woe betide anyone who said a word against Maurice Leyland after that. The offender became the target for dust bombs. Maurice was accepted as a 'fair dinkum pommie.' They rooted for him.

Bill Bowes, *Cricket Heroes*, Phoenix Sports Books, 1959.

It was 11 o'clock on the first morning of the [1991] Barbados Test – I'll never forget it. Dessie snicked this ball onto his back hip and through to me for a catch. After I threw the ball up I looked up and he's telling the umpire it only hit his hip. That type of thing frustrates us worse than anything. I said to Haynes, 'Let the effing umpire do his own effing job.' Haynes took his helmet off and came at me saying, 'I don't have to take that from you,' and I said, 'You have to take whatever you get out here, mate.' He said, 'I'll see you after the game,' and I said something like, 'You're a big man, aren't you?' When I came off at lunch my heart was still pumping through my chest because the crowd was into me – it was his crowd, remember. All through the game I coppied it from the crowd.

Ian Healy, quoted in the *Good Weekend,* January 1996.

Cricket

I couldn't wait to bat. I never suffered from stage fright. The bigger the occasion, the tenser the atmosphere, the more I liked the game. It just happened to be part of my make-up.

Sir Donald Bradman, quoted by Roland Perry in his book *The Don*, Macmillan, 1995.

Queensland won't win the Sheffield Shield until the day they raffle it and Queensland buys all the tickets.

Bill Tallon, Queensland cricketer. Quoted in various references.

How can you miss? They're all bloody full tosses.

Stan McCabe, after he was complimented on hitting the ball three times deep into the outfield in a baseball match between the Australian cricketers and a South African baseball team during the Australians' tour there in 1935–36. Quoted by Jack McHarg in *Stan McCabe – The Man And His Cricket*, Collins, 1987.

When my father came to Australia in 1950, he realised quickly that an understanding of cricket was the hallmark of successful assimilation. Being a Pole recently extracted from the wreckage of post-war Europe, he knew nothing of the five-day game that often failed to produce a result. Stuck as he was, by government order, in an open-cut coalmine in Leigh Creek, 450 kilometres north of Adelaide, there wasn't much opportunity to observe the white-flannelled ritual. He set about learning the hard way.

Books were the thing. He ordered dozens of them and spent his evenings pouring over the differences between a leg glance and a cover drive. His friends thought he was mad ... but my father persevered. Before long he was able to sidle up to the managerial gatherings where the fate of the Australian XI was a regular topic of conversation. 'I would have brought in a third slip at least an hour earlier,' he might say. Or, 'Why didn't they take the new ball when they had the chance?' Within weeks he had been promoted to an administrative position, the first 'New Australian' in Leigh Creek to make the grade.

Wanda Jamrozik in a *Sydney Morning Herald* article, 11 August 1989.

Though we never stop for shell-fire we're not too keen on planes,

Cricket

But when the Stukas start to hover round
You can sometimes get a wicket, if you're game
   enough to stay,
By bowling as the batsmen go to ground.

Hugh Paterson, *Tobruk Test*, 1941.

He just belts the hell out of anything within reach.

Jack Ryder, Australian captain in 1928–29, on being asked about the batting methods of a new Australian player, Don Bradman. Quoted by Denis Compton in *Compton On Cricketers*, Cassell, 1981.

I don't care what my bats weigh as long as they are given to me.

Sid Barnes on being questioned about his preference for light bats. Quoted by Ray Robinson in *After Stumps Were Drawn – The Best of Ray Robinson's Cricket Writing*, compiled by Jack Pollard, William Collins, 1985.

I wish I could bowl to myself.

Stan McCabe, displaying surprise on being complimented

on his handy medium-pace bowling. Quoted by Jack McHarg in *Stan McCabe – The Man And His Cricket*, Collins, 1987.

A couple of years ago I was in a sports depot in Sydney and a wiry sunburnt young bush chap came in, and started looking over the goods. I've had so much to do with athletes I can generally pick a man fairly well, and I said to the salesman, 'That's a hard-looking young fellow and he's very light on his feet. I should say he had done some boxing or was accustomed to riding rough horses. They have to be pretty active for that game.'

So the salesman laughed and said, 'No, you're a bit out. But he's a somebody all the same.' I said, 'Who is he?'

'Oh,' he said, 'that's Don Bradman, this new boy wonder cricketer they have just discovered.'

You see he was only Don Bradman, the Bowral boy then, and hadn't been to England. He's Mr Bradman now, and many congratulations to him.

So the salesman brought the boy over – he seemed only a boy to me – and after we had exchanged a few remarks, Bradman went out. So then I asked the inevitable question: I said, 'How good is this fellow? Is he going to be as good as Trumper?'

Now, the salesman had been a first-class cricketer

himself and he gave me what I consider a very clear summing up of the two men.

'Well,' he said, 'when Trumper got onto good wickets he developed a beautiful free style, like a golfer that plays a full swing with a good follow-through. He trusted the ball to come true off the wicket, and if it bumped, or shot, or kicked, he might be apt to get out. But this Bradman takes nothing on trust. Even after he has got onto good wickets, he won't trust the ball a foot, and he watches every ball till the last moment before he hits it. His eye is so good and his movements are so quick that he can hit a ball to the fence without any swing at all. That makes him look a bit rough in style compared with Trumper, and he hits across his wicket a lot. They say that's a fatal thing to do, but I never saw him miss one of them.'

So I said, 'You wouldn't remember W.G. Grace, can you remember Ranjitsinhji?'

'Yes,' he said, 'Ranji had a beautiful style, but he was a bit fond of playing to the gallery. If he'd liked to stone-wall, they'd never have got him out, but he used to do exhibition shots – late cuts, and tricky little leg glances – and out he'd go. There's no exhibition shots about this Bradman.'

I said, 'How will he get on in England? Will he handle the English wickets?'

'Yes,' he said, 'don't you worry about him on

English wickets. He'd play on a treacle wicket or on a corrugated iron wicket. He's used to kerosene tin wickets up there at Bowral. He'll never be the world's most artistic cricketer, but he'll be the world's hardest wicket to get.'

Well, it's not often that a prediction works out as well as that, is it?

A.B. (Banjo) Paterson. From a radio talk reproduced in *Song Of The Pen: Collected Works 1901–41*, Lansdowne, 1983.

Colonial society is low – shockingly low. You have plenty of money, no doubt, but your gentlemen are yet unborn. I suppose, including yourself, I met about three during the whole of my trip. As to the promoters, they worked like demons to hide the split in our camp, but I heartily despised them, and put them in the hole nicely in the Adelaide match. And now, goodbye. I don't expect a very pleasant voyage home, for we are at daggers drawn among ourselves, and there will be a fight or two before it is all over. As to Australia itself, it is a fine country, but wants steeping for 24 hours in the sea to rid it of the human vermin crawling over it. So with kind regards to yourself, and hearty contempt for the cads, bullies, and fools who exist among you in profusion, I am, dear M., yours truly, W.G. GRACE.

Cricket

From a hoax letter allegedly written by W. G. Grace to a friend during his first visit to Australia in 1873–74 but almost certainly created by an Australian journalist. Many Australians believed the letter to be genuine.

The Australians came down like a wolf on the fold,
The Marylebone cracks for a trifle were bowled,
Our Grace before dinner was very soon done,
And Grace after dinner did not get a run.

From *Punch*.

Licking the Poms was then, as now, a national ambition; and yet I sometimes think that, even though the game is and has been every bit as much Australian as English, the Australians could never have invented it. Indeed many in my school thought it a sissy's game; and as for tennis . . . ! Rugger, yes; and they went on to develop Australian Rules. Possibly it was all part of beating the Pommies at their own games, cricket, tennis, that is very much Australian.

Leo McKern. From an essay in *Summer Days – Writers On Cricket*, Oxford University Press, 1983.

We batted first, hitting up 228 runs and we thought we were in a very strong position. Two local players opened the innings for them and one of them was out quickly and Bradman came in. Soon the other opener was out and Wendel Bill came in and he and Bradman really got going.

When Bradman was about 50, George Thorn, who was captain, threw the ball to me and said, 'Here you are. Try your luck again.'

I stood at the bowler's end and while I placed my field Bradman was talking to the wicketkeeper, Leo Waters. Later Leo told me this conversation took place.

Bradman: What sort of bowler is this fellow?

Waters: Don't you remember this bloke? He bowled you in the exhibition match at Lithgow a few weeks ago and has been boasting about it ever since at your expense.

Well, my first over to Bradman provided him with 33 runs. The next bowler was the late Horrie Baker – later Lithgow Town Clerk – and he had no less than 40 runs hit off his over. There were 29 runs hit off my second over, 27 of them by Bradman, to give him an almost unbelievable century in just three overs. I pleaded with George Thorn to take me off and he did.

Bill Black, one of the Lithgow players who bowled to

Cricket

Bradman when he scored 100 runs in three consecutive (8-ball) overs at Blackheath in November 1931. From an article in the Sydney *Sun* in 1969 by Tom Downes.

When Don was in his early twenties I saw him give a demonstration of bouncing a golf ball with a cricket stump and he did it twenty times easily. 'When my luck's in I get towards a century,' he said. I found that other cricketers when their luck was in struggled to double figures.

Bill Bowes, *Cricket: The Great Ones*, Pelham Books, 1967.

Bramall Lane, now, alas, surrendered to football, was the ground for lively wit. The Sheffield spectator had no equal anywhere in the world, and it was a treat to field near the boundary and listen to the comments. One handed down in the Yorkshire dressing room involved George Macaulay, and there is a moral to it.

Don Bradman had been batting only a short time and, as usual, looked to be in ominous form. Macaulay, who had been known to quail batsmen with a glare and a mutter, asked for the ball and in a loud voice declared: 'Let me 'ave a go at this booger.' His first over produced the considered achievement of a maiden to Bradman, but in the next he was hit for five boundaries, and a further 16 runs in his third over. As silently he took his sweater, a voice with the strength of a loudhailer came from the crowd: 'Tha should have kept thy bloody mouth shut, George.'

Len Hutton, *Fifty Years Of Cricket*, Stanley Paul, 1984.

So much has been written about Bradman that no superlatives are left. I said yesterday that he is a menace to English cricket. Today, I go further. I think that he will be the death of it. If he comes over more than once again we shan't be able to spare the time to get him out, and English cricket will quietly fade away.

Chapman Jocose, London *Daily Mail*, 1930.

The late intense weather has been very favourable to the amateurs of cricket, who have scarcely lost a day for the last month. The frequent immoderate heats might have been considered inimical to the amusement, but were productive of very opposite consequences, as the state of the atmosphere might always regulate the portion of exercise necessary to the ends this laborious diversion was originally intended to answer.

This is the oldest known reference to cricket in Australia. It appeared in the *Sydney Gazette*, 8 January 1804.

It's Australia I want us to beat. More than anyone and all the time. As you'll realise I have had a very frustrating life in this respect. The lust to beat them bites in very deeply. The other year, after a sad defeat at the bats of our antipodean friends, I had a drink or six with a few cricket-lovers in the Earls Court area before proceeding in an easterly direction to Mayfair to meet my wife and accompany her to the Curzon Cinema. Ingmar Bergman's *Scenes from a Married Life* was showing. Now I esteem Mr Bergman so highly that I would defend him as the best film-maker alive today. But his made-for-television condensed-for-cinema piece did not catch my interest. In the comfort of the Curzon and rather cast down by another inglorious English defeat, I dozed: well, slept. My wife tells me that she prodded me several times before the last prod got through and I woke up instantly, shouting 'Bloody Australians!'

The audience, by then enwrapt in Liv Ullmann's long monologue, were surprised, I think, judging from the freeze which came in from all about me. But as I explained to my wife again and again – it's all very well to try to gather up insights on the deeper currents in contemporary relationships, and painful, profound and moving it certainly is: but what were we going to do about the bloody Australians winning all the important matches?

Melvyn Bragg. From an essay in *Summer Days – Writers On Cricket*, Oxford University Press, 1983.

Those synthetic pitches were rewarding to play on if you happened to be a fast bowler, because the ball whizzed off the surface. On one fairly overcast day, I found myself bowling particularly fast on a synthetic wicket in a match between my state school and a Catholic school, Ipswich Brothers. I had bowled a few overs and hit two or three of their batsmen – mainly on the hands, as I recall – when, to everyone's amazement, their coach walked onto the field and announced, 'That's it – the game's over.' Our coach, Don Rucker, objected. Rucker was an outstanding teacher of the game who, incidentally, still comes to see me occasionally when I play at the Gabba. He joined us on the field and said, 'You can't do that – you can't call the match off just because a kid's bowling fast.' Their coach was adamant. 'I don't care what you say,' he said. 'I'm not leaving my kids out there any longer.' So that was that.

Craig McDermott, *McDermott – Strike Bowler*, ABC Books, 1992.

The infamous Bodyline Cricket Series was played in Australia against England in 1932–33. By then I was aged nine. My father became interested in that series, as I recall, because it was 'us' against the 'Poms' – but more particularly because there were four Irish-Australian Catholics in the side. Not that he was biased . . .

They were Stan McCabe, Bill O'Reilly, Jack Fingleton and Leo O'Brien.

I remember Dad telling me in his soft brogue, 'Fingleton had his rosary beads crushed in his pocket by Larwood.'

To Dad, that was an unforgivable deed – even more monstrous than the misdeed of Cromwell.

I kept the story to myself until 1985 – by then McCabe and Fingleton were dead, so I decided to check the story out with Bill O'Reilly before it was too late.

I wrote to Bill giving him all the above explanatory details about my father. Bill replied – 'You sold your father to me in a few words, Pat. I cannot vouch for the story's accuracy but I can say that Jack always had his rosary beads in his pocket when he went out to bat against Larwood.'

You will all recall how important it was for our parents to carry rosary beads and wear holy medals – and how they tried to teach us the habit. It was understandable that Fingleton would carry his beads because I can recall that his brother who was a Marist Father had written a CTS pamphlet – 'A Fistful of Beads'.

Bill then told me another story, which he was not clear about – but I checked it out with Leo O'Brien.

The fourth Test of that series was played in Brisbane following the notorious Test in Adelaide where Woodfull and Oldfield were injured. In Brisbane the four Irish Catholics met Archbishop Duhig at a function and he gave each of them a 'Holy Medal' (St Christopher Medal) to wear to protect them against injury by Larwood, Voce, Bowes etc.

They left Brisbane and went to Sydney for the fifth Test and O'Brien and 'Fingo' were batting.

Suddenly 'Fingo' raised his hand and stopped play because O'Brien had lost his holy medal. The players went searching for it – and the Englishmen joined in the search even though they did not know what they were looking for.

Cricket

Can you imagine either Benaud or Ian Chappell being able to describe the human side of that story. The men who played for Australia were different in those days.

Pat Mullins, from a family history.

He doesn't do much with the ball but he is a bit quick.

Stan Sismey, wicketkeeper for the Australian services team in 1945, on being asked by the incoming batsman, Denis Compton, about the bowler, Keith Miller, then unknown to Compton. Compton said Miller's first ball whistled past his ear before he had even raised his bat.

He is compounded of tea, leather, patience and subtlety.

R.C. Robertson-Glasgow, English cricket writer, on Clarrie Grimmett.

He was unique, a batsman appearing not just once in a lifetime but once in the life of a game.

Denis Compton's assessment of Don Bradman, *Compton On Cricketers, Past and Present*, Cassell, 1981.

I have a wife and family. No more of that stuff for me.

Johnny Brown of Yorkshire in 1896, standing his ground at the bowler's end and refusing his partner's call to go for a second run. Brown had been facing the Australian express bowler Ernie Jones, who had narrowly missed hitting him in the head with his two previous deliveries. Quoted by Clem Hill in a newspaper article, 1920.

When England batted in that same Sydney Test, they got away to a reasonable start to be humming along at 1–128.

Then Miller decided to take a few wickets. I say 'decided' because that is largely the way he operated. When he was really determined to do so, he could make inroads almost at will. He had Hutton, Simpson and Compton in quick succession. England slumped from 1–128 to 4–137 and in came Freddie Brown to stop the rot. On his way to the wicket, Miller accosted him.

'Hey Freddie,' he offered. 'There's a big crowd here looking for some action, why don't we give them a bit?' Brown looked at him quizzically. 'I'll give you three half volleys outside the off stump,' Miller continued. 'Make sure you hit 'em.'

True to his word, Miller served up three juicy deliveries which Brown duly crashed through the covers. Three balls, 12 runs. The fourth ball Miller dug in viciously, and it caught Brown fair on the forehead. Stunned, Brown glared at his 'mate' who had been so full of compassion and good humour just a moment before. A wry grin came to Miller's face once he had been assured Freddie was okay. 'I said three balls, Freddie,' he explained. 'Not four.'

Alan McGilvray, *McGilvray – The Game Is Not The Same . . .* , ABC Books, 1985.

Boarding a passenger train leaving Sydney's Central Station for Goulburn one Saturday morning in December 1925, I travelled peacefully for 80 miles, blithely unaware of what was to happen to me before I arrived at my little home town, situated 104 miles south. As the train came to a halt at Bowral, an attractive township popular as a health resort and holiday mountain town, I was startled out of my peaceful reverie by the weird sensation of imagining that I heard my name being called. I jumped up, leaned my long frame from the carriage window and called out 'Here I am.'

It was the stationmaster from Wingello doing the bellowing. His instructions were terse and forceful. 'Grab your bag and get out.'

My reluctance to obey him must have been plain for him to see, for he added in explanation, 'We are all down here to play Bowral this afternoon and you are going to get the new ball.' I jumped out smartly. And that was a dreadful mistake, I must admit.

The stationmaster, with the same organising ability which had induced the Railway Commissioners to promote him to his dizzy height of responsibility, put my fears to rest by informing me that he himself had been in close contact during the week with my dear mother, who had packed my cricket gear and given it to him to set me up for the afternoon. Misguidedly I silently gave three hearty cheers for the good luck which had given me such a welcome start to the Christmas holidays.

On the way to the Bowral Oval in an old 1918 T Model Ford truck I was well and truly briefed on the growing reputation of a kid named Don Bradman who had been showing such unusual skill that they had decided to enlist my services at short notice.

We were a motley looking crew I suppose as we began to peel off under cover of a clump of gum trees beside the ground. Young and old, all shapes and sizes. Moustaches were popular with the more mature members, but no youngsters dared then to run the risk of wholesale criticism by encouraging the reluctant growth of a few goose-down hairs on the top lip to give the false impression that he had entered the state of manhood. It wasn't done then. There were no beards. It was long since the days when cricketers found it necessary to add to their ferocity, glamour, sex appeal – call it what you will – by hiding behind a thatch of fearsome whiskers.

Bowral won the toss and batted. I got the new ball.

You might well ask, 'Why did O'Reilly get the new ball? He wasn't a fast bowler who thrashed them down at headlong speed. There has never been any suggestion that he could move the new ball in the air sufficiently to claim recognition as a worthwhile new ball operator.'

Quite true.

O'Reilly got the new ball regardless. The reasons were basic. O'Reilly could bowl consistently at the stumps. He had earned himself a noticeable reputation as a wicket-taker in the Sydney Moore Park Saturday morning competition. Furthermore the Wingello captain and the entire team – including O'Reilly himself – thought that O'Reilly was a good bowler.

Play began.

In my first over I hit the stumps of one of Bowral's openers. That warmed me up for the entrance of a diminutive figure, approaching with what appeared to be the diffident gait of a stop-gap performer sent in to hold the fort long enough for the real number three in the batting order to get his pads on. What struck me most about him was the difficulty he seemed to be having in taking normal steps as he approached. His pads seemed to reach right up to his navel. His bat was small and had reached the sere and yellow stage, where the yellow was turning to dark tobacco.

Still, he shaped up as though he knew what the game was all about, and the expression on his face publicised the fact that he felt quite at home and was ready to cope with anything that I had in store for him.

The battle was joined. As the game proceeded I was quick to realise that I had come into contact with my very first 'problem child'. My training as a prospective primary school teacher was supposed to have prepared me for dealing with the occasional hard case who would turn up from time to time, but nothing could have prepared me for the confrontation with this particular youth.

As the precocious lad began to handle my quickish leg breaks, bouncing high off the coir mat which always favoured spin, I was made aware that here at last I had a real job of work on my hands, and I wondered what I should have to say to Len Kelsey the next time I saw him.

I had a bit of bad luck early in that memorable afternoon. Twice before he had reached 30 the youngster was dropped in the slips off my bowling. To elucidate, it is necessary that I give an honest pen-picture of the captain who led Wingello in that great struggle.

Selby Jeffery was a railway fettler. He had worn the Australian uniform which proudly displayed the big brass 'A' denoting the fact that he was present on the Sunday morning of 25 April 1915, when the Australian and New Zealand forces went into action at Gallipoli in their attempt to open up the Dardanelles. Selby was an Anzac, and as such held the unbounded respect of every man on the field. He sported a fairly robust black moustache. His face was rosy with blatant good health and his persistent good humour was heralded by the most pleasant smile one could wish to see.

His snow-white shirt and duck trousers were immaculate, as were his rubber boots. He wore a black waistcoat, unbuttoned, over the shirt. The idea of the waistcoat was quite original – it held his pipe, his tobacco and his matches. It was not unusual in those far off days for a country cricketer

to light up and take a few draws on a pipe or cigarette. Nobody took umbrage at it. I saw it happen
outback many times. Indeed I once saw it in first-
class cricket on the Sydney Cricket Ground, when
Freddie Mair, the gifted all-rounder and Balmain
captain for many years, playing for New South
Wales against Victoria, let his craving for a few
draws get the better of him at the fall of a Victorian
wicket. And I seem to recall that he had to get a
match from the man fielding at short leg, but I can't
remember who that was.

Selby used to slip his big-bowled bent-stemmed
Captain Peterson pipe into the top pocket of his
unbuttoned waistcoat. His tobacco pouch fitted
snugly into the other top pocket, with the tin box
holding his Wax Vestas matches in the bottom
pocket along with a penknife for cutting the plug of
dark 'Conqueror' tobacco.

It would have been senseless for him to field in
any position where it might have been necessary to
raise an occasional canter. Had he run there would
have been a scattering of smoking paraphernalia in
all directions. Wisely therefore he placed himself
invariably at first slip where he was splendidly
covered by a magnificent 'keeper named Tommy
Lynam and always supported by an active and
mobile second slip.

Very early in the day I got one to lift and bite.

Cricket

Young Bradman edged it and the ball travelled speedily and straight in the direction of Selby's midriff. It would have been an extraordinary effort had the catch been taken. It struck him in the solar plexus just at the moment when he was, with both hands well and truly occupied, lighting his pipe.

Bradman soon gave our skipper a chance to redeem himself by snicking my quicker ball straight to him again. This second time Selby made a manful attempt with both hands to make the catch, but he had blown such a dense cloud of bluish smoke from his startled lungs that he must have lost sight of the ball well before it reached him.

'Sorry Bill,' he called, as if nothing untoward had happened. Selby's inconsistencies in the slips were part and parcel of the Wingello team's programme. I was probably the only one among us who felt that he might have been wise to deny himself just a little longer.

Who in the name of all that is holy could ever possibly hope to get away unscathed when Don Bradman had been given two lives. If I said earlier that I experienced some early worries as the boyish Bradman started his innings by methodical employment of the middle of his bat, I could certainly go much further in describing my own mental reactions as this young man tore the Wingello attack apart. Even though his size suggested that he would have been better fitted physically to have been riding winners at Randwick racecourse, he summoned up the energy required to land the ball right over the fence on half a dozen occasions. One wondered where he was hiding the battery that generated the power.

To draw a convenient veil over the desolate scene, Selby Jeffery's team finished the day a crestfallen crowd who listened more to the rattles of the old Model T Ford than to any animated flow of conversation on the thirty mile return trip by road to Wingello. Their chief bowling hope had nothing whatever to say. The boy Bradman was 234 not out.

Back at home I questioned my mother's wisdom in aiding and abetting my downfall by so carefully collecting my gear, but she seemed to think I had come to little harm, really, and that I should have considered myself lucky to have spent such a lovely day out in the fresh air playing cricket.

As the game was to be continued on our Wingello wicket the following Saturday afternoon, I could not help feeling that I was due to face up to another hammering from this pint-sized powerhouse a week later. I saw no hope ahead for me. All was gloom. I began to count my blessings in that I had other sports to choose from. As an athlete I had spent two happy years with Botany Harriers, where I had done reasonably well without ever having really tried to train assiduously for the three events – high jump, triple jump and shot put – in which I competed. I had done well enough in tennis to promise myself some sort of a future there if I cared to concentrate. All these thoughts went through my troubled boyish mind, but it was difficult to find one alleviating premise upon which to base my deep-dyed love for cricket. Having been belted unmercifully by a schoolboy was a pill too bitter for me to swallow. My pride had been badly injured.

The next Saturday afternoon arrived. I lined myself up manfully for another serve of what the game I had loved so much might have to offer.

The first ball again was mine to bowl, and the not out Bradman was there to deal with it. I let go my accustomed leg break, aimed at the leg stump. It spun sharply past the Bradman bat and crashed into the top of the off stump. Suddenly, I thought, the grass round our Wingello ground began to look greener than ever it had done before. The birds began to sing. The sun shone becomingly. One ball changed my whole sporting outlook. Gone were the dismaying plans to give the game away forever. I was prepared to go on and take whatever it had in store for me, and I made the personal pledge that as I was taking it on the chin in future I would be unsparing in my efforts to deal out as much as I could of what I was getting.

Bill O'Reilly, *'Tiger' – 60 Years of Cricket*, Collins, 1985.

There was a good deal of sledging during the World Cup in Australia in 1992. Not all of it could be understood. It has become common for players from certain non-English speaking countries to abuse opposing players in their own language. The idea is that they call you anything they like without your realising it, so they get away with it. They would not get away with it with me. Even if a player was speaking Outer Mongolian, I would know when I was being sledged.

Ian Botham in an article in the *ABC Australian Cricket Alamanac, 1993*.

There's Neil Harvey standing at leg slip with his legs wide apart waiting for a tickle.

Brian Johnston, quoting a remark he made inadvertently during a Test telecast at Headingley in 1961, *Rain Stops Play*, Unwin Paperbacks, 1979.

Well, O'i doant think mooch of their play, but they are a wonderful lot of drinking men.

Cricket

Roger Iddison, a Yorkshire batsman who toured Australia with H.H. Stephenson's side in 1861–62, giving his impression of Australia's cricketers. Stephenson's team was the first to visit Australia. Quoted in *Cricket Walkabout – The Australian Aborigines in England* by John Mulvaney and Rex Harcourt, Macmillan, 1988.

Couldn't half do with a cuppa tea, couldn't you, Bert?

A remark by genial Maurice Tate to Bert Oldfield during a Test match. Tate had had an LBW appeal against Oldfield turned down and, at the end of the over, walked down the pitch and spoke to him. The press thought he was complaining about the umpire's decision, whereas, as Oldfield later reported, he merely made this harmless remark. Quoted by John Arlott in *Cricket Heroes*, Phoenix Sports Books, 1959.

Well, goodbye. Vic is taking me for my little walk again.

Reg Duff, who was for several years Victor Trumper's opening partner. According to Clem Hill, Duff used to say this to his team-mates before leaving the dressing room with Trumper.

Bradman and Barnes each made 234 and it was during their stand of 405 that Len Hutton put his hand on my shoulder and said: 'You know, Godfrey, there's nowt for it but run the bastards out!'

Godfrey Evans, England wicket-keeper, writing of the second Test of the 1946–47 series in his book *The Gloves Are Off*, Hodder and Stoughton, 1960.

I have three baskets on my desk – one marked IN, another marked OUT and the third marked LBW. That stands for 'let the buggers wait'.

Bill O'Reilly in a speech at a book launch in 1987. He was explaining his failure to reply quickly to a certain letter.

In the many pictures that I have stored in my mind from the 'burnt-out Junes' of 40 years, there is none more dramatic or compelling than that of Bradman's small, serenely moving figure in its big-peaked green cap coming out of the pavilion shadows into the sunshine, with the concentration, ardour and apprehension of surrounding thousands centred upon him, and the destiny of a Test match in his hands.

Cricket

H.S. Altham, *The Heart Of Cricket, The Cricketer*, Hutchinson, 1967. Sir Donald Bradman said he found this paragraph more moving than any other he had read about himself.

Why oh why didn't La Perouse get here first and save us from centuries of cricket? Just think, we would still have all the football, fabulous food, no republican debate and those citizens inclined towards unhurried sport could play boules in our public squares.

M. S. Daly in a letter to the *Sydney Morning Herald*, August 1993.

The grunts and screams of female tennis players drive me from the TV when my wife is in tennis-watching mode. However, if cricketers were encouraged to grunt or scream when batting or bowling, TV cricket could be much less of a deadly boring spectacle.

Bruce Schumacher in a letter to the *Sydney Morning Herald*, January 1996.

That was the first time I had ever seen Russell

Drysdale. We were getting ready to go when he asked us to hang around. I remember him sitting with a queer frame in front of him. Us two skinny kids, we just didn't understand that sort of thing. Artists – they were the type of people we weren't used to. It was unusual to see someone sitting around painting or drawing, sort of unheard of. We had seen paintings but had never seen anyone doing painting. We couldn't work out how this artist made a living painting when people we knew had to swing picks and shovels.

Teddy Woolard, one of two boys playing cricket at Hill End in 1937 when asked by Russell Drysdale to pose for him. The painting, titled *The Cricketers*, is one of Drysdale's most famous works. Quoted by Jocelyn Freeman in the *Sydney Morning Herald*, 13 May 1969.

I can't believe this kissing business which Merv Hughes is involved in. If someone had come up and tried to kiss me after I had taken a wicket, I most probably would have put my knee up.

Bill O'Reilly, quoted by Suellen O'Grady in the *Good Weekend*.

Cricket

On one of those occasions when Hobbs threatened to spend the weekend with us, I entered into a pact with Jack Gregory during the lunch interval. The idea was that my first ball to Jack in the second over was to be an obvious 'wrong 'un' pitched, if possible, on the middle or leg stump. The moment this ball was bowled Gregory was to spring round the back of Oldfield and wait at leg-slip for Hobbs to snick an easy catch.

Gregory remembered the scheme but *I* forgot it, and instead of the planned ball being a 'wrong 'un' it was a perfect leg-break on the *off* stump. When I saw Gregory dashing behind the wicket I realised the blunder I had made. But Gregory, keeping his eye on the ball in flight, saw it spinning the opposite way to what he had expected, hurtled back to the slips, and was just in time to grab the ball almost off Jack's bat.

Gregory wasn't particularly pleased about the incident. He said that I was trying to make a fool of him.

That night I asked Jack Hobbs if he knew what had happened.

'Not quite,' he said. 'But I heard a devil of a scramble going on behind the stumps.'

Arthur Mailey, *10 For 66 And All That*, Phoenix Sports Books, 1958.

O'Reilly, Jack Fingleton and I drove Denis Compton home on our way back to London for the Oval Test. Precisely why Denis was with us I can't remember, but I vividly remember O'Reilly and the Compton dog. Denis invited us in and his wife Valerie came into the room, holding two dear little white Maltese terriers, one with a pink bow around its neck and the other with a blue bow.

Now, as a White Cliffs boy who grew up chucking gibbers at kangaroo dogs, O'Reilly was never one to dote on dogs, and certainly not in the manner the English are wont to do. 'Say hello to nice Mr O'Reilly all the way from Australia,' said Valerie to the dogs. Realising what was expected of him, O'Reilly put out a tentative forefinger to pat one of the animals. Like a flash the dog lifted its head and clamped its fangs on Bill's finger, whereupon rich Irish blood began spurting from it. Valerie dropped the dogs, and she and Denis rushed out of the room for band-aids. 'Come here you little bastard,' said O'Reilly. Grabbing the dog he executed one of the finest drop kicks one would ever wish to see. The dog hurtled through the air, struck a wall several metres away with a resounding thwack, then slid to the floor.

Jack Fingleton and I stood with open mouths through the performance. When the Comptons returned with the first-aid repairs, we commiserated with Bill and joined the cry of 'Naughty dog!'

Cricket

Strangely enough, the dog was then crawling back on its stomach looking up at O'Reilly with adoration and respect. Thirty years after the flying-dog incident I told Denis Compton what happened. He said, 'I wish I'd known. Those two dogs drove me bloody mad.'

Arthur Morris, from a tribute to Bill O'Reilly in the *ABC Australian Cricket Almanac*, ABC Books, 1993.

I was staying at Elwood. When I got onto the St Kilda station – there was a kiosk there – the old chappie who ran the kiosk said, 'Hello, Mr Alexander. Aren't you playing today?' I said, 'Yes. Why?' 'Well,' he said, 'they're seven down.' I said, 'What!' I nearly fell over. Anyhow, I got into town outside Young and Jackson's and I got on the tram and asked the conductor, 'Didn't hear any scores, did you?' He said, 'Yes. They're all out.' I nearly fell of the tram. When I came down to the ground I could see up on the board 'Alexander – absent'. Oh, the rumours that went around after that. I was supposed to have been blind drunk and . . . But that's the true story.

Harry Alexander explaining his failure to turn up to bat in a Sheffield Shield match against NSW in Melbourne in December 1931. Victoria had barely begun its innings when play ended on the previous day, so Alexander, a tail-ender, had decided not to arrive until lunch, not expecting the rapid collapse that occurred. Quoted in the *Good Weekend*, February 1993.

When World War II broke out Bradman was given twenty-one lines in *Who's Who* – eight fewer than the more topical Hitler, seventeen more than Stalin.

R S Whitington, *Bumper*, Latimer House Ltd, 1953.

Give him 300 and ask him to go out!

A remark shouted by a spectator at the Australians v Worcestershire match in 1934 during Don Bradman's innings of 206, the second of three consecutive double centuries Bradman scored against that county. Quoted by Trevor Wignall in the *Daily Express*, 1934.

Why don't they let someone else have a turn? I'm sick of looking at him.

A remark by the mother of a Sydney sports writer, Eddie Kann, while she watched young Don Bradman score 452 not out in 415 minutes for New South Wales against

Cricket

Queensland in January 1930. Quoted in *The Grand Old Ground*, Cassell, 1981.

Anything can happen.

A favourite saying of the Australian radio commentator, A.G. Moyes. He often used it to qualify his predictions about the play.

I felt sorry for those bowlers who were, and will be tomorrow, up against Bradman. Breaking through the defence is even more difficult than getting a clearance from the Taxation Department. I've tried both.

Arthur Mailey's newspaper commentary on the Kippax-Oldfield testimonial match in Sydney, February 1949.

Good riddance – we could never get the cow out.

By a cricketer in the Bowral area on hearing Don Bradman had moved to Sydney for good. Quoted in a newspaper, 1930.

It's much harder to win a big pigeon race than it is to make a Test hundred.

Bill Lawry, quoted in *Inside Sport*, February 1994.

Often Barnes seemed to get bricked up inside his own run factory.

Ray Robinson, writing about Sid Barnes's safety-first approach to batting. Quoted by Jack Pollard in *After Stumps Were Drawn – The Best Of Ray Robinson's Cricket Writing*, William Collins, 1985.

Now, I spurn the halls of history and the company
    of the mighty.
No more do I long to be a toff – I'd rather go to
    Blighty.
I scoff at names like Marlborough, Marco Polo and
    Kate Leigh;
Nor do I pine to rise to fame like Sister Ligouri.
I scorn the honours time has brought to Gladstone
    and Disraeli.
I'd rather sit out on the Hill and urge on Bill
    O'Reilly.

Barney McCooe, Australian soldier in New Guinea in World

Cricket

War II, from *Saga Of A Sucker* circa 1944.

Frank Woolley, Kent's incomparable left-hander, even went to the length of choosing a World XI in his book without giving Bradman a place, because of doubts about his ability to play on sticky wickets. To me, it would be safer to put Don in and chance the weather.

Ray Robinson, quoted in *After Stumps Were Drawn – The Best of Ray Robinson's Cricket Writing*, compiled by Jack Pollard, William Collins, 1985.

So many old players . . . see the game through a fog of their own experience. They remember facing Lindwall and Miller, or Hall and Griffith, remember doing well and then suppose they could bat just as well now. But it is not so easy. They don't realise they'd be playing Lindwall and Miller every day of the season and every hour in the series. At the start of our series against the West Indies in 1984 the press asked me if I was going to wear a helmet. I said, 'Yes.' They said, 'Why?' I said, 'Because I'm twenty-eight and I've got a family and I want to see tomorrow.'

Ian Botham, *It Sort Of Clicks*, Willow Books Collins, 1986.

I think he [Norman O'Neill] will play a great innings without being as good all round as he once promised to be. But for all that, I would sooner travel fifty miles to watch an O'Neill innings than cross the road to see some of the record-breakers in action.

Denis Compton, *Denis Compton's Test Diary 1964*, Rigby Ltd, 1964.

Up to this period I had only been a slow leg-break bowler, very accurate and with plenty of spin, but that was all. It was during this season of 1905–6 that I worked out the method of bowling the googly or 'Bosie', after its inventor, Bosanquet. I had to *work it out* as there was no one to show me; I cultivated it in private with my nephew F.E. McElhone (who later became a fine varsity and representative player) and eventually reached a stage when I thought it might be tried against somebody else. Practising one afternoon at the Sydney Cricket Ground, I asked my old friend A.C.K. Mackenzie would he mind if I tried something on him. He was one of the state's best players at the time and only out of our friendship did I have the courage to ask him. He kindly said:

'Bowl anything you like.'

Cricket

I started my usual leg-breaks and then timidly tried my newly discovered 'wrong-un.' It was a full toss and was promptly hit from one end of the ground to the other. Another period of leg-breaks and then my googly full toss again, with the same result. But, just before his practice was over, I made my third effort; luckily this time it hit the ground first and *he played the wrong way for it!* I rushed up and said:

'Why didn't you hit that one, Alec?' And he said:

'I don't know, I just missed it.'

But I knew then that if such a fine player had played the wrong way for the break, well, I had it. I said:

'That was what I wanted to try on you.'

He gave me every encouragement, and in my next grade match I tried it. What a delicious thrill went through me when I collected my first victim – it so obviously 'had' the poor devil, that I knew I had acquired the genuine article.

The acquisition of this ball really enabled me to become a first-class player; and as I evolved a top-spin some two years later, I then had quite a nice little repertoire up my sleeve for the unwary.

H. V. Hordern, the first Australian bowler to develop the 'wrong 'un', describing how he first tested the delivery. From *Googlies*, Angus & Robertson, 1932.

Vic Trumper, beautifully clad in creamy, loose-fitting but well-tailored flannels, left the pavilion with his bat tucked under his left arm and in the act of donning his gloves. Although slightly pigeon-toed in the left foot he had a springy athletic walk and a tendency to shrug his shoulders every few minutes, a habit I understand he developed through trying to loosen his shirt off his shoulders when it became soaked with sweat during his innings.

Arriving at the wicket, he bent his bat handle almost to a right angle, walked up the pitch, prodded about six yards of it, returned to the batting crease and asked the umpire for 'two legs', took a quick glance in the direction of fine leg, shrugged his shoulders again and took up his stance.

I was called to bowl sooner than I had expected. I suspect now that Harry Goddard changed his mind and decided to put me out of my misery early in the piece.

Did I ever bowl that first ball? I don't remember. My head was in a whirl. I really think I fainted and the secret of my mythical first ball has been kept over all these years to save me embarrassment. If the ball *was* sent down it must have been hit for six, or at least four, because I was awakened from my trance by the thunderous booming Yabba who roared: 'O for a strong arm and a walking stick!'

Cricket

I do remember the next ball. It was, I imagined, a perfect leg-break. When it left my hand it was singing sweetly like a humming top. The trajectory couldn't have been more graceful if designed by a professor of ballistics. The tremendous leg-spin caused the ball to swing and curve from the off and move in line with the middle and leg stump. Had I bowled this particular ball at any other batsman I would have turned my back early in its flight and listened for the death rattle. However, consistent with my idolisation of the champion, I watched his every movement.

He stood poised like a panther ready to spring. Down came his left foot to within a foot of the ball. The bat, swung from well over his shoulders, met the ball just as it fizzed off the pitch, and the next sound I heard was a rapping on the off-side fence.

It was the most beautiful shot I have ever seen.

The immortal Yabba made some attempt to say something but his voice faded away to the soft gurgle one hears at the end of a kookaburra's song. The only person on the ground who didn't watch the course of the ball was Victor Trumper. The moment he played it he turned his back, smacked down a few tufts of grass and prodded his way back to the batting crease. He knew where the ball was going.

What were my reactions?

Well, I never expected that ball or any other ball

I could produce to get Trumper's wicket. But that being the best ball a bowler of my type could spin into being, I thought that at least Vic might have been forced to play a defensive shot, particularly as I was almost a stranger too and it might have been to his advantage to use discretion rather than valour.

After I had bowled one or two other reasonably good balls without success I found fresh hope in the thought that Trumper had found Bosanquet, creator of the 'wrong 'un' or 'bosie' (which I think a better name), rather puzzling. This left me with one shot in my locker, but if I didn't use it quickly I would be taken out of the firing line. I decided, therefore, to try this most undisciplined and cantankerous creation of the great B. J. Bosanquet – not, as many may think, as a compliment to the inventor but as the gallant farewell, so to speak, of a warrior who refused to surrender until all his ammunition was spent.

Again fortune was on my side in that I bowled the ball I had often dreamed of bowling. As with the leg-break, it had sufficient spin to curve in the air and break considerably after making contact with the pitch. If anything it might have had a little more top-spin, which would cause it to drop rather suddenly. The sensitivity of a spinning ball against a breeze is governed by the amount of spin imparted, and if a ball bowled at a certain pace drops on a certain spot, one bowled with identical pace but with more top-spin should drop eighteen inches or two feet shorter.

For this reason I thought the difference in the trajectory and ultimate landing of the ball might provide a measure of uncertainty in Trumper's mind. Whilst the ball was in flight this reasoning appeared to be vindicated by Trumper's initial movement. As at the beginning of my over he sprang in to attack but did not realise that the ball, being an off-break, was floating away from him and dropping a little quicker. Instead of his left foot being close to the ball it was a foot out of line.

In a split second Vic grasped this and tried to make up the deficiency with a wider swing of the bat. It was then I could see a passage-way to the stumps with our 'keeper, Con Hayes, ready to claim his victim. Vic's bat came through like a flash but the ball passed between his bat and legs, missed the leg stump by a fraction, and the bails were whipped off with the great batsman at least two yards out of his ground.

Vic had made no attempt to scramble back. He knew the ball had beaten him and was prepared to pay the penalty, and although he had little chance of regaining his crease on this occasion I think he would have acted similarly if his back foot had been only an inch from safety.

As he walked past me he smiled, patted the back of his bat and said, 'It was too good for me.'

There was no triumph in me as I watched the receding figure. I felt like a boy who had killed a dove.

Arthur Mailey, *10 For 66 And All That*, Phoenix Sports Books, 1958.

Mr Augustine Birrell, QC, MP, lectured on Dr Johnson at the London Institute. Some time ago he (the lecturer) met at a supper of the Johnson Club, in Fleet Street, two guests. One was an Irish patriot, who had languished in gaol during a recent political régime. He had asked the Governor of the prison for some book to read – not the Bible – and the Governor gave him *Boswell's Life*. The patriot immediately forgot all about his country's woes and his prison dress, and spent his period of incarceration joyfully. He was now no longer a 'patriot', but he remained a Boswellian. The other guest was Bonnor, the Australian cricketing giant. He declared he had never heard of Johnson till that evening, whereupon somebody was rude enough to titter. The huge cricketer got up and said: 'And, what is more, I come from a great country, where you can ride a horse at sixty miles a day for three months and never meet a soul who has heard of Dr Johnson either. But I can say this much, that if I weren't Bonnor, the cricketer, I should like to have been Dr Johnson.' At this retort a solemn conviction seized his (Mr Birrell's) soul that had the doctor been resurrected in the flesh that night he would have preferred the talk of the Australian cricketer to that of any of the Fleet Street critics gathered round the supper table.

From the *Referee*, February, 1896.

Soon after leaving Malta an army officer was talking about throwing the cricket ball 100 yards. Bonnor, in his usual grandiloquent way, said: '100 yards! 100 yards! Why, I could jerk it!' And so he could. After a little talk, it culminated in a wager of £100 that Bonnor would not throw 115 yds or more with the first throw, and on the first day he landed on English shores. I remember Bonnor coming down on board ship and telling me he had made the wager. Old Caleb Peacock, of Adelaide, was stakeholder. We got to Plymouth, and it was a fine day, so Bonnor, Murdoch, Tom Garrett, and myself got off the boat, the others going on. We tried to get a 5¼oz ball, but could not get any lighter than 5½oz. Before finally agreeing to the ground we went to several places, including The Hoe, but that was down hill – all right for Bonnor, but it did not suit the other party. Then we went to the Racecourse, but that was slippery, and, of course, did not suit us, so at last we arrived at the Barracks in Plymouth. As it was gravel, and there was no wind, all agreed that the conditions were fair. We got hold of the quartermaster – he happened to have a record in the army, for he had thrown 107 yards, I think. When we told him what the event was he became deeply interested. Bonnor got the quartermaster to put a pile of newspapers down as a target, about two feet high, at a distance of 120 yards, to aim at. He was going to throw without taking his waistcoat off. It showed you the cool belief he had in his powers. I insisted on his stripping to the singlet, though he didn't like the idea. He was toying with the ball. 'A man of my inches not being able to throw this little thing 115 yards!' Well, he threw 119 yards 7 inches, and won the wager. I remember the old quartermaster begged for the ball, and we gave it to him. He never dreamt that anyone could throw so far, and he wanted the ball as a souvenir. You ought to have seen 'Bon' the centre of admiration at Plymouth Barracks after that throw. It was a pretty good throw, seeing that Bonnor had been six weeks on board ship.

Cricket

Charles Beal, manager of the 1882 Australian Touring Side, from the *Referee*, November 1914.

The result of a match can depend on the toss of a coin. I always called heads because of a humorous slogan I once saw on a garage wall. It read, 'God gave us two ends: one to sit on and one to think with. Our success depends on which one we use most. Heads we win and tails we lose.' I liked that so I preferred to call heads.

Brian Booth, former Australian captain, *Cricket And Christianity*, Scripture Union Publishing, 1985.

If I could only remember that balls hit on the ground can't be caught, and make it my pet proverb, I'd have these English bowlers looking both ways for Sunday in every match I played.

George Bonnor, quoted by George Giffen in *With Bat And Ball,* Ward Lock, 1898.

A gentleman asked the hitter [George Bonnor] who were the three best batsmen in the world. 'Well,' said Bon, 'you cannot get away from W. G., Billy

Murdoch is not far behind, and,' he concluded, 'I would rather you did not ask me the name of the third one.'

By JW, *Australasian*, January 1921.

When [George] Palmer came over for the first time his accomplishments as a bowler were heralded in the most extravagant fashion by Bonnor, whose unstinted praise struck terror into the hearts of a small circle of acquaintances to whom the great man was holding forth. Bonnor, however, was the most boastful of men, and he nullified – or, rather, considerably lessened – the effect of the impression he had made by adding arily, 'So far as I myself am concerned, I could play him all day with a tooth-pick!' The confession came as a great relief to his hearers, but Palmer was nevertheless destined to obtain numerous triumphs.

F.S. Ashley-Cooper, London *Evening Standard*, April 1919, writing of the 1880s Australian bowler George Palmer – and his team-mate George Bonnor.

I was the fastest bowler that ever lived and so great was my pace that in a match at Orange, after sending down one of my fastest deliveries, which I knew would be snicked in the slips, as I bowled it I ran down the pitch, chased the ball after it had been played and caught it at deep first slip. I could not do it always, but on that day I could do anything.

George Bonnor, quoted in the *Australasian,* 1927.

A pure game that nobody watches is a dead game.

Andrew Caro, the managing director of World Series Cricket, soon after Kerry Packer launched his one-day cricket tournaments, quoted in *The Players*, 1988.

Have nothing to do with coaches. In fact, if you see a coach coming, go and hide behind the pavilion until he goes away.

Bill O'Reilly's advice to a 14-year-old spin bowler who sought his advice at the Sydney Cricket Ground in 1985 on how to improve his game.

The top of my mouth got sunburned while I watched the ball go over.

Bill Tallon, Queensland leg-spin bowler, describing how a New South Wales batsman, Cec Pepper, drove the first ball he bowled to him back high over his head. Quoted by Lew Cooper in a speech, 1988.

We had to travel down south to Adelaide to play the Croweaters. We knocked over the first bastard and we had them one for one. We were bloody excited. Then out came Bradman. Everyone was full of expectancy. Everyone was doing their best, moving in with the bowler, really keen. Bradman was in a fair bit of bloody trouble. His timing was off, and the boys were rubbing their hands with glee. Eventually Phil Hurwood came on and Bradman hit the bloody thing so high in the air that every bastard tried to get under the catch, including the Queensland manager. We caught it. Two for 400!

A story told by the Queensland bowler Bill Tallon and quoted by Lew Cooper, 1996.

I guess, if I'm really honest, that to hold the Sheffield Shield record means I didn't play as much Test cricket as I would have liked.

David Hookes, quoted in the press on the day after he broke

the record for runs scored in Sheffield Shield cricket.

If you play in pyjamas you should expect an occasional nightmare.

Ian Melville in a letter to the *Sydney Morning Herald* on 24 March 1992, after South Africa was eliminated from the World Cup in farcical circumstances because of the tournament rules on rain interruptions.

During our winter of 1892–93 it was recorded that in the course of a game at Bunbury, Western Australia, a player skied a ball into a three-pronged branch of a tall jarrah tree. The umpire declared that, as the ball was in sight, it could not be lost. No axe was procurable to fell the tree, and the ball was eventually brought down by a shot from a rifle, but not before the batsmen had run 286! So far as we are aware this stands as the largest number of runs obtained in the course of an over.

From an editor's note in *Cricket: A Weekly Record Of The Game*, 10 June 1911.

At Laidley, Queensland, on New Year's Day, a bowler named James Higgins, of the Milton CC, bowled a bail 51 yards [nearly 47 metres]. The distance was measured by four of the players.

An item in *Cricket: A Weekly Record Of The Game*, 27 February 1908.

By the way, we hear that the Melbourne barrackers say JWHT stands for 'Johnny Won't Hit Today.' This is ingenious, but rather unkind.

A gossip item in *Rugby Football And Cricket*, 2 December 1911. This seems to be one of the earliest references to the nickname which the England player J. W. H. T. Douglas acquired in Australia and by which he was universally known when he captained the first England side to tour Australia after World War I in 1920–21.

A peculiar accident happened to a batsman in a match Sackville v Windsor, on the former's wicket, a few days ago. He failed to strike a ball, which struck one of his pockets wherein reposed a box of wax matches, igniting them; but, beyond consuming a portion of his clothing and singeing his side, no damage was done.

Cricket

An item in the *Referee*, 17 November 1909.

The Aboriginal cricketers are this week trying their skills against an eleven of the Albert Club. This is a novel match, but a useful one. Fellow cricketers must be recognised as fellow men, and it may be discovered, even through the medium of an amusement, that colour does not destroy humanity and that 'blackfellow' is fit for something better than to be shot down or killed by the vices of civilisation.

An item in the *Sydney Mail*, 23 February 1867.

England achieved the impossible here yesterday. They got even worse.

Ian Todd in the London *Sun* after yet another England batting collapse against Australia in the fourth Test at Old Trafford, 1989.

I opened once with Charlie Macartney, and as we walked out he said, 'Keep your eyes open for the first ball, son. I'll take strike.' I thought he meant that there would be a quick, stolen single and I was doubly anxious to respond to the Great Man's call. But the first ball came hurtling back like a meteorite and was crashing against the fence while the umpire, the bowler and I were still prone to the grass as if in an air-raid. I picked myself up and met Charlie in the middle. 'It's always a good idea,' he confided, 'to aim the first ball right at the bowler's head. They don't like it. It rattles them.'

Jack Fingleton, *Masters Of Cricket*, William Heinemann, 1958.

Don, Don, lay the willow on;
there was none like you before you;
there'll be none when you are gone.

Come and bat again before us
till the arching sky that's o'er us
rattles with the mighty chorus:
'Don, Don, Don!'

From a *Sunday Sun–Guardian* supplement, November 1936.

My life has been peopled by great cricketing names – and great characters. This book is about most of them.

Cricket

They include the peerless Wally Hammond, who, I suspect, vetoed my one real chance of a Test place, and Don Bradman, who figures in the title of this book. At Taunton in 1938 he gave me his wicket. He took a blind swipe and I bowled him. Hence the light-hearted greeting I've used ever since when meeting someone for the first time, 'Shake the hand that bowled Bradman'.

Perhaps I should add that he had scored 202 at the time.

Bill Andrews, a Somerset all-rounder in a preface to his memoirs, *The Hand That Bowled Bradman*, MacDonald, 1973.

We have no objection to a little *humorous* chaff, either in the field or out of it, but we certainly condemn that low slang and insulting remarks, so often resorted to by the Australians – it is much to their discredit.

Possibly the first reference to sledging in Australian cricket. From a report of a match between the Australian and Union clubs in Sydney, *Commercial Journal*, February 1838.

I reckon (said Dad) that the country's pests
Is this here wireless an' these here Tests.

Up to the house and around the door,
Stretchin' their ears for to catch the score,
Leavin' the horses down in the crop.
Can you wonder a farmer goes off pop?

I'm yellin' at Jim or I'm cursin at Joe
All hours of the day; but it ain't no go –
Leavin' their work and hangin' around
When they think I'm down by the fallow ground;
Sneaking away when I start to rouse,
An', as soon as me back's turned, back at the house.

'Who got Wyatt? Is Sutcliffe out?'
Wot do they care if I rave an' shout?
Bribin' young Bill for to leave his job
To twiddle the switches an' twist the knob.
'Has he made his century? Who's in now?' . . .
And I bought that machine for the price of a cow!

There's a standin' crop, an' the rain's not far,
An' the price is rotten, but there you are:
As soon as these cricketin' games begin
The farm goes dilly on listenin' in;
Not only boys an' the harvester crew,
But Mum an' the girls gits dotty too.
An' I reckon (said Dad) that a man's worst pests
Is this here wireless an' these here Tests.

Cricket

C. J. Dennis, *Dad On The Test.*

Ev'ry morning on the radio, the news comes from
    Australia
The English batsmen once again have had a ghastly
    failure
It was Lilian Thomson's bowling once again caused
    the collapse
I always thought Test Cricket was intended just for
    chaps
But Lilian Thomson is Australia's finest flower
A maiden bowling overs at a hundred miles an hour.

She's the fastest lady bowler that the world has ever
    seen
Her bumper's awe-inspiring and her language far
    from clean
Just imagine the reaction of Greig or Knott or Amiss
As this six foot six of Sheila runs up, do you wonder
    they miss?

She hit Randall on the ankle, then she hit him on
    the forehead
She finds the happy medium she could hurt him
    something horrid.

She's Lilian Thomson, the first of cricket's dames

A mixture of Joan Sutherland, Rolf Harris, or Clive
  James
She'll hit you on the temple, in the groin or knee
  and kidney,
To prove that liberated Adelaide's as good as Sydney.

Richard Stilgoe, 'Lilian Thomson', *Bat & Pad*, Oxford University Press, 1984.

I remember playing in a match and batting with
Macartney when cover point came within fifteen
yards of him. Charlie issued an ultimatum to him
to get back, otherwise Charlie would not be responsible if the fieldsman was seriously injured.

Hunter 'Stork' Hendry, from an article in *Middle & Leg –
Memorable Cricketing Moments From The Game's Cavaliers*, edited by Jack Pollard, Macmillan, 1988.

While the England team was touring Australia in
1994–95 and losing match after match, Sir Donald
Bradman was asked what he thought he would
average against the current England attack. After
thinking for a moment, Sir Donald replied: 'Probably about fifty.' Surprised, the other said: 'But
surely, Sir Donald, you'd average more than that.

Cricket

After all, you averaged nearly 100 in Tests, facing bowling attacks that were much stronger than this one.'

'True,' Sir Donald said, 'but you must remember – I am eighty-five years old.'

A version of a fictional story of unrecorded origin, which circulated widely during the England tour.

I said nothing to him at any time and I was very surprised when he came up behind me and kicked me. I was lucky I wasn't badly hurt because he was wearing spikes.

Javed Miandad, speaking about his famous confrontation with Dennis Lillee at Perth. Quoted in the *Cricketer*, January 1982.

If she bowled as fast as Thomson, with the guile of Lindwall, the hostility of Lillee, batted with the panache of Ian Chappell and the grace of Greg Chappell and kept wickets as well as Marsh or Knott, the dear lady would still not play in my cricket team.

Don Chipp, MHR, in reference to Senator Ruth Coleman's

request to play in the Parliament's cricket team in Canberra. Quoted in the *Cricketer*, March 1976.

If they [the Australian Cricket Board] don't cooperate, they'll walk straight into a meat mangler.

Kerry Packer during the World Series Cricket revolution. Quoted in the *Cricketer*, May 1977.

In the ten years I was in the centre, I was so fit I could have won the Melbourne Cup.

Bill O'Reilly. Quoted in the *Cricketer*, January 1980.

Australia is bright, brash, noisy but friendly but the country is all the same. They are nice people but there is no variety. I have a fancy to write a book about Australia. The Australians would hate it but I would be out of the country by then.

John Arlott in a letter from Australia to his secretary in England during the 1954–55 Ashes tour. Quoted by Timothy Arlott in *John Arlott – A Memoir*, Andrew Deutsch, 1994.

Cricket

The problem at the moment, from our point of view, is that [John] Howard is like a batsman who pushes and prods and bores everyone to sobs because he's so careful. Give him a rank full toss outside the off stump and instead of hitting it for four he pushes it past point for a single. Yet the real problem isn't that he's boring: it's that he's hard to get out. And he's hard to get out because he doesn't make mistakes. Some time in this election campaign the new ball will have to be taken to try and blast him out.

Michael Duffy, former Labor minister, during the 1996 federal election campaign. Quoted by the political writer Alan Ramsey in the *Sydney Morning Herald*.

We've lost a couple of wickets. One bloke got out after an impressive 75 and there was another one who had to retire hurt because when he went to tea one of our supporters slapped him too hard on the back. The opposition tried Carmen Lawrence for an over, but she had to be taken off for tampering with the ball. Ralph Willis ... had a few very sloppy overs with the new ball and he's now been confined to fine leg.

John Howard describing the first week of the 1996 federal election campaign.

One-day cricket's fine to play, but in a week's time you won't remember who's done what.

Allan Border, quoted in *Inside Sport*, November 1992.

It will be wonderful if England wins, not least because no one crows quite like an Australian when the Poms are getting a stuffing. Unlike England, Australia has a unique safety valve to losing: it pretends it isn't happening. The Test score suddenly gets relegated to the small print, alongside the Too-woomba tiddlywinks results or the Alice Springs small-bore rifle shooting.

Christopher Martin-Jenkins, *The Independent*, 1994.

I just hope they don't shake a coconut tree in the Caribbean and a black Shane Warne drops out.

Robin Smith, quoted in *Inside Sport*, March 1994.

I recall a supposedly true story that my father related to me long ago about an Australian cricket fan who travelled to England to watch Bradman in his heyday and was billeted at an English cricket fan's home. He and the Pom were at one of the Tests and Australia was batting when he realised that he had left his wallet at the house, so he excused himself and went back to the house. On his return he said to the Pom that he had bad news for him and it was that when he went back to the Pom's home he had caught the Pom's wife in bed with the bloke next door. The Pom turned to the Aussie and said he had even worse news for the Aussie. 'How do you mean?' said the Aussie. 'Bradman's out!' replied the Pom.

James R. Quested of Lightning Ridge in a letter to the *Sydney Morning Herald*, August 1993.

I never saw a technical weakness in Bradman except that he did not like the really fast stuff, particularly if it was lifting a bit, but, then, nobody does. I don't think Bradman would have liked batting against the West Indians, but I think he would have made runs against them.

Bob Wyatt, England vice-captain on the bodyline tour 1932–33, when asked in a 1987 interview how he thought Don Bradman would have fared against the current West Indian pace attack.

A fair impression of a typical Bradman innings may be gained by thinking of all the best strokes one has ever seen, all played by one man in the course of an afternoon.

Ian Peebles, *Talking Of Cricket*, Museum Press, 1953.

[Monty] Noble, the Australian skipper, tells an amusing story of the way he, as a young man, specially noted and worked out an attack against the single weakness of Vernon Ransford. Ransford, an immovable batsman, had an Achilles heel in a certain pull to square-leg. Noble spent hours and hours perfecting a ball to take advantage of it, and then, in an interstate match, after bowling six overs of ordinary stuff to soothe the sticky left-hander into unsuspiciousness, bowled that ball. Ransford fell headlong into the trap – but square-leg was dozing, and the ball hit him on the head. Ransford then went on and made a century.

Learie Constantine, *How To Play Cricket*, Eyre & Spottiswoode, 1951.

As a captain, this man has transformed Australia from a team which used to struggle against battlers like New Zealand and Sri Lanka to a team which today can struggle against really good teams.

Andrew Denton, speaking at an Allan Border tribute dinner in Sydney, January 1994.

Australians will always fight for those twenty-two yards. Lord's and its tradition belong to Australia just as much as to England.

Prime Minister John Curtin, speaking during World War II. Quoted by Denzil Batchelor in *The Changing Face Of Cricket*, Eyre & Spottiswoode, 1966.

When I first saw Keith Miller bowl, he was a member of Lindsay Hassett's services side playing in the Victory Test at Old Trafford against Hammond's team in 1945. As a boy of fifteen, I had to lie on the grass because of a capacity crowd and peer between the straddled legs of a policeman at the awesome sight of Keith Miller in full flight. In those days he was a fearsome prospect. He ran like his beloved gee-gees the length of the Randwick straight and bowled like a willy-willy in an enveloping halo of hair. He made George Pope and

Bill Edrich look like the maiden aunts of carthorses in comparison to his ferocity and athleticism.

Frank Tyson, *Cricket And Other Diversions*, Newspress, 1978.

I went around to the Australian dressing room to say how sorry we were he had been so badly hurt. Our reception was freezing. Woodfull had just taken a shower-bath, and we found him with a towel wrapped around him, and the following conversation passed. We said how sorry we were, and Woodfull replied, 'I don't want to see you, Mr Warner. There are two teams out there. One is trying to play cricket and the other is not.' I replied, 'Apart from all that, we most sincerely hope you are not too badly hurt,' and he answered, 'The bruise is coming out,' and there certainly was a very livid mark over his heart. We then left the room.

Pelham Warner, England team manager on the 'bodyline' tour of 1932–33, describing how he was rebuked by the Australian captain, Bill Woodfull, who had earlier been struck a severe blow in the chest by a Harold Larwood bumper in the third Test at Adelaide. From *Cricket Between Two Wars*, Sporting Handbooks, 1942.

Cricket

Bradman is a living witness to the very important truth that men are not equal.

St Pancras parish magazine, Chichester, UK.

Through all, his play reflected that inner enjoyment which, rarely seen in Test matches, expresses the chief purpose for which cricket was invented.

R. C. Robertson-Glasgow writing of Keith Miller in *More Cricket Prints – Some Batsmen And Bowlers 1920–1945*, T. Werner Laurie, 1948.

Don Bradman was very nervous before going into bat for at least the first half of his career, and I think it was always the same, but he contrived to hide the signs later. The first time I ever saw him on a cricket field, in a match on our 1928–29 tour, he was playing for New South Wales and I remember asking Pat Hendren who the slim boy was. 'Oh, he's a lad from the backblocks called Bradman – bats a bit, they say. But he looks too frightened to do much today!' was what Pat answered. We were to learn better before the game was over, for young Don scored 87 and 132 not out.

Wally Hammond, *Cricket's Secret History*, Stanley Paul, 1952.

Cricket has this command over people like me, not because it produces statistics (heaven knows I see enough of those every day), but because it produces a million things of beauty for the eye. It is not only a game – it is a fine art. Whenever I get the chance, and in recent years it comes all too seldom, of going to a cricket match, I reserve a particular place in Hades for the wretched fellow who wants to sit with me and talk about politics when all my attention is rivetted upon the beautiful artistry with which Lindsay Hassett can get his feet into position to a ball that swings and drops at the last moment.

Robert Menzies in a foreword to *Bumper*, Latimer House Ltd.

An Australian batsman, famed for his souvenir hunting, attended a reception at the Duke of Portland's palatial Welbeck Abbey. Noticing two of the famous Australian racehorse Carbine's hoofs mounted in gold resting on the mantlepiece in the duke's 'sports museum' he asked his host, 'How about letting me have a couple of those hoofs?' 'My dear man,' responded His Grace, 'Carbine was a horse, not a centipede.'

R. S. Whitington, *Bumper*, Latimer House Ltd, 1953.

What a pity. I was just dropping into a length.

'Chuck' Fleetwood-Smith, on learning that England had closed its innings at 7 for 903 in the Oval Test, 1938. Fleetwood-Smith had taken 1 for 298 in 87 overs. Source unknown.

If I happen to get hit out there, keep Mum from jumping the fence.

Stan McCabe to his father before going to pad up during the first 'bodyline' Test in Sydney, December 1932. McCabe had been sitting with his parents, who had come down from Grenfell to see their son play. McCabe played his famous innings of 187 not out in this match. Quoted in *People*, November 1952.

It was impossible to keep one of them straight, he was useless altogether, owing to his drinking propensities . . . More than once I had to defend myself from the attacks of drunken brutes, and threats were made galore.

Victor Cohen, manager of the Australian team that toured England in 1893, speaking of his unruly players. Quoted in the *Argus*, December 1893.

In 1893, when the Australians were playing against eighteen of Blackpool, an amusing incident occurred during the local men's innings. Arthur Coningham was fielding in the 'country'. It was a cold, raw day, and the Australians were playing in their sweaters. The batting not being too brilliant or lively, the outfields had little to do, and the idea evidently struck Coningham that he would like to get warm, so he gathered up some bits of sticks and grass, piled them up, and then asked one of the spectators for a match. Having obtained this, he set fire to the little pile of grass and commenced to warm his hands. It amused a section of the spectators, who applauded him, and one wag suggested he should go inside and get a couple of hot potatoes to put in his pocket.

C. T. B. Turner, *The Quest For Bowlers*, Cornstalk Publishing, 1926.

Cricket

Getting out to a girl may have been an issue at the back of his mind.

Zoe Goss, Australian woman cricketer, after bowling Brian Lara in a charity match at the Sydney Cricket Ground, December 1994. Quoted in the *Age*, 19 December 1994.

The Australians were quartered in a marquee, 1878 belonging to the pre-pavilion days so far as many English grounds were concerned. With a characteristic want of knowledge in colonial matters, an imprudent spectator tried his idea of 'black-fellow' talk upon our boys. Sauntering into their enclosure, he began, 'You talkee Engliss allee same?' 'Certainly,' replied Conway, 'and we act English, too.' He thereupon seized the astonished Britisher and tossed him over the pickets.

Nat Lee, *Tasmanian Mail*. Lee was writing about John Conway, manager of the Australian team that toured England in 1878, after Conway's death in 1909.

One of the leading sections of Lawson's squadron followed Lieutenant Burton as they raced at the trenches. The four troopers and Burton were old Gallipoli men; all were shot dead as they flung themselves from their horses within a few feet of the enemy. The mounted stretcher-bearers rode forward, as they always did, with the advanced light horse lines, and worked coolly in the midst of the dismounted fight round the earthworks. While so engaged Private A. Cotter, the famous Sydney fast bowler, was shot dead by a Turk at close range. As has already been recorded, he had at the second Gaza engagement been singled out for fine work under heavy fire; he behaved in action as a man without fear.

An account of Tibby Cotter's death in the *Official War History Vol VII.*

When 'Johnny-Won't-Hit-Today' Douglas comes to write his memoirs, 'My 97 Years of Cricket at Home and Abroad', I bet he won't remember a certain cricket match played on the sands of the Mediterranean coast of Southern Palestine between the British Yeomanry and the Australian Light Horse. Both divisions were having a short rest and a clean up on the coast. The Yeomanry, led by Gentlemen from the Very Best Families of England, sent the Light Horse Commander a challenge to a game of cricket. Our scouting parties had seen the Tommy officers sporting themselves in flannels in the cool of the evening. Anyhow, we took them on.

Douglas was a Colonel of the Yeomanry, although I never rightly knew whether he was in the Warwicks, the Worcesters, or the Gloucesters. He was always there when it came to a cricket match or a fight according to the Marquis of Queensberry.

We had a few sets of cricketing tools bought out of certain regimental funds – never mind whose funds. The desert sand, watered and stamped with tibbin by the Kamleelah wallahs, made a pretty fair concrete pitch.

The Yeomanry team, all officers, was a treat to see in spotless flannels. The officers were always punctilious about appearance and cleanliness even in the desert. How they carried their boudoirs about the desert was a marvel.

Our team looked like a mob of Murrumbidgee whalers who had lost their swags. A few of the officers were in khaki slacks and shirts, and the other ranks wore their old blue-grey flannel shirts, riding strides with the knees out for the most part, no leggings, and their knitted socks hanging down over their ankle boots.

Our fellows won the toss, and had a bat. They put up only 57, Douglas getting most of the wickets.

Then the Yeomanry took block. That's about all they did take. Tibby Cotter, a trooper in the 12th Light Horse Regiment, bowled with the wind behind him, and the Tommy officers never saw which way he went. They just walked in and out in a dazed manner. We had four men behind the stumps to stop any risk of byes getting into double figures.

Clive Single, Colonel of our ambulance, bowled from the other end. He had been high in Grade cricket in Sydney and had a good University career – as far as cricket went, anyhow. He bowled a mixed over of slow and medium balls breaking in from both sides.

Cotter and Single bowled the Yeomanry all for 4, including one bye.

'Who is this Cotter man?' they kept asking. Douglas had spotted Cotter the first time he made his characteristic long run before bowling, but thought it wise not to break the news to the batsmen beforehand.

They took it like sportsmen when they knew. It hardly seemed fair. They squared it off with us later – but that is another story.

Poor old Tibby Cotter was given out at Beersheba later. He was in the front of the mounted charge.

By 'Sergeant', Melbourne *Evening Sun*, November 1924.

I was 'Tibby' Cotter's cobber in the 12th Light Horse

and on the night of 30 October 1917, we were at Khallassa, in Southern Palestine, the most remote portion of the southern position. We watered our horses there, and prepared to move off in the attack on Beersheba.

'Tibby' was one of the best foragers in the AIF. He would come to light with a bottle of champagne in the middle of the desert, and the lads in the section all looked to him to turn up with something unusual.

About 1.30 on the morning of the attack, 'Tibby' who had received instructions to report to Echlon on a guard, turned up at the unit. He said to me: 'Bluey, I've skittled a Turk in one hit; and what do you think he had on him? Here it is – a yard of ling.'

He wasn't going to Echelon, he insisted, but said he would treat the boys to a Stammell fish supper in Beersheba, and be damned to the consequences.

We moved off at 4.30 a.m. from Khallassa, and attacked Beersheba that afternoon. 'Tibby' was next to me on one side in the charge, and Trooper Jack Beasley on the other. Rex Cowley was there also. The other three were skittled by a machine-gun, and after we had cleared the Turks out, the troops went back half-an-hour later to bury the dead.

'Tibby' was still alive when I got to him, and he recognised me. 'Blue', he said, 'You can have the fish supper on your own.' He died shortly afterwards.

He should never have been in the charge. Had he obeyed orders, he would probably have been alive today.

Just before we left Khallassa, 'Tibby' – who, in a bowling competition at Tel-el-Fara, bowled over 18 single stumps at full pace out of 24 – took up a ball of mud, and throwing it into the air, said: 'That's my last bowl, Blue; something is going to happen.'

By 'Blue'.

So much guesswork by the media over this so-called 'hoodoo' among the batsmen has prompted this despatch. Among a lot of guesses it is now the popular belief that it is 13 less than 100. The true story is a simple one.

When Don Bradman was hitting centuries, double and triple centuries, I saw Victorian fast bowler Harry Alexander bowl Bradman for 87 in the Vic.-NSW match when I was a kid sitting in the outer. It stuck in my mind – what a great delivery to bowl the great man with when he was scurrying to get another century-plus.

Looking through various scores in all grades of cricket, somehow the dismissal at 87 often appeared. Later, when playing for South Melbourne

Cricket Club, Ian Johnson, now Secretary of the MCC, was dismissed at 87. I remarked that I expected it. I then told him the story.

Johnson and I later played together for Australia usually fielding together in slips. A few more dismissals at 87 and we were laughing at this odd dismissal number. Soon it caught on among the other players, with no explanation for this strange dismissal number.

The TV, radio and press in recent years have put more emphasis on this hoodoo number, with wild guesses as to its origin.

To check my facts, I recently looked up the record books. Thumbing through, there it was – the year 1931. Vic. versus NSW at the MCG Bradman bowled Alexander 89. What – not 87!!

Obviously, as a kid, the last time I looked at the scoreboard, Bradman was 87. Obviously a couple of runs went unnoticed before his dismissal. So 87 should in effect be 89. Let it stay 87.

Keith Miller, *Bat & Pad*, Oxford University Press, 1984.

CRICKET (crikk-itt in England, criggit in Australia). Like living in igloos, skateboarding and eating tripe, unless taught at birth it remains forever as unfathomable as nuclear physics.

Keith Dunstan.

When I made the Shield team at the age of sixteen my first captain was the mighty Keith Miller. I will never forget my first match with him. He had always been a boyhood hero of mine and I was delighted at the prospect of playing under him. As we walked onto the field I stuck close to him thinking, 'Well, here I am beside a great man.' I followed him to the centre and waited to be sent to my position. He stood by the pitch surrounded by the crowd of players. Suddenly he looked around. I thought, 'Now he'll really show me what to do as a captain and set the field.' He said just one word – 'Scatter'. And that's what the fieldsmen did – they scattered to their positions.

Bob Simpson, *Captain's Story*, Stanley Paul, 1966.

It was another club match at Chatswood against Gordon. Sid Carroll, a fine player, was batting against a young Alan Walker, who in these days before he went to England was very, very quick.

Dud Fraser was keeping, Eddie Robinson at first slip, Miller at second slip, and Philpott in the gully. Fraser, Robinson and Miller were talking about the races, Keith with his usual animation on that subject, and I was frozen in terror-stricken concentration as Walker hurtled his thunderbolts short of a length, and Carroll slashed hard at every one of them. A full-blooded cut or jet-propelled snick was due any ball.

When it did come, Miller was in mid-conversation with Robinson. He barely missed a word. As the ball flew at a thousand miles an hour, Keith casually reached out a left hand, caught it, flicked it to the keeper, and continued his discussion of the horses.

Disconsolate, Carroll trailed off the ground, while a very young gully fieldsman still could not quite get his jaws back together.

Peter Philpott, *A Spinner's Yarn*, ABC Books, 1990.

I met Trumper in opposition in a grade match on the Chatswood Oval. If I had ordered the wicket it could not have been more to my liking. It was what we get so rarely in this country, a fiery one; in other words, fastish, inclined to kick, and the ball easily turnable on it. No slow bowler could ask for better, and I was in absolute top-hole form. Trumper collected some 12 runs off my first over. My second was delivered to the late F.A. Iredale (at that period still a fine batsman) and 'tied him up' very badly. My third was to

Trumper. He started to operate on me again, and one ball in particular stands out in my memory, because, for the fraction of a second, I thought it had bowled him. It was a perfect length leg-break, pitched some three or four inches outside the leg-stump, and broke sharply into the wicket. Trumper played so late that I almost saw it hit his wicket, but within a few inches of the stumps his bat flashed, and he cut the ball to the boundary past point.

Now, what could one do? That individual ball could not have been better if a *machine* had delivered it, and yet it was brilliantly hit for four! As I sorrowfully watched it speed on its way to the boundary, Frank Iredale said to me:

'You never bowl me any of that "tripe" when I'm down that end.' I turned to him and said:

'My dear Frank, it's the same "tripe" that's got you tied up, which Victor is hitting for four.'

H. V. Hordern, Australian leg-spin bowler, *Googlies*, Angus & Robertson, 1932.

My God, that must have been the most boring innings you've ever had to sit through.

Bob Cowper, speaking in the dressing room after he took twelve hours and eleven minutes to make 307 against

Cricket

England at Melbourne in February 1966. Quoted by Ian Wooldridge in the *Daily Mail*, 1984.

Gee, what a beauty! That's the best ball I've ever seen bowled.

An exuberant Alan Davidson early in his career, after he bowled Ken Archer with a beautiful, late-swinging delivery in a Sheffield Shield match. Quoted by Keith Miller in *Sporting Life*, February 1954.

Keith Miller could be a down-to earth realist when the occasion justified it. At Manchester, Jim Laker had placed England in an unassailable position. Australia was 375 runs behind on the first innings and the cause was lost. Ian Johnson, however, endeavoured to rally the team. He said with some feeling. 'We can fight our way back. We need guts and determination. We can still save the match.' Miller, sitting in the corner of the room, lifted his head from a racing guide and commented indifferently: 'Bet you 6/4 we can't.'

Alan Davidson, *Fifteen Paces*, Souvenir Press, 1963.

Alec Bedser was to dismiss me eighteen times in Tests and once, when somebody asked me why, I remember saying, 'Well, he must be a better bowler than I am a batsman.'

Arthur Morris, *Sydney Morning Herald*, December 1965.

The original plan had been to go to England on the *Chimborazo,* but when this vessel was wrecked on Point Perpendicular we had to make a rush to Sydney to catch the *City of Sydney* to San Francisco. This was the only hope we had of getting to England in time to play our first match. We had about three days in which to make the journey from Melbourne. Leaving at six in the morning we got as far as Wodonga by the mail train. Thence we went to Albury, where a special coach awaited us. Thirty hours later we caught the train at Bowning and arrived at Sydney at seven o'clock in the morning. That afternoon at three o'clock we sailed on the Frisco boat.

We arrived at Frisco on a Friday about eight in the evening, and left on the following morning on a seven-day train journey to New York. The day we arrived there we went aboard the *City of Berlin*, and nine days later arrived in Liverpool. That was on a Monday night, and as our first match was against Notts on the Thursday we proceeded at once to Nottingham. We had a big reception at the railway station, and evidently the locals expected a team of black men. One of them remarked to his neighbour. 'They bain't black, Bill,' but as he spoke Dave Gregory, Bill Murdoch and Blackham appeared on the scene, and he exclaimed, 'But those three chaps have black blood in them.' We were rather badly beaten in this opening match. Not knowing any of the fine points of the game, we fielded in the rain, and naturally our bowlers were unable to do any good with a sodden ball.

Tom Garrett, a member of the first representative Australian side to visit England, in 1878, describing the rush to arrive in time for the opening match in an article in the *Sunday News* (date unknown).

Quite a sensation has been caused in the Queensland cricket world by the resolution of the Kilkivan-Murgon Cricket Association to debar Eddie Gilbert, the Aboriginal fast bowler, who has represented Queensland in Brisbane and southern states, from bowling on concrete wickets. The ground for the decision was that his bowling was too dangerous for any but turf wickets. The Barambah Club, of which

Gilbert is a prominent member, has advised the Kilkivan-Murgon Cricket Association that if such a ban
is held on the Aborigine it was practically certain
they would withdraw from the competition. An
effort was made at a delegate meeting of the Association to secure a promise from the Barambah Club
that Gilbert would bowl at only half pace in competition matches. The promise was refused in view
of the fact it would prevent Gilbert getting the
proper practice for interstate and international
cricket.

An item in the *Australian Cricketer*, October 1931.

Gilbert then took the ball. It came over so fast that
Wendell Bill edged a catch to the wicket-keeper.
Bradman then came in and fell over backwards in
trying to dodge the second ball of Gilbert's over. It
clipped the peak of his cap and knocked it off his
head. The next ball smashed the bat clean out of
Bradman's hands for the first and only time in his
career. He swung at the next two balls and was completely beaten by each. Gilbert's sixth delivery
struck the batsman on the body. Attempting to hook
the seventh ball Bradman nicked a catch to the
wicket-keeper and Gilbert had taken 2–0. When
someone sympathised with Bradman about his

dismissal when he returned to the pavilion he smilingly said, 'It was the luckiest duck I ever made.'

From an article in the Sydney *Daily Mirror*, 1982.

George Giffen was playing first-grade cricket at sixteen. To encourage the boy's development, his father had a rule that unless he made a good score in the afternoon he went to bed on Saturday night without dinner. By the time he was twenty Giffen was one of the best players in South Australia.

From an article in the Sydney *Sun*, November 1975.

I take cricket a bit more seriously these days. I think it's because I realise I'm a better player than I thought I was.

Gary Gimour, quoted by the Sydney *Sun*, October 1976.

An appeal was made for a catch at the wicket against Charlton, and [the umpire] Briscoe disallowed it, whereupon Grace said to him, 'You'll not give anyone out; it is unpardonable; we might as well go home tomorrow.' The remark was grossly offensive, and Briscoe, when the innings was over, reported the matter to McDonnell, the New South Wales captain, and declined to go out again. If McDonnell had acted as he should have done, he would have insisted on Grace apologising for the remark and refused to allow the match to go on until it was forthcoming. As it was, the umpire, who had merely done his duty, was snubbed, another was appointed in his place and the match went on without him. Remembering Grace's offensive expression to Bruce on the cricket field in Melbourne not long ago, Australians will be justified in concluding that the England captain is not becoming more courteous as he grows older, and we have a strong suspicion that much of the complacency exhibited towards him here is due to the fact that it is considered he may have something to do in making or marring the success of the tour of the next Australian team in England. What a fine homily would be delivered by the English papers upon the 'uncouth Australians' if a colonial had said such a thing on an English cricket field, and what would be thought of the English captain who backed down before the offender?

An article in the *Sydney Mail*, February 1892, after W. G. Grace questioned an umpire's decision in a match in Sydney between his English team and New South Wales.

Cricket

John McCarthy Blackham was born at Fitzroy, Melbourne, on 11 May 1855. His height is 5 feet 11 inches; weight, 11 stone 3 pounds. I was very much tempted to put him at the head of the Australian cricketers I have met; for it can be said of him, as it can be said of no other Australian, that he is without a rival in his own particular branch of the game. Blackham has a genius for wicket-keeping, but it is a genius that has been built up by stern hard work and pluck. He has been a member of every team that has come to us. Before he had been a month in England in 1878 his quickness with the gloves was the theme of admiration; today he has still no equal behind the sticks.

Above all other wicket-keepers he is noted for standing close to the wicket, and taking the ball and knocking off the bails as one action. He is marvellously quick, taking shooters between the wickets and the pads with comparative ease. The quality of the bowling makes no difference to him, for he is equally at home with fast or slow. I believe he was the first to teach us at home to dispense with a longstop against fast bowling, but it must be remembered that he has always been used to good bowling, and has had no occasion to look out for erratic balls. He never funks, and seems partial to hard knocks, but it is his stamina that has elicited our admiration most. The wear and tear he has gone through in the last twelve years is without parallel. I have no need to say that he has kept wickets more than once in a fairly long innings without giving a single extra.

W. G. Grace's appreciation of Jack Blackham, *Forty Years Of Cricket*, 1890. Grace erred with Blackham's date of birth. It was 11 May 1854.

The world has not seen his equal, nor anybody approaching his equal, in the consistency and degree of his big scores. I particularly stress the word consistency. Some of aesthetic tastes might have preferred the cultured charm of a Kippax or a Jackson to Bradman's flaying piece; I saw Macartney and knew his genius to be of a different mould from that of Bradman. Repute also has Trumper to be of a different mould; but, in the sheer consistency and robust profligacy of their respective arts, Bradman far outshone all others, the English eras of Grace, MacLaren, Hayward and Hobbs not excluded.

Other individuals might have been noted for fast footwork, unerring judgment or brilliant eyesight. Bradman possessed all these; but, if there was one faculty which made him superior to others, it was in being able to judge, almost as soon as the ball left the bowler's hand, the length, spin and merit of that particular delivery. Therein lay much of his greatness – a quicker brain, a quicker judgment than any other batsman I have seen.

But a batsman does not place himself on a pinnacle such as Bradman occupied by virtue of any one, two or three outstanding gifts. Bradman was richly endowed in all that went towards making the champion, and in none more so than in his twinkling, magical feet. I have tried to dissect their movements from the distance of the pavilion and from the closeness of the opposite batting end; but Bradman's feet were almost too quick for me, especially against slow bowlers.

A friend of mine once had an interesting conversation with Ponsford about Bradman's batting. When asked why it was that Bradman made batting look so easy, Ponsford, with his usual modesty, replied: 'The reason is very simple. Don sees the ball about two yards sooner than any of the rest of us.'

Ponsford meant by that exactly what I have written – that Bradman was able to judge the merits of the ball two yards or so sooner than any other batsman. This, in turn, gave him what I consider the greatest advantage he possessed over all contemporary batsmen. He played forward more, he played up the wicket more than any other first-class batsman I knew, and no bowler likes to see a batsman coming forward with confidence and attacking good length balls. Unusual height with its long reach enabled Woolley to cover by forward play ordinarily good length balls; Bradman, a smallish man, got to where he wanted by quick footwork. J.M. Taylor hit Tate hard off his back foot; Bradman hit him hard off his front, delighting in the fact that Tate's excessive pace off the pitch gave him additional speed off the bat. Where most batsmen instinctively swayed on to the back foot to cope with this Tate pace off the pitch, Bradman went forward gleefully to make the most of it.

His batting stance was unique. His bat touched the ground between his feet, not behind them, like every other batsman and photograph I have seen. He stood perfectly still as the bowler approached; the end of his bat did not act as an escape conductor for energy with that nervous tap, tap, tap on the pitch so common to most batsmen as the bowler ran to deliver the ball.

Bradman at the wickets was completely at ease and at rest until the ball began its apologetic advance towards him. His lithe, compact body was a power-house of latent electricity until the switch of a ball released was turned, and then his brightness flashed in all directions. His feet took him into immediate position to offset swerve, swing or break bowling; his running feet took his three and even four yards up the pitch to slow bowling to kill the break and take advantage of the gap in the field which his eye had detected. He was at his best in making the placement of a field look foolish. He was at his greatest against slow bowling (he took 30 off a six-ball Freeman over at Folkestone in 1934), for he moved far out to the ball on the full or drew back to destroy its length and pull in that unorthodox manner which grew with him on the concrete wickets of his country youth.

I remember Bradman in his first appearance at the Sydney nets. There was a breeze of the bush and bygone years in the braces he wore, but there his rusticity ended. He was the cynosure of all eyes, and well-intentioned critics, as they always do, converged on him at the finish of his net and talked to him of his stance, his unorthodoxy on the leg-side. They would have had him change this or do that, but Bradman gave them a polite ear and then promptly dismissed them from his thoughts, internationals and ex-internationals though they were. Even at that age Bradman possessed pronounced qualities. Confidence in his own ability and interpretation of the game was one of them.

The story is told of him in those years when he was first chosen, a mere slip of a country youth, in the New South Wales touring team. An admirer had presented him with a touring cricket bag and he had gone to choose it.

'I want something big to carry plenty of equipment and I also want something that will last a long time. It is going to have a lot of work to do,' airily said Bradman to the storekeeper, and that story quickly went the rounds.

His selection, like that of others at the time, was purely in the nature of an experiment, a commendable New South Wales experiment of the period which paid and repaid handsome dividends. Mere lads were chosen in first-class games. Some fell by the wayside, others bore rich fruit (Jackson and McCabe were two), but Bradman did not consider that there was anything problematical in the scattering of his seed and its ultimate harvest. Youths walked blushingly and full of awe into the precincts of Macartney, Taylor, Andrews, Kippax, and others, but Bradman came supreme in his own confidence, determined to go his own way. And he did!

In a few short years he had the Australian sporting firmament at his feet. No Prime Minister, no inventor, no medical genius of the calibre of McCormick and Hunter, no South Polar explorer like Wilkins or world-acclaimed airmen like Kingsford Smith, Ross and Keith Smith, Hinkler or Ulm knew the publicity from the Australian Press that Bradman received.

He rose to the heights in a period of world

uneasiness, the depression years and the early rumblings which were later to develop into the avalanche of European troubles. Hitler had just commenced his rise to power; economic conferences were being held in London; gold standards were crashing; Wall and Throgmorton streets were dizzy with speculation, and one of the representatives of world finance, Sir Otto Niemeyer, had just delivered to Australians a depressing lecture on how to run their country – a lecture dictating financial belt tightening in a land of primary abundance. As the Iris poet and author, Eimar O'Duffy, had it:

> *The banker in his counting-house counting out his money;*
> *The land was overflowing with bread and milk and honey;*
> *The shops were full of good things, the factories likewise;*
> *The banker shut his books and said we must economise.*

Bradman's colossal feats with a piece of willow gave editors a chance to depart from their usual mournful run of depression news. His deeds were so remarkable that they spilled over from the sporting pages and gave the window-dressers of the Press an infrequent opportunity in those days to instil a little brightness, some light relief, into their usually gloomy leader columns.

He became the most discussed person in Australia, conceding the limelight for a short period only to the then New South Wales Premier, John T. Lang, when that turbulent politician became embroiled in a Government Bank crash, a constitutional tilt with Governor Sir Philip Game and a ribbon-cutting episode at the opening of the Sydney Harbour Bridge.

Bradman became the continent's number one idol, not merely because of his prodigious batting feats, but, in a sense, because they happened at a time when Australian national life was sick and apprehensive. Business men on the verge of bankruptcy said, 'To hell with business' (it invariably finished there, anyhow, in those days!), closed up their doors and went out to forget their woes and themselves with Bradman. It was usual to see thousands leave the ground when Bradman was dismissed. The atmosphere and most of the interest in the game walked back with Bradman to the pavilion, a bitter pill for previous headliners to swallow and none too happy a prospect for those who had the interests of the game at heart; but circumstances and his own genius surrounded Bradman with an atmosphere and a publicity value no other player could approach.

Cricket

People who had never been to a cricket match before, who did not know a bat from a ball, flocked to see Bradman. A carnival spirit hung over every ground on which he played, and the first sight of him as he emerged from the pavilion was sufficient to send the whole ground into ecstacies of delight. No other batsman in my time, which corresponded with Bradman, could approach his terrific skill with the bat or his unlimited popularity with the crowd. He was the planet, solely inhabited; the others revolved around him, shining intermittently in the early 1930s in his reflected glory.

His colleagues frequently felt that they were mere lay figures or items of scenery to be arranged to provide a background for the principal actor, but, from a public point of view, Bradman was responsible for a very great percentage of the enormous public interest in cricket between the two wars.

He seemed to bring out through the gate with him a breath of power and a confidence which made everybody feel that the whole fortunes of the game would be changed by him – as they invariably were. He walked slowly to the wickets with a slight rolling gait, the slowness so that he could accustom his eyes from the dark of the pavilion to the light of the ground (a gentleman named Lyon took him to task for this slow walk, in England, in 1930, but as Lyon had also played the game he should have known better).

Where 99 batsmen out of a hundred make their last few yards to the wicket with a grim, haunted look on their faces, determination alternating with nervous hopefulness, Bradman's mien when at last he reached the creases was one of supreme and disarming happiness. A few seconds' business with the umpire and then he looked about him with a huge grin. That grin was the cheekiest, the most challenging, and the most confident thing I have seen in sport. It was such as to rip the innards out of any bowler, sending him hurtling down to spreadeagle the stumps of this cocky young man, but always the tale was the same, Bradman opened his score with the cheekiest and most confident of shots, and there he was at the other end or walking back down the pitch from a boundary shot, grinning, grinning, grinning!

The crowd loved and adored him for his tradesmanlike activities at the wickets. His worth was apparent and intrinsically honest. He gave them even more than they asked for their admission money.

He was at once the despair of the bowler, the captain and his fieldsmen, the batting worthy struggling at the other end and his comrades in the pavilion. He made it all look so easy, so simple, so prearranged. He always made the onlooker feel that a loose ball would be lifted for four to the very place on the boundary to which batting science required that that ball should be sent.

He was the genius absolute. To bat with him was an education and revelation, not given by any other batsman of the period. Great artists like Trumper and Macartney varied the direction of the shot for sheer artistic satisfaction, but Bradman was implacable. He was more interested in runs than art, and in the days when he was playing for Australia you would have searched a long time before you found an onlooker who seriously disagreed with him. He was the undisputed hero of the new-found public, the broadcasting public. He was the darling of the spectator's heart – and justifiably so, because no batsman in history had been so prolific and none of the moderns could approach the standard he set for consistency and sheer honesty of batting purpose.

Sydney citizens asked the visitor whether he had seen our Harbour, our Bridge and our Don. It was embarrassing to walk down the street with Bradman, to ride in a street car or dine with him. He was instantly recognised and acclaimed, even staid professors permitting themselves a childlike chuckle as they obtruded a pen and a piece of paper on Bradman for an autograph. The life of the champion seemed to be one long succession of autographs. The post disgorged hundreds of them at him daily, and almost the only peace he knew from them

was while he was at the wickets – which was probably a reason why he stayed there so long.

In all this adulation, in all this hero worshipping,
which came at its flood when he had just passed his
21st birthday, Bradman never lost his balance. He
never allowed his head to expand in the vapourings
of flattery. The ground was always in contact with
his feet, though once established he did not tempor-
ise with any challenges against his domain.

Once in a game in Sydney against Victoria there
had been the bold claim in a newspaper that Ironmonger, who had taken his wicket in the first
innings, had the measure of the champion. It was
dangerous for Ironmonger that such stuff should
have been written. Bradman made a close study of
what the critics wrote. His most spectacular innings
in Australia was played in Sydney (Fleetwood-
Smith being the chief operating medium) the day
after a leading critic had written that he did not
possess the spectacular flair of a Trumper or a
Macartney.

As he opened his huge mail this other Sydney
morning he casually asked several of us if we had
seen the particular article about Ironmonger and
himself.

'Yes,' somebody answered, 'we did.'

'It will be quite interesting,' said Bradman, with
a smile, 'to see what happens today.'

Cricket

The tone in Bradman's voice suggested that he himself was in no doubt. Ironmonger was to be put through the Bradman hoops, but Bradman was not boasting. In his 'it will be interesting to see what happens today,' he was letting us know that he had accepted the Ironmonger challenge, and he wished us to note how he accepted it.

Until he reached the sobriety or comparative sobriety of his late twenties, Bradman was always impish in his batting. It amounted almost to a point of honour with him, as I have written, to take at least a single from the first ball bowled to him, but in this innings against Ironmonger, the innings which was to prove whether a mere bowling mortal could hold a cricket god in chancery, Bradman's audacity took on the flavour of contempt.

It was not sufficient for Ironmonger first to be subdued and then flayed. A Jackson or a Kippax might do that. Ironmonger, or rather the critic, had to be put in his Bradman place.

From the very first ball Bradman took the most daring risks. He cut Ironmonger fine off his middle stump, he flicked him off his stumps to the fine leg fence, he on and off drove him, hit him high to the outfield (always difficult with Ironmonger), and then, in a final flourish of contempt for the critics, Bradman hit Ironmonger over the fence. No batsman could have done more against a bowler, and in all this it was difficult not to believe that Bradman was laughing hugely, not at Ironmonger so much, but at those critics who suggested Iron-monger held an option over him.

Bradman returned radiant to the pavilion. 'What was in that article again?' he asked.

That was Bradman's nature. He liked nothing better than slaughtering bowlers and critics alike.

There was another occasion, on the eve of a charity game in which Mailey and Bradman were opposed, when a statistician found that Mailey, then a cricket veteran, had taken Bradman's wicket several times. The newspapers displayed the fact. It was an interesting news item, but for Mailey it could mean only one thing, even though the game was a charity one. It meant for Mailey his offering on the sacrificial altar of Bradman's greatness, for the little chap never missed a cricket item in the newspapers.

I lunched with Mailey that day and he was obviously ill at ease.

'They shouldn't write stuff like that,' he said, referring to the newspaper item.

Mailey knew his Bradman. He knew, as a consequence of that item, that there would be a hot Bradman reception awaiting him.

Thousands thronged the small ground, and there was a buzz of excited expectancy as

Cricket

Bradman made his customary slow walk to the wickets. The test was to be immediate, Mailey was bowling. As Mailey apprehensively twiddled the ball from hand to hand at the other end, Bradman meticulously took his guard and looked about the field as if to say: 'So Mailey, one of the Old School, has my measure. Well, well! Let us see if there is anything in this rumour. I'm ready when you are, Arthur.'

Mailey began his ambling run, his arm came up and over – and Bradman was running yards down the wicket with his bat poised aloft. There was a succulent swish of Bradman's bat and away in the distance, as if fearing what was to come, the ball lost itself in the crowd.

Then followed cold and deliberate cricket murder. Mailey's deliveries speeded to the fence and over the fence, and from one of the latter soaring hits came the tinkle of falling window-glass, the orchestral accompaniment to a stage plot of murder that had thousands calling for blood, blood, still more Mailey blood. Bradman put Mailey in the stocks that day for all to see. Then he hanged, drew and quartered him. Mailey was butchered to make another Bradman holiday.

That was another glimpse of Bradman. He was the dominant cricket figure of his age, and if fate delivered to him one of an older generation, then his treatment would be such as to suggest that Bradman was the dominant cricket figure of all the ages. Mailey had then retired from the first-class stage and was far past his best, but had he been in his prime I venture to say the story would have been much the same. Bradman paid respect to no bowling save bodyline.

All bowlers, with the possible exception of O'Reilly, whom he first met in a country game, came alike to Bradman. At one time or another he took up Tate, Larwood (before bodyline), Geary, Voce, Freeman, Verity, Constantine, Francis, Griffiths, Grimmett, Fleetwood-Smith, Ebeling, Blackie, Ironmonger, Oxenham, Quinn, Bell, Morkel, McMillan and the rest of the world's best. He was wary and respectful always with O'Reilly, but the others he closely analysed and then slashed them apart before he left them bewildered, abashed and out of breath.

By Jack Fingleton, *Cricket Crisis*, Cassell & Co. 1946.

Not once did I take my eyes off a batsman, even he was relaxing. Any little idiosyncrasy was noted. I was like a cat watching a mouse. In a Test trial at the SCG I bowled Tommy Andrews, and as he walked from the wicket he gestured with his arms to the incoming batsman, Alan Kippax, that I was turning the ball sharply. This information proved costly. I made sure my first ball to Kippax did not turn an inch. It bowled him, and he missed out on a tour of England.

Clarrie Grimmett as told to Alan Trengrove. Quoted in the *Sydney Morning Herald*, 1966.

Clarrie Grimmet was the best bowler I have ever seen.

Bill O'Reilly in a *Sydney Morning Herald* tribute after Grimmett's death in 1980.

Buzz off, mate. My preference hasn't changed – I still prefer girls to boys.

Wally Grout, telling Bob Simpson at first slip to stand wider. Quoted by Simpson in the *Sun-Herald*, 1984.

The hardest thing about taking over from Bradman was that you didn't have him in the side.

Lindsay Hasset who replaced Don Bradman as captain in 1949. Quoted by Dick Tucker in the Sydney *Mirror*, 1975.

Well, Stork, if you think I'm good, Vic to me was as
the ceiling to the floor.

Charlie Macartney, on being asked by his team-mate Hunter
'Stork' Hendry, about Victor Trumper. Quoted by Hendry in
an interview, 1986.

Henry, the Queensland Aboriginal fast bowler,
whose death from consumption at Yarrabah,
Queensland, on 13 March is reported, fell far short
of making the reputation in first-class cricket that
it was hoped at one time that he would achieve. In
all he played in seven of Queensland's big matches
during the four seasons 1901–2 to 1904–5 inclusive,
taking 21 wickets ... In Mr B.J.T. Bosanquet's
Impressions Of The MCC Tour Of 1903–04, in
Wisden, Braund's account of his experience of Henry
is thus given: 'I took the first ball from the Aboriginal, Henry, supposed to be the fastest bowler in the
world, and certainly I will say that the first three
balls he gave me were indeed the fastest I have ever
seen. I got him away for two on the leg side, but the
next ball, in cutting him, I was spendidly caught at
point.' Mr Bosanquet's own account differs from this
in amusing fashion. 'Queensland ... produced a fast
Aboriginal bowler. Leonard Braund was selected to
open the innings for us, and didn't much fancy it.

Cricket

The first ball hit the bat somehow and went to fine-leg for two; the second passed batsman, wicket-keeper *and long-stop*, and hit the screen about the time Braund finished his shot. The third was slower, and the batsman, retiring gracefully, put it gently into point's hands.'

From an obituary on the Aboriginal fast bowler Albert Henry (1880–1909) in the 24 June 1909 issue of *Cricket: A Weekly Record Of The Game*, quoting the two English players Braund and Bosanquet.

With all his greatness the crack right-hander was superstitious. Bowlers had no terrors for him, sticky or fiery wickets did not unnerve him, but he had a decided objection to members of the cloth. At Manchester on one occasion after he had missed the bus, he came back into the dressing room and said, 'I knew I wouldn't score with all those parsons hanging round our pavilion; why don't they keep to the collection plate, or marry people, instead of coming worrying us Australians?' Trumper always wore an old Australian Eleven cap. It was bottle green, but nevertheless he stuck to it to the end, and there was always no end of bother if Duff or some of the other humourists of the side got hold of the cap and hid it. He could make runs with any old bat. Just as we were beginning a county contest on one occasion an amateur bat-maker came along with a most unwieldy piece of willow, which weighed over three pounds, and asked Vic whether he would try it. Trumper said, 'Yes, so long as it's got a spring in it.' He made 100 with it straight away. He had wonderful wrist power, and could almost bend the spring of a bat in two.

Clem Hill, writing of his old team-mate Victor Trumper in the *Australasian*, 1920.

There wasn't much difference between bowling and throwing for a good bit. I remember one match it was all throwing, so I thought. Tommy Wills and Wardill threw for Victoria, and we had two men to throw for us – one of them was a black fellow. Twopenny we used to call him, and he was a good thrower. But they got more particular after a time.

Harry Hilliard (1826–1914), who played for New South Wales in the 1850s. From an interview in the *Australasian*, 1893.

Still dressed in his cricket creams, sipping a lemon squash and wearing an Australian pullover, he fielded questions at the regular post-match press conference, speaking earnestly about the good things to come out of the game for Australia and joking about whether a back injury might temper his costly desire to hook. Then, with no indication of the stunning news to come, he said: 'Gentlemen, before we go I have something to read.' He then unfolded two sheets of notepaper written in his own hand. 'The Australian cricket captaincy is something I have always held very dear to me,' he said firmly. 'However, playing the game with total enjoyment has always been of greatest importance. The constant speculation, criticism and innuendo by former players and sections of the media over the four to five years have finally taken their toll. It is in the interests of the team . . . ' There was a poignant pause as Hughes' lips quivered. Then, encouraged by team manager Bob Merriman, he tried again. ' . . . and Australian cricket . . . ' After another pause Hughes rose from his chair and in a high-pitched, broken voice asked Mr Merriman to finish reading the statement. His head down, those famous blond curls looking just a little bedraggled, he walked out through the TV cameras and microphones, out of the players' lunch room at the Gabba and out of the Test captaincy.

Warwick Hadfield's account in the *Australian* of Kim Hughes's tearful resignation as Australian captain after

Australia lost to the West Indies in Brisbane, November 1984.

I am leaving shortly to take up residence in Brisbane and though this may seem unduly harsh on the NSWCA after helping me through my illness the position is this. I feel the Queensland climate will do me an infinite amount of good and that ultimately I will regain perfect health. If such is the case I hope to return to this state and again don the blue cap.

From a letter written by the young Australian batsman Archie Jackson to the New Cricket Association on 19 September 1932, explaining his departure for Brisbane – where he was to die of tuberculosis less than five months later.

His late Majesty King Edward VII (then Prince of Wales) visited one of the grounds where the Australians were playing, and as they were presented to His Majesty he shook hands and spoke a few words to each of the team. When Jones was introduced, it was noticed that no word was spoken but tears came to the Prince's eyes, and on someone remarking on the fact to Jones that worthy replied, 'I made up my mind that if ever I got the opportunity to shake hands with the Prince, each of us would have good cause to remember it.'

From an article in *Australian Cricketer*, December 1933, about the former Australian fast bowler Ernie Jones.

Jones was my cabin companion on the way to England. After the first few days of seasickness the trip was a merry and bright one. Poor old Jonah was very ill with mal de mer, and his anguish was pitiable. One morning he exclaimed, 'Oh, to goodness that I could find the man that first put a cricket ball in my hand.'

Clem Hill, writing about Ernie 'Jonah' Jones, Australian fast bowler before and after the turn of the century. *Australasian*, October, 1920.

Sorry, doctor. She slipped.

A remark reputedly made by the Australian fast bowler Ernie Jones to W. G. Grace after Jones had bowled a bumper through Grace's beard in 1896.

On one occasion he [the England player Patsy Hendren] was fielding on the boundary by the famous Hill on the Sydney Cricket Ground. The batsman hit the ball high in the air towards him. As it soared higher and higher into the air a raucous voice from the Hill shouted, 'Patsy, if you miss the catch you can sleep with my sister.' Later Patsy was asked what he had done. 'Oh,' he replied, 'as I hadn't seen his sister, I caught the ball.'

Brian Johnston in *Rain Stops Play*, Unwin Paperbacks, 1979.

Let me tell you something of that most remarkable experience, the tenth-wicket partnership of 307 runs which Halford Hooker and I shared against Victoria in Melbourne in 1928. It was Christmas Day, and we were in a very bad way when play started. It was about ten minutes to one when Hooker joined me with nine down for 113. We were still together at the end of the day, and the score had grown to 367, our stand having put on 254. Next day, when thousands came to see the end of the partnership, we took three overs to score the ten runs necessary for a first-innings lead, which eventually gave us the game. Hooker had reached 62 when Jack Ryder caught him off Ted a'Beckett with out total 420! You should hear Hal Hooker telling the story of that Christmas Day. He says there were times when he felt he could hardly breathe because of the press of fieldsmen around his bat. They formed a funnel, down which the ball came. Hooker, our number eleven, did a miraculous job. It was steadfast batting, marked by rare judgment. He played to give me the strike. We had frequent conferences, as did Jack Ryder and his bowlers and fieldsmen as this Hooker nuisance continued. When the last ball of the day was due, Hal and I agreed we should run as soon as I played the ball, because I wanted the strike next morning. The fieldsmen had their ideas, but when I tapped the ball Hooker was down the pitch like a greyhound. I remember when we gained the lead on Boxing Day, Hooker asked me, 'Can you use the long handle now?' I agreed, and he had his lash. In no time there were three of four fieldsmen on the boundary.

Alan Kippax. From an article in *Sunday Herald*, February, 1949.

A corpse with pads on.

A English journalist's description of Bill Lawry referred to by Bob Simpson in a *Sun-Herald* article, November 1983.

Strike again, Lightning!

Shouted by a Sydney Cricket Ground barracker to Bill Lawry after Lawry ended a long period of tedious batting by hitting a boundary. Quoted by Ray Robinson in *People*, March 1968.

Watching the fifth Test against England on TV I used a mirror. Instantly, Bill Lawry became a right-hander in the mirror, and I could see what a magnificent batsman he is and could understand all his shots.

F. B. Walker, a Canberra cricket enthusiast, quoted in the *Sydney Morning Herald*, March 1966.

I have got to be aggressive to be a good player. Look at history. There has never been a non-aggressive fast bowler who has been successful.

Geoff Lawson, quoted in the *Age*, May 1985.

Maybe I could play for another two or three years physically, but mentally out on the field there were too many times, there were three or four occasions, when I thought, 'Gee, I wish I was out on the beach.'

Dennis Lillee, explaining his decision to retire from international cricket, January 1984.

Cricket

Can't you get him out without riling him?

A remark by the England opener Dennis Amiss to Tony Greig in 1974–5, after Greig had dismissed Dennis Lillee with a bumper, thereby stirring Lillee into a visible rage. Quoted by Greig in a newspaper interview, October 1981.

Look, I made the Victorian Sheffield Shield side and was dropped. Then I made the Australian Test side and was dropped. I don't like it and it's not going to happen again.

Dean Jones, quoted by Rick Allen in the Sydney *Sun*, January 1985.

I shall never forget one instance on Lord's ground. I was bowling and W. G. Grace batting at the other end. W.G. stepped out to a ball from me and apparently W.G. was six inches or probably more [over the line]. He missed the ball and Blackham had the bails off like a shot. W.G. waited for the appeal but none was made. On crossing I asked Blackham why W.G. was not out. He said, 'I did not appeal.' To the question why, he said, 'I was in such a hurry to get W.G. out that I took the ball a couple of inches in front of the wicket.' I wonder how many wicket-keepers would not have left that matter to the umpire?

William Cooper (1849–1939), an Australian player of the 1880s, writing about the famous Australian wicket-keeper Jack Blackham in a private letter in 1935. The incident he refers to occurred in 1884. The letter was one of several written by Cooper to Les Hill, which were published in *Wisden Cricket Monthly*, 1983.

This will be the last time I'll play here. Tell the crowd they have only two days to get stuck into me.

Ken Mackay speaking to a journalist before his final appearance at the Melbourne Cricket Ground, December 1963.

He became such a hero that when he batted in his first Brisbane Test the standing ovation lasted so long that an official announcement had to be made to everyone to sit down so the match could continue.

From an article about Ken Mackay by Hugh Lunn in the *Australian*, December 1980.

You quite flatter me when you put my abilities in

the same street as his. The comparison, I should say, was as the electric light to the tallow candle.

James 'Sunny Jim' Mackay in a letter to the *Referee* about Victor Trumper's death, August 1915. Mackay, a brilliant NSW batsman before an eye injury ended his career, was replying to a *Referee* article which likened his ability to Trumper's.

Well, I bowl the ball where I want to, and he hits it where he wants to.

The England bowler L. C. Braund when asked for his opinion of Victor Trumper. Quoted by H. V. Hordern in *Googlies*, Angus & Robertson, 1932.

Jim Phillips was a good companion to travel with and always entered into any of the practical jokes with no end of zest. Going home with the '99 team, McLeod, Trumble and Johns had an exceptionally big four-berth compartment – the envy of us all. However, after leaving Ismalia, Phillips decided that he would upset the occupants of that berth by imitating a dying consumptive man. He put Trumble, the purser and myself in the joke, and muffling himself up in a great heavy overcoat he rolled into the bottom bunk and soon afterwards began coughing. This developed into the apparent cough of a person in the advanced stages of consumption, and he accompanied it with the usual retching and expectoration. Every time he would flick the bottom of the berth and thus gave the impression that he did not care very much where he was spitting. He continued this throughout the night, much to the annoyance, in fact disgust, or shall I say absolute fear, of the other occupants. At daylight Alf Johns turned out, first consulted the purser (who expressed deep regret and said the man had got in there by mistake), and then he even went to the skipper of the boat about the incident. He got some consolation when he was told that it was a second-class passenger who had got into the wrong compartment. While this was going on Charlie McLeod was getting dressed and was shaving when Jim Phillips gave an extra cough and gurgle and apparently expectorated on the glass. McLeod, looking out of the corner of his eye, cried out, 'You dirty devil,' but not for some time after did he know the strength of the joke.

Clem Hill writing of the famous umpire Jim Phillips in the *Australasian*, 1920.

Cricket

A cricket match which aroused considerable interest was played at the Mullion (Yass, NSW) cricket ground on December 18th, between a team of ladies selected and captained by Miss Nonie Styles and the gentlemen of the Mullion CC. The gentlemen wore skirts, batted, bowled and fielded left-handed, and used pick handles instead of bats ... The men won by 14 runs.

Cricket, A Weekly Record Of The Game, February 1910.

As a captain Vic Richardson was a great believer in practical psychology. Once in 1935–36 Australia was having difficulty in clinching the fifth Test against South Africa at Durban. On the morning of the last day Bill O'Reilly could not get turn with his wrong'un or leg-break. He seemed to lack his usual killer instinct. So Richardson purposely took him off and kept him out of the attack for the rest of the first session of play. Vic also asked Stan McCabe and Len Darling to keep baiting him about having to field on the fence. 'Aren't you playing in this match, Tiger?' asked Stan. 'Doesn't ... well look like it, does it?' growled O'Reilly, pulling his cap harder down over his right ear and swinging his arms about as he strode impatiently this way then that in the outfield. By lunch O'Reilly was boiling with anger. Richardson deliberately lunched apart from the team and the baiting process was continued by the other players. After lunch Vic threw the ball to O'Reilly to take the first over. The angry O'Reilly took seven wickets in less than two hours and the match was won by tea.

People, 1953.

On one occasion two schoolboy friends of mine, of whom Norman Gregg (later Sir Norman, eminent eye doctor) was one, were watching Trumper batting from alongside the fence in front of the old grandstand, when a drunk alongside them remarked (as told me by Sir Norman afterwards), 'He only has one stroke.' They asked what that was, and he replied, 'Hitting the ball where there is no fieldsman.'

By Frank McElhone, who played for NSW with Victor Trumper before World War I, in a private tribute to Trumper that he wrote in 1981.

The funeral of Victor Trumper on Wednesday was one of the largest and most impressive ever accorded a sportsman in Sydney. It left his residence at Chatswood and was met at Fort Macquarie by many hundreds of cricketers and other friends of the deceased, who marched four abreast, thence along Macquarie Street and Oxford Street. Near Regent Street, Paddington, the procession halted and those who had marched joined special trams and went as far as Charing Cross. There they left the trams and formed in line again, leading the procession to the cemetery and down through the winding paths to the beautiful spot chosen for the grave on a height not far from the cliffs, overlooking the broad, blue Pacific. A very peaceful scene.

C. J. Davis, *Referee*, 7 July 1915.

One of our earlier Australian elevens was playing a country match, and the country folk had come from far and wide to see the bowler with the dread name of Spofforth. It was a two-day match, and the local men were doing badly; in fact, so much so that the Australian captain said to Spoff: 'It's no good bowling these fellows out like this Spoff – there will be no play tomorrow. We can't lose, so I think you had better come off.' Spoff thought a while and finally agreed. A few minutes later – when it was found that the demon bowler had been given a rest -- there came a voice from the crowd: 'Hey, I've travelled 300 bloomin' miles to see that long cove bowl, and ain't yer goin' to put 'im on?' and the spectators brawled loudly for Spoff to go on again. 'It's no good,' said the captain to Spoff. 'You'll have to bowl.' 'All right,' returned Spofforth, 'but I'll show them something they've never seen before,' and with that he took a run of about twenty yards and sent down a ball at terrific pace. The ball went high over the batsman's, wicket-keeper's, and shortslip's heads, and reached the fence almost without touching the ground. This struck great terror into the minds of all, and then came the first voice. 'Hey, take that long feller off. We've seen enough of 'im.'

From the *Sydney Mail*, December 1899.

Our first sight of Jeff Thomson at Lord's was just before the 1975 World Cup. The Australians had agreed to play a warm-up match in aid of John Murray's benefit. It is traditional in such games to allow the beneficiary the luxury of a single off the mark. Ian Chappell's instructions to Thommo were clear: 'When J.M. comes in, you must let him have one.' Emphasis on the last word. Thomson's first ball to Murray, which was greeted, in anticipation, with a languid forward prod, turned out to be a vicious bouncer. Thommo, acting on orders, had missed the emphasis.

Mike Selvey, former England player, *Sydney Morning Herald*, May 1985.

After the 1878 tour of England, the two Bannerman brothers, Charles and Alick, played for Australia against the Rest and were batting together. After an apparent mix-up, Charles found himself at the same end of the pitch as Alick. He said, 'You're better out than me,' and, stepping across Alick's crease, gave his younger brother a shove out.

Source unknown.

Australian Test all-rounder Richie Benaud has been studying television with BBC studio and outside transmission crews for the past week. The *Evening Standard* says Benaud intends taking a job in Australian television when he returns from England.

An item in the Sydney *Sun*, September 1956.

The match took place at the Jolimont ground where the wicket was as fine as any I have played on. Lou Woolf, the well-known barrister, was long-stop, a position in which he was champion. He said, 'I'm getting nothing to do, Jack,' and suggested he should field fine-leg, which he did. This was when the alteration was made. At first I did not like being deprived of the safety valve. It was a great surprise to them in England where they had a long-stop to fast and fast-medium bowlers. Then they followed our idea.

By Jack Blackham, describing in the *Referee* in December 1915 how he became the first wicket-keeper to dispense with a long-stop.

It was an embarrassing day in more ways than one for Australian left-hand batsman Allan Border in the first Test at the WACA Ground yesterday. Border survived a caught-behind appeal, only to be given out leg-before to Ian Botham two balls later and making only four runs. The dejected batsman left the field, walked into the dressing room and dropped his bat on the floor, much to the amusement of David Baistow, England's number-two wicket-keeper. Only then an embarrassed Border realised he had mistakenly walked into the England dressing room. He bent down, picked up his bat and left, cap in hand, for the room next door.

AAP newspaper story, December 1979.

I went through a stage where I really didn't give a hoot about cricket or anything. I just wanted to lie on the beach or bum around for a while.

Allan Border, quoted by John Webb, *Australian*, February 1982.

Throughout my career people used to say I was overweight. The barbs about my being too fat were always sharper when I failed. But I was always told I had lost weight when I scored runs. The fact was that my weight rarely varied.

Peter Burge, quoted by Dick Tucker, Sydney *Mirror*, January 1977.

Watching cricket is as near as I'll ever get to meditating.

Kate Fitzpatrick, *Sydney Morning Herald*, 1983.

Really, Bill? Don't you think I was like an old maid defending her virginity?

Douglas Jardine remarking to Bill O'Reilly after O'Reilly had complimented him on his batting in the Brisbane Test of the 'bodyline' series.

[On 'Chuck' Fleetwood-Smith] I regard him probably as the most gifted spin bowler ever I set eyes upon. If I'd been behind him with a bullock whip I reckon I could have got him to put up the greatest performances Test cricket has ever seen. But I wasn't his captain and I didn't have the bullock whip.

[On Stan McCabe] If I had an Aladdin's Lamp and could use it, said my prayers each night for a month assiduously, I would say this: if I were reincarnated, I'd come back as a cricketer and I would be Stan McCabe. Take the rest – doesn't matter.

[On arriving with the Australian team in Ireland, 1938] The excise man came rushing through our carriages – 'Open your bags. Where are they? Open your bags.' I decided I wasn't going to take this. I said, 'This is a beaut way to welcome a man who's coming back to the land of his forefathers, and you're asking him to open his bags and declare himself. What's going on over here?' 'What's your name?' he said, and I said, 'O'Reilly.' 'What are you doing here?' I said, 'I'm with the Australian cricket team.' 'Hey, you're not that fella who's been knocking those Englishmen about over there, are you?' I said, 'Yes, I am.' So he took out a lump of green chalk and did every bag in the section.

[On Douglas Jardine] In London, I was invited by Bob Menzies, who was a good old mate of mine, to a dinner at the Savoy Hotel. I accepted the invitation and when I got there I found that I had sitting on my left Douglas Jardine, the captain of the English bodyline team who later became a friend of mine. Douglas had a bad time out here. Nobody liked him. Everybody detested him. Douglas Jardine was an Englishman, tough, red-faced – Hiawatha I used to call him – who later turned out to be, I thought, a very kind bloke. I went to dinner with him quite a few times. Well, here was Jardine sitting on my left side at the dinner at the Savoy. On this side I had Gubby Allen. Over here was Freddy Brown. These three were English captains and I'm right in amongst them, so you can imagine what I copped. They really gave it to me, boots and all, but I think I held my own. I had to call on a few parts of the Australian vernacular to help me out. But Bob Menzies, tremendous host and great after-dinner speaker, was introducing to his guests a man who was just about to become Governor-General of Australia on Bob's invitation. His name was Hector

Morrison. He was the Speaker of the House of Commons. Now Bob was really going flat out. He was talking about how happy he was about the way the English people accepted him, how nice it was to be an Australian Prime Minister and to be so welcome. He said, 'It's not the same at home, you know. They don't think much of me out there at all. What's more, I'm certain that there are very many Australians who think I'm the greatest bastard that ever stood in their country.' I got a dig in the ribs from my mate Douglas. 'Bill,' he said, 'the honourable gentleman is misinformed. He could never possibly be more than number two.'

[On Don Bradman] There's never been and never will be in my estimation a batsman so good as that fella. I don't care how many you like to pour into one – all the Chappells, the Borders and so on. Forget them, they're just child's play compared with Bradman, and I've seen them all. Bradman was a bloke whose ability with the bat was absolutely inconceivable. The Yanks talk about Babe Ruth and all that. To hell with Babe Ruth. This boy was a modern miracle.

Bill O'Reilly from a speech to a Catenian Association meeting in Sydney, October 1986.

Cricket

Even cricket – that dullest of games – becomes murder when Australians are involved. For several years England had dominated play for the Ashes, cricket's mythical Davis Cup, but in the 1920s one of the world's most remarkable sportsmen appeared in a small Australian town. He was Don Bradman, cricket's Babe Ruth, Ty Cobb and Joe Di Maggio rolled into one. He mesmerised the opposition. Sometimes he batted for days, scoring double and triple centuries. He was knighted by the King for having practically murdered English bowlers.

James A. Michener, *Return to Paradise*, Random House, 1951.

We would prefer Sri Lanka to win, of course, but we do like Shane [Warne] and we would like a visit.

A prostitute from Lahore's red-light district on the eve of the 1996 World Cup final.

We had to get off the mini-bus called disaster and on to the streetcar named desire.

Windies manager Wes Hall after his side bounced back with

a win against Australia during the 1996 World Cup.

Without doubt, Border is the toughest man I've ever seen play cricket.

Greg Matthews, quoted by Martin Blake in the *Age*, 1990.

Merv Hughes does some strange things, but underneath he's a pretty caring sort of bloke.

Steve Waugh, quoted by Gideon Haigh in the *Australian*, November 1994.

Warney looks as though he is the sort of bloke who will turn on most pitches because he really gives it a rip. I think he'll eventually play [for Australia].

Allan Border, December 1991, quoted by Phil Wilkins in the *Sydney Morning Herald.*

It's unbelievable that they could pick a guy like Shane Warne, who is just an average club leg-spinner.

Geoff Lawson, complaining about Greg Matthews' treatment

by the Australian selectors. Warne had made his Test debut earlier that year. Quoted by Sam North in the *Sydney Morning Herald*, October 1992.

Punk? I've never been a punk in my life. I'm a capitalist, man. Punks are anti-capitalist. People say I have a punk haircut, but there's nothing much I can do with my hair because there isn't much left.

Greg Matthews, quoted by Martin Blake in the *Age*, November 1990.

Doug Walters was a legend. David Boon's no legend.

David Boon, quoted by Paul Kent, *Herald Sun*, October 1993.

We picked Warne as a surprise packet but never thought he'd turn out quite so surprising.

Allan Border during the tour of England, 1993.

He does not seek to entrap each batsman in a web of deceit, building up the tensions with bluff and counter-bluff. He just runs in and rips it, like a quickie trying to kill the batsman with every single delivery. Each extravagant, wildly turning leg-spinner is Warne's own kind of throat-ball, intended as an utterly destructive ball, aimed viciously at the batsman's mind.

Simon Barnes writing about Shane Warne in *The Times*, August, 1993.

You're here to xxxxing bowl. Why don't you xxxxing get on with it?

Steve Waugh's reported remark to Curtly Ambrose during their celebrated eyeballing confrontation in Trinidad, 1995. Quoted in various sources.

GOLF

Jim Webster was a senior sports writer with the *Sydney Morning Herald* and the *Herald Sun* for more than thirty years. He covered five Olympic Games, six Commonwealth Games, four Wallaby rugby tours and nearly 200 rugby Test matches and numerous Wimbledon and British Open golf championships. In 1987, he was honoured with the Diploma of the International Amateur Athletic Federation. He officially retired in 1988, but has not been allowed to rest. He is consulting editor of *Golf Australia*, was media attaché for Australia's team at the 1992 Barcelona Olympics and media director for the 1996 Atlanta Olympics. He is the author of seven books on sport.

GOLF, A GOOD WALK RUINED

Mark Twain

Greg Norman has the word SHARK printed on his golf balls. It stops him ever hitting the wrong one.

Steve Elkington has made the remarkable revelation that whenever he lines up a putt, he doesn't aim at the hole!

Don't bother rubbing your eyes or wiping your reading glasses, because you did read what you thought you did.

The Elk aims all his putts to the left of the hole.

Many people felt that putting was the only part of his game holding him back and so in America he went to Dave Pelz, recognised as the world's foremost expert in golf's short game. Pelz used to be a NASA scientist and has since applied that analytical mind to the many secrets of putting.

'Dave said I was one of the best putters technically that he had ever seen,' said Elkington. 'Having said that, he discovered I was aiming my putts too far to the right. My eye saw the hole to the right of where it actually was. From six feet away, I was aiming about three inches to the right of the hole.

'After a while I got it too perfect and over-corrected so that I began aiming too far left. Finally, I got it spot on and now I aim all my putts inside the cup.'

Apparently Elkington's problem is not uncommon among golfers, as Pelz reckons 90 per cent of all amateurs under-read the break on their putts.

That aspect of his game corrected, Elkington went on and won the 1995 US PGA championship at Riviera in Los Angeles on some of the worst greens ever seen in a major championship. He closed with a seven-under-par 64, the lowest-ever final round in the championship's history, to tie with Scotland's Colin Montgomerie and then beat him in the playoff.

No doubt Kel Nagle ranks among the finest of Australian golfers, having won the Open championships of Britain, Canada, Australia, France, New Zealand, Hong Kong and Switzerland and a swag of other titles in-between.

Two teams successes also occupy a very special place in his heart, for he teamed with his good pal Peter Thomson to win the Canada Cup in Montreal in 1954 and they repeated this success in Melbourne in 1959, when they won before record crowds by ten shots over the celebrated American duo of Sam Snead and Cary Middlecoff.

Nagle was always immensely popular, forever willing to chat to all and sundry, give advice or share a cup of tea (he's a teatotaller). He's so well liked and respected by fellow professionals that Bruce Devlin even named his son, also a tournament professional, after him.

The secret of Nagle's success was his compact, machine-like swing, beautiful chipping game and one of the silkiest putting touches imagineable. He was a chip-and-one-putt legend, able to rap the ball into the hole with uncanny repetitiveness.

Remarkably, Nagle used the same rusty old Bullseye putter throughout his long career. After picking it up from a fellow at the Tam O'Shanter tournament in America in 1954 it became his feared partner. He has re-gripped it only once since, in 1965, and no club has ever served any golfer longer or more faithfully.

On 27 August, 1995, with his dramatic playoff

victory in the World Series of Golf in Akron, Ohio, Greg Norman received $US360 000, thus passing American Tom Kite to become the all-time leading money-winner on the US Tour with earnings of $US9 493 579.

He did it with a certain amount of panache, chipping in for a birdie with a 7-iron from twenty metres to beat Nick Price and Billy Mayfair at the first extra hole.

Born in Carmyllie, Scotland, Dan Soutar lived there until he was five before his parents moved to the nearby seaside resort of Carnoustie. Soutar was the second eldest of a family of eleven and the difficulty of keeping such large families forced him to leave school at twelve years of age and earn a wage.

He became a regular caddie on the Carnoustie links and, by studying the methods of the many great players for whom he worked, developed in no time at all a very sound swing. He went on to become a club member and win a number of trophies.

At the age of twenty, and accompanied by a friend, he migrated to Australia. Just three months after his arrival he went across to Adelaide, where he succeeded in winning the 1903 Australian amateur championship.

In 1905, Soutar turned professional and went into partnership at Rose Bay with fellow Scot Carnegie Clark, with whom he had been good friends ever since his early days at Carnoustie. That same year he won the Australian Open championship, beating the defending champion, the Hon. Michael Scott, by ten shots.

This was to be his only national title, although he should have won the 1907 Open and might have won the 1912 Open.

Even the Rules Committee at St Andrews was adamant that the Hon. Michael Scott, should have been disqualified instead of being declared the winner of the 1907 Open. Scott, who finished eight shots ahead of Soutar, accidentally played outside the discs at the 12th tee on the second day, which was at once drawn to his attention by J. Victor East, his playing partner. Soutar's protest was thrown out by the Royal Melbourne Golf Club. The club submitted the case for opinion to the R & A. It replied that it could see no reason why Scott should not be disqualified. Nevertheless, Royal Melbourne chose to take no further action and Scott, not Soutar, remains in the records as the 1907 Australian Open champion.

Again, in the 1912 Open at the same course, the club's favourite and most illustrious member Ivo Whitton received a committeeman's ruling on the

12th hole when he hit his ball into an unplayable lie and amid thick tea-trees. He was allowed to take a penalty of two strokes and move his ball to the fairway in line with the spot where the ball had lodged. Playing on with his penalty, Whitton finished with a six for the par-3 hole.

Professional golfers grumbled that the ruling favoured Whitton because he was such a stalwart amateur and that the ball should have been played from behind where it entered the tea-trees. While they remained neutral, a Rules official, W. Windeyer, lodged a written protest to the match committee.

When play was about to commence in the amateur match-play section of the championship which followed the Open, officials caused a delay while they deliberated whether Whitton should have been disqualified from the Open. Eventually they ruled in Whitton's favour.

Soutar had tied for second behind him.

He was to be runner-up in the Open no fewer than seven times in 1906, 1907, 1908, 1909, 1910, 1912 and 1920 and was placed third in 1904 and 1911, although he was only ever credited with having won the title once.

Sam Ginn is the wife of prominent Tour player Stewart Ginn. Sam? Her real name's Lynne, but she reckons she couldn't go through life with the married name of Lynne Ginn.

Perhaps the most infamous Australian Open ever played was that at Royal Melbourne in 1987 when Greg Norman led a player walkoff, the first in the history of Australian tournament golf.

The final round had to be abandoned and the final reassembled on the Monday to complete the tournament.

The reason for the chaos was the third green where, quite unbelievably, the hole had been cut in the wrong place.

Under the hot breath of a searing northerly, this particular green had dried out and become so glassy that it provided no more than a roller-coaster ride for any ball unfortunate enough to land upon it.

Sandy Lyle threw down his putter in anger on the third green and refused to play on. Left-hander Russell Swanson took eight putts to run up a 10 on the hole. Other players took five and six putts.

The farcical situation was reached whereby caddies were racing up the slope after putts and as soon as the ball was about to return from whence it came they would slip a marker beneath it. The hope then was that their master could replace the ball and make the downhill putt from there.

Four groups were banked up on the third tee when Greg Norman finally instigated a player walkoff at 2.15pm – at a stage when he held a seven-stroke lead.

When normality was restored the following day and the final round replayed, the Shark won by 10 shots – breaking the previous winning margin achieved by Jack Nicklaus, who had won by eight strokes in the 1971 Open at Royal Hobart.

But his dominance will always be clouded by one of the most monumental foul-ups in Australian Open history.

When Wayne Grady won the 1990 US PGA championship by three shots at Shoal Creek in Alabama, the impish Queenslander with the blond hair and infectious grin told an international television audience, 'You bloody bewdy!'

Among the many courses Greg Norman has designed worldwide is one near Chicago named Royal Melbourne. The Australian course of the same name is his favourite piece of golfing real estate.

He seemed very much at odds with the touted image of the professional golfer, for he enjoyed the delights of classical music, painted with a delicate touch, very much enjoyed the writing of Kazantsakis and Tolstoy, was a talented journalist and eventually stood for parliament as a Liberal candidate.

Yet he enjoyed more successes in terms of major successes than any other Australian golfer.

Peter Thomson won five British Open championships and, while many might point out that his earlier victories were achieved against predominantly European opposition, the last of them in 1965 saw him repel the might of America as well. He had countless other triumphs in Australia, New Zealand, the Orient and Europe.

His game always was a delicate voyage around the course, rather than a launching pad of power.

As Ken Bowden relates in *The Masters of Golf*, 'He is invariably at his best when playing the small ball in wind and/or on bone-hard fairways and greens. No matter how badly he is outgunned – and he has been frequently outgunned very badly – he continues to drive for safety and position, often with a three or four-wood (he won at least two British Opens without ever drawing the driver from the bag).

'The harder the conditions underfoot or the stronger the wind, the more adept he has been at trundling the ball along the ground, often to within one-putt range from vast distances off the green.

'Always he has a game plan and always he sticks to it until his instinct or serenely observant eye tells him that here is the opportunity, the climactic moment, of a tournament. Then, when trying to grasp that opportunity and under the greatest pressure, he will dig into his reserves and produce his most telling strokes.'

While Thomson's swing exuded simplicity of motion and economy of effort, he never wrote about the mechanics of the game, saying that what he had to say wouldn't occupy more than two sheets.

When his game waned, Thomson gave his attention to the game's administration becoming the strong and influential president of the Australasian PGA Tour.

He also immersed himself in the course design business and before very long had risen in proficiency to where his designs, all with a naturally strong British feel to them, are considered among the best of contemporary works.

That marvellous old player and personality, Dan Cullen, who won the West Australian Open championship in 1937 and 1938 and was still breaking par well into his seventies, may well be the only golf professional with a service decoration.

He was awarded the Distinguished Flying Cross after flying bombers in raids over Germany during World War II.

When Greg Norman won his second British Open at Royal St George's in 1993 his score (267) was the lowest in the history of the Open championship, his 64 was the lowest final-round score by a champion and he was the first champion to shoot four sub-par rounds – 66–68–69–64.

Born at St Kilda in Melbourne on 23 May, 1946, David Graham grew up amid much unhappiness. Eventually, his family split down the middle, with David going to live with his mother and his sister going with her father.

At fourteen, he quit school to become a professional golfer. As a sixteen-year-old he worked in a golf shop in Melbourne and, after his apprenticeship, took a job at a nine-hole course in Tasmania.

Returning to Melbourne, one of the first things the wily old teacher George Naismith told him was that, as a natural left-hander, he'd never be any good. So Graham converted himself from a left-handed to a right-handed golfer, hitting literally thousands of golf balls in the process.

That penchant for practice never stopped. More than once the eager young Graham would practice until blisters developed on his hands. Then they'd burst and he'd practice some more. And when his hands started bleeding he'd still keep practising.

The result was that he developed a swing as mechanical and methodical as a metronome, never missing a beat. It was unnatural looking, but rigidly effective. He enjoyed success in every corner of the globe, eventually winning two of the world's major championships.

In 1979 he won the US PGA championship, beating Ben Crenshaw with a birdie on the third extra hole. He followed this in 1981 with victory in the US Open. He trailed George Burns by three strokes on the last day, but then played a final-round three-under-par 67 on the demanding Merion course, which still ranks among the greatest single rounds of golf ever played. It was near-perfect in the purity and technical excellence of his shots, allowing him to win by a stroke from Burns and Bill Rogers.

This soundness in Graham's technique had been ground into him on the practice fairway many years before as he successfully turned himself from a left to a right-handed golfer.

Jack Newton was doing the television commentary

on the last day of the 1983 NSW Open when Bob Shearer hit a wide at the 17th hole. Shearer's wife, Kathie, thinking it was a bird whizzing by, ducked and the ball hit her friend, Newton's wife Jackie. 'It has hit a spectator,' Newton told viewers. 'It looks like my wife. It is my wife!' Luckily, Jackie was unhurt.

Dame Joan Hammond's operatic career might never have been were it not for her golfing prowess. A member of Sydney's Avondale Golf Club, she was three times NSW amateur champion, runner-up to New Zealand's Oliver Kay in the 1933 Australian championship and represented Australia against Great Britain and New Zealand. The Australian Ladies Golf Union raised funds to send her to Vienna and Italy to study and years later she repaid them by giving concerts to raise funds to send Australian women golfers abroad.

During Greg Norman's Holden Classic in 1995 at The Lakes, he split the 14th fairway with his drive and then tried to clear the water on the par-5 hole with a two-iron.

But the ball disappeared into a clump of bushes near the green. He walked right along the fairway, over the bridge and back along the other side to where it had disappeared, only to discover that it had rolled back into the hazard.

So he had to make the long march back from where he had come.

He hit another from the same spot using the same club and it plopped into the water. He tried again. Same result. By then pride had taken over, for he could have saved himself some metres by hitting from the water's edge but declined to do so.

Finally, at his fourth attempt the ball cleared the water only to land in a bunker. He exploded out and two-putted for an 11.

Those watching took comfort in seeing the tournament host and world's number one golfer play as badly as them.

It was still not Greg Norman's worst score. He once took 14 on the 17th hole in the final round of the Martini International at Lindrick in Yorkshire to finish with a closing 82.

Graham Marsh may well have followed his brother Rodney – one of Australia's outstanding Test wicket-keepers – into cricket had it not been for a broken arm.

The injury kept him out of the game for a while after having represented Western Australia in its under-15 team as a batsman. To rebuild the strength in his arm, he turned to golf and from thereon it overtook his love for cricket.

The former mathematics teacher has since won tournaments all around the world and at one stage in 1973 he was the current holder of five Open championships, those of Switzerland, Germany, India, Thailand and Scotland.

Norman von Nida was many things during his career. He was enormously talented. He was impudent. He was volatile. He was determined. And Peter Thomson salutes him as the pathfinder for Australian golfers going overseas.

More than any other Australian golfer, The Von succeeded in pushing his sport into the newspaper headlines in the years immediately after World War II.

Part of golfing folklore is the tale of fourteen-year-old von Nida, only 162 centimetres tall, approaching the legendary Walter Hagen on a visit to Brisbane for a series of exhibition matches and asking could he carry his clubs. When he saw the doubt on Hagen's face, he quickly chirped: 'Mr Hagen. I'm to carry your clubs. I'm the best caddie in Brisbane.'

'Okay, son,' said Hagen, looking down at him.

'Then you and I are a winning pair, for I'm the best golfer in Brisbane.'

Several years later, in 1936, the equally famous Gene Sarazen, who had only recently won the British Open, was also playing a series of exhibition matches in Australia when von Nida challenged him to a £50 winner-take-all match. The fact von Nida didn't have that much cash didn't worry him in the slightest. He borrowed it and beat Sarazen!

Thereafter, The Von went on to win more than 100 titles around the world, despite his career being interrupted by World War II when he spent five years in the AIF. He won three Australian Opens in 1950–52–53 and was runner-up on six other occasions.

Although not evident on the course, his tempestuous and outspoken nature often saw him at loggerheads with the media, particularly in Britain, and sometimes with other players. During the 1948 Lower Rio Grande tournament in America, he got into an altercation with American golfer Henry Ransom, who had allegedly altered a five to a four on his card. The matter was referred to the tournament director. Ransom took exception and let fly. Typically, The Von retaliated.

In his later years, many famous golfers came to him for instruction and advice – Gary Player, Bruce

Devlin, Bruce Crampton, David Graham, Peter Thomson and the greatest of them all, Jack Nicklaus.

Greg Norman was born on 10 February, 1955 in the mining town of Mt Isa.

His mother Toini is Finnish. Her parents Seth and Tyyne Hovi were married in Finland and migrated to Australia around 1930. His father's ancestors were a mixture of Norwegian, Danish, German and English. It's from this combination that he derives his Nordic looks.

American professional Marty Bohen needed only nineteen putts in his closing 10-under-par 63 in the 1977 South Australian Open at Royal Adelaide, thus equalling the world record. His only chip-in occurred at the 9th hole.

Watching Jack Nicklaus play on one of his numerous Australian visits, Melbourne golf writer Don Lawrence pondered on the rotund build and blond hair and came up with the nickname 'The Golden Bear'. The name stuck and Nicklaus adopted it as the trademark for his golfing empire, which manufactures clothing and equipment, and builds golf courses around the world.

Lawrence never received a cent from his inspiration, although Nicklaus readily acknowledges that he was its source.

'(Ian) Baker-Finch now thinks par is what you call your grandfather.'
– Patrick Smith, writing on the sad decline of the former British Open champion.

Until this day, Horace Henry Alfred (Ossie) Pickworth carries the distinction of being the only man to win three successive Australian Opens (1946–47–48). He tagged another to that treble in 1954.

Undoubtedly, his most memorable victory was when he completed his hat-trick of Open wins at Kingston Heath in 1948, when he beat Jim Ferrier by three shots (71 to 74) in a playoff. Ferrier, the reigning US PGA champion, had irked Pickworth's many followers by recalling the pre-war days when Ossie had caddied for him at Manly.

After the playoff, Ferrier urged Pickworth to try his luck in America, but Ossie wasn't interested. Having spent five and a half years as a cook in the army in World War II, during which he saw action in Borneo, he didn't fancy spending any more time away.

Pickworth scored many wonderful victories, but none finer than his defeat of South Africa's Bobby Locke on Royal Melbourne's West Course in October 1950. Locke, who had won the British Open the previous year, had a stroke score for the round of 65, yet was defeated 2 and 1 in matchplay by Pickworth, who zipped around in 12-under-par 63 in what has been described as 'the greatest par-shattering exhibition of golf ever seen in Australia.' Yet Ossie three-putted the last green!

Greg Norman once owned a house at Paradise Point, just north of Surfers Paradise, named Divot and had a cruiser named Divot II.

Despite Peter Thomson's course record of 63 in a qualifying round of the 1958 British Open at Royal Lytham and St Annes, a gatekeeper failed to recognise him when he arrived for the first round.

'What are you?' asked the gateman, wondering if Thomson was a player, official or spectator.

'Presbyterian,' came Thomson's reply.

Golf

When the world's greatest cricketer, Sir Donald Bradman, stored away his bat for the last time, he turned to golf, becoming a scratch-marker at Kooyonga in Adelaide.

In his early golfing days he found himself by accident playing in the club's Saturday competition with the *Adelaide Advertiser* sports writer, Sylvester Phelan, himself an accomplished golfer. Thereafter, Bradman insisted that they continue to play together, which they did on a weekly basis to the virtual exclusion of all others for several decades until Phelan's death.

Phelan's lament was that he spent hundreds of hours listening to cricketing yarns and controversies from Bradman – who otherwise refused to talk to the press – and yet was honour-bound never to write a single word of it.

'I am not a machine all the time and sometimes I get a little squeaky.'
– Greg Norman

In 1954, two players who had been team mates for Victoria Golf Club in Melbourne brought the club a unique distinction, Peter Thomson became Australia's first British Open champion and Doug Bachli was the first Australian to win the British amateur championship. For a year, the two trophies adorned the same mantleshelf at the club.

'Lady, the problem with you is you're arguing too much out of emotion and not enough about golf course architecture. Trees are for the Botanical Gardens.'

– Mike Clayton, to a lady who questioned the removal of a number of trees in his restoration work of Victoria Golf Club.

The amazing scoring skills of Billy Dunk were never more in evidence than in the 1970 North Coast Open tournament at Coffs Harbour. His round roared into life with birdie, birdie, par, birdie, birdie, birdie, birdie, birdie, birdie, eagle, par, birdie so that he was a phenomenal 11-under-par after 12 holes!

The fire in his putting then extinguished itself somewhat and he added four more pars before bogeying the last two holes.

Still, his nine-under-par 63 remains among the finest rounds in Australian golf history.

Royal Melbourne has seen some spectacular golf over the years, but none quite as phenomenal as the left-handed member whose drive from the first tee of the West Course holed out on the 18th hole of the East Course. As an admiring spectator remarked, he had covered 36 holes in one shot.

After winning the 1995 Canon Challenge at Terrey Hills Golf & CC, Craig Parry sped from the course to the international terminal at Sydney Airport, where he caught a flight to Los Angeles and then a connecting service to Orlando, Florida, where he lives while playing the US Tour.

Thanks to the international dateline, he arrived home that same Sunday night.

After just a few hours' sleep, he rose at 4 a.m. Monday for the four-hour drive to the Doral Ryder Open in Miami.

Three hours down the road he suddenly had the sickening feeling that he had forgotten something. So he pulled over, phoned the tournament office and had his worst fears confirmed.

He had forgotten to submit an entry!

'I felt such a fool,' said Parry, who spun the car around and drove cursing all the way back to Orlando.

In 1977 at Sydney's Chatswood Golf Club, 19-handicapper Sue Prell created a world record by having successive holes-in-one. She got her first ace by holing a six-iron shot which hit the pin before dropping in at the 122-metre 13th. She popped the ball in her bag as a souvenir. Then with a brand new one, Miss Prell smacked a four-wood shot to the 167-metre 14th. It landed a metre short of the cup and rolled in.

The 1969 Australian Open was rostered for Royal Sydney and the crusty atmosphere and old, refined furnishings of this splendid and exclusive old club on Sydney's Rose Bay rattled with controversy from the very first day.

Indeed, the rumpus attained almost the same volume as that in 1911 which led to the formation of the Professional Golfers' Association.

In fairness to the club, which has an extremely large membership and inordinately small car parking space, it must be pointed out that it has to place restrictions on its own members during the playing of major tournaments. So competitors in the Open were required to park their cars in a side street near the first green and tote their equipment up the first fairway to the clubhouse.

A large marquee was set up adjacent to the

clubhouse for players to have meals, but they were permitted to use the locker rooms and have drinks in the bar.

Severe reaction to these conditions came from overseas players and the following is from Mark H. McCormack's *Golf Annual* of 1970: 'Signs at the clubhouse door read 'Members and competitors only' and an army of grey uniformed guards stopped golfers' wives, business managers and guests from setting foot in the domain of Australia's aristocracy. Australian PGA officials were also turned away. 'I've got to get into the locker room to talk to the players,' tournament director (Bob) Wilson explained on one occasion. 'Do your business while they are on the course,' he was told sternly. Qantas, which was sponsoring the tournament (to the tune of $50 000), also had its officials turned away. Orange-blazered Qantas men had to use the outdoor privies, which were two blackened cans and a length of roof gutter behind the 17th tee.'

To add to this criticism, Peter Thomson discovered that the cups on all the greens were too small.

Thomson measured each with his putter, which has a four and one quarter inch blade (the lawful diameter of a hole). Not one was the correct size and Thomson, to prove his point, sent his putter to a nearby manufacturing plant to be measured. It was found to be within 1.1000th of an inch of what he claimed. The next day the cups were cut to the proper size.

To make things even less agreeable, a gale developed on the final afternoon, blew over the main scoreboard and generally created awful havoc.

The Australian Open did not return to Royal Sydney for another nineteen years. On that occasion in 1988 it was staged without any of the acrimony, or restrictions, of the previous championship held there.

'This game is about 90 to 95 per cent in the head and anyone who says it's not is stupid.'

– Robert Allenby.

Jack Newton's influence on Australian golf has been wide-ranging, firstly as a marvellous player and more recently as a television commentator, course designer and foster parent of junior golf.

After a fine amateur career, he turned professional in 1970 and headed for the European Tour the following year. He won his first tournament, the Dutch Open, in 1972 and continued to enjoy success both there and later in America.

His most famous tournament was the 1975 British Open, in which he shot rounds of 69–71–65–

74 at Carnoustie to tie Tom Watson, then the greatest player in the world. They went out again the following day for a 18-hole playoff and he was nipped at the post, with Watson shooting 71 to his 72.

Jack won the Australian Open at Metropolitan in 1979 with a score of 288. The next year he had six birdies in the first seven holes of the US Masters at Augusta before finishing equal second to another of the game's greats, Seve Ballesteros.

In July, 1983, he had a near-fatal accident when he walked into the whirling, chopping propeller of a light aircraft he was attempting to board at Sydney airport. From the shocking mess it made of him, he lost his right arm and eye and suffered serious abdominal injuries. For days he lingered between life and death, but slowly began to recover. Among his first visitors was then Prime Minister Bob Hawke.

With his golfing career finished, Newton turned his attention to TV commentary and became the most respected expert in this field, providing not only a deep knowledge of the game and rules, but interesting insights into the personalities of the players. Jack also gives much of his time to junior golf. He's founder and chairman of the Jack Newton Junior Golf Foundation, which introduces children to golf and cultivates their interest in it.

Even the loss of his arm has not stopped him

returning to playing golf. He continues to amaze other golfers by being able to comfortably play to a handicap of sixteen, a level most able-bodied golfers would be extremely happy to achieve.

The 1995 US PGA champion Steve Elkington has a most unwelcome complaint for one of the world's finest golfers. He's allergic to pollen, dust and grass!

Fortunately he only ever encounters any real problems in certain places at certain times of the year – in Melbourne in November/December, in Houston in April/May and at the British Open each July.

'The sinus operation I had (in 1995) doesn't make me any less allergic to anything,' he said. 'It just gives me a wider passage to breathe through. Where I used to have a one-way street I now have a four-lane highway.'

Whenever the bad time approaches at home, or he's going to Melbourne or Britain, he has an asthma specialist in Houston check what flowers are blooming, mix up an antidote and he injects himself with it each morning.

Despite his vast number of successes, Greg Norman's mastery of the golfing world was never more apparent than in 1986.

He won twice on the US Tour, was second four times and had ten top-ten finishes in nineteen starts. Elsewhere, he won the British Open at Turnberry (including Friday's 63, with an eagle, eight birdies and a three-putt on the last!), the European Open at Sunningdale, the Suntory World Match Play title and then the Queensland, NSW, South Australian and West Australian Opens.

In the world's four majors that year, he was the leader going into the final round.

He led by one stroke going into the last day of the Masters and finished equal second. He was one in front after three days of the US Open and finally tied for 12th. He led by four at the US PGA and finished second. He was ahead by one after three days of the British Open and went on to clinch his first major by five strokes.

Australians were eager to watch Lee Trevino when the flamboyant and enormously talented American came to play in the $450 000 Chrysler Classic at Royal Melbourne in 1974.

After viewing the famous layout during four practice rounds. Trevino commented, 'This is a tremendous golf course, one of the best in the world. It's a course on which you have to play defence golf – it's impossible to attack it. The greens are so fast – and they could be faster by the end of the tournament – that it's impossible to go for birdie putts outside of four or five metres.'

After opening rounds of 75–75, he found his stride and returned a 66 in the third round. In the final round, however, the Dear Old Thing took her revenge and he returned a humiliating 77 to finish equal third. Trevino signed his card, walked briskly across the practice green and, without so much as removing his spikes, dived into his courtesy car and issued directions to get him out of the place.

On the run he made a virtiolic attack on the course to the media representatives hurrying alongside him, describing the greens as 'the biggest joke since Watergate' and saying that 'the people of Royal Melbourne are proud of the greens . . . so they can have 'em!' He then suggested that the media photographers get a snap of him driving out the club's gates because he wouldn't be coming back.

Trevino's outburst brought a $500 fine from the PGA and, in due course, he paid this and also tendered a letter of apology.

'I don't know how the hell that happened.'
– American John Daly, after shooting six consecutive birdies in the second round of the 1995 Australian Open at Kingston Heath.

Golf

The Vardon Trophy is the most prized award on the US Tour, for it is awarded annually to the player with the best scoring average.

Greg Norman won it in 1989 (69.49), 1990 (69.10) and 1994 (68.81).

He was also the moral, if not official, winner in 1995. He finished with an average of 69.06 strokes from fifty-eight rounds, but was ineligible for the award because he pulled out during a round earlier in the year.

Norman, who hit just the opening tee shot in the second round of the Heritage Classic in April before back spasms forced him to withdraw, was an unintended victim of a rule designed to stop players from quitting during a bad round to protect their average.

Norman said it was the only award he really cared about. 'I don't care about all the other stuff. (The Vardon Trophy), that's the most important thing to me,' he said.

Gary (Smokey) Dawson did what so many golfers yearn to do when he spent a whole week playing golf – literally.

He just kept going round and round Northbridge golf course in Sydney night and day from one Monday to the next in a fundraising marathon drive to help sick kids. Eventually, he completed 1180 holes.

During his marathon he lost over three dozen balls, wore out eight pairs of golf shoes, twenty-one pairs of socks and, naturally, ended up with blistered hands and feet.

In all, he hit 5141 strokes, played 65 rounds (plus 10 holes) and finished with the impressive scoring average of 78 per round. He walked 331 477 metres and had a hole-in-one.

He smashed the previous record, set in America, of 1128 holes. He even stumbled across a couple in the dead of night in the most intimate of poses and, in the process, raised more than $50 000.

Jan Stephenson has caused more than a few ripples and newspaper headlines during her illustrious career. Bred in working-class Balmain, she was an amateur sensation in the 1960s and early 1970s, winning many schoolgirl, junior and senior titles while surviving the occasional spat with officialdom.

She made a blistering attack on the national selectors and the NSW Ladies' Golf Union in a magazine article in January 1971, but would have been in boiling water had she not convinced authorities that she was a bona fide trainee journalist.

The following year she rang this writer and over lunch asked whether she should stick with journalism or turn professional. Putting down my glass of bitter flagon reisling, I advised her of the far greater financial rewards to be had from golf. Within a few months, she turned professional and in July 1974 headed for America to join the US LPGA Tour.

Jan had three qualities which set her aside: she was an extraordinarily talented golfer, with a looping follow-through which ended with her resembling a tangled ball of wool; she possessed enormous competitive spirit and ambition; and she was strikingly attractive, with long, bouncing locks setting off a wholesome, embracing smile, sparkling teeth and the softest of complexions.

In America, Jan was an instant attraction with the media and showed that she had the talent to complement her looks. Within two years, she registered her first Tour win and from there her career took off in spectacular fashion.

She became the Tour's ninth millionaire in 1985 and won three of the four majors, including the 1983 US Women's Open in blazing heat at the Cedar Ridge Country Club in Broken Arrow, Oklahoma. It was so hot that the Governor of Oklahoma declared a heat emergency as five residents of nearby Tulsa expired from the heat. An unofficial thermometer indicated the temperature was 140°F in some bunkers and 115°F in the rough.

After four energy-sapping days Jan held a three-stroke lead with just three holes to play. But it was not all over. She then bogeyed both the 17th and 18th holes, but maintained her shot to spare to win the US national crown.

Over the years her name has seemed permanently stuck in the news for her off-course activities as well, for she stirred up a nest of criticism for some provocative calendar poses in slit dresses (*Playboy* even offered her $US55 000 to do some minus the slit dresses), had some flawed, mixed-up romances, produced an exercise video for people with arthritis, flies her own plane, designs golf courses (becoming the first woman pro to do so), was honorary chairman of the National Multiple Sclerosis Society and sold over 50 000 of her golf video.

A little over a century ago golf was largely unknown outside Scotland, where sufficient is known of the early game to suggest that until about 1650 it may have resembled the Dutch game of colf. At that time it began changing to resemble the modern game.

Then the Scots began spreading the gospel from Perth (where the six-hole links on the city's North Inch was the first recognisable course), St Andrews, Prestwick and Dornoch to every corner of the earth.

They became the game's disciples, taking it firstly to England and then to every corner of the world where the Empire held sway.

Among those itinerant Scots was Alexander Reid, who migrated to Australia in the 1820s, settled in Tasmania and, using clubs and 'feathery' balls, played golf on some cleared land at his property, Ratho, at Bothwell some seventy-five kilometres from Hobart. The Ratho homestead was completed in 1834, and soon after Reid established a course and invited friends to play on it. Play was by invitation only until 1904 when the nine-hole Bothwell Golf Club was formed.

Thus golf came to the shores of our continent.

Tom Ramsey in his book *Discover Australia's Golf Courses* says, 'Driving past it, one could easily miss Australia's oldest golf course. No wonder, its club probably has the smallest membership of any in Australia – eleven playing members. They wouldn't want to work up too much of a thirst either, at least for alcohol, because liquor is not allowed in the clubhouse or on the course.'

The greens at Ratho are fenced off, and for good reason, says Ramsey. Assisting the solitary caretaker in keeping the fairways well trimmed is a mob of thirty or so sheep. Players hitting the fence with their approach shots are permitted another try if they wish. The reason for the cohabitation is that the club does not own the land, but pays a peppercorn rent of ten cents a year.

'Most of the history of Ratho has been lost, and

what is known had only been passed down by word of mouth,' says Ramsey. 'It seems a shame that, with golf flourishing in this country, the scene of its beginnings should remain so humble.'

In the first 500 weeks that the Sony world rankings were in operation, Greg Norman held the position of the world's number one golfer for 231 of those weeks. In that time he was the only player never to have been out of the top-ten.

The darkest clouds of anger and despair hung over Wayne Grady on the last green of the 1992 SxL Sanctuary Cove Classic on The Pines course at Sanctuary Cove. His putting had let him down.

So in a moment of pique, he tossed the putter to a group of small boys standing alongside the green and told the lucky one who caught it, 'Here, keep it.' The kid was gone in a flash.

It perhaps didn't dawn on Grades at the time that he had just lost the putter with which he had won his only major, the 1990 US PGA championship at Crooked Stick, Alabama, and that at any auction it would have attracted a vast sum of money.

'Nicklaus's courses are like Jack himself – grim and humourless, with sharp edges.'

– Peter Thomson on courses designed by the Golden Bear.

Royal Melbourne's composite course is considered among the finest courses of the world. Indeed, in the most current rankings compiled by the authoritive *US Golf* magazine it comes in sixth behind Pine Valley, Cypress Point, Pebble Beach, Augusta National and the Old Course at St Andrews. Very august company.

Yet the layout upon which such votes are cast is unavailable for play even to members.

Royal Melbourne has two courses, with twelve holes from the West Course and six from the East Course combining to form the composite course, which has been the scene for many great tournaments, including the Canada Cup and its successor the World Cup, the Eisenhower Cup world amateur teams matches and many Australian Open and amateur championships.

Yet it's incorrect to assume that they represent the finest eighteen holes at Royal Melbourne. Rather, those holes used in the composite course have been chosen because they lay within the main enclosure surrounding the clubhouse, which facilitates the control of spectators and avoids crossing roads.

Robert Allenby fulfilled his immense promise by winning the 1994 Australian Open at Royal Sydney, although history will remember the occasion more for the finish.

In a remarkable final hour's play, Allenby lurched home with a bogey, double-bogey, bogey, bogey finish (and then dared any media type to label him a 'choker', which everyone promptly reported). He fell across the line by a shot from an equally jelly-legged Brett Ogle, who played the last eight holes in four-over-par. Between them, they surrendered eight shots to par over the final four holes!

The prominence placed on winning the world's four majors has unfairly clouded the achievements of Bruce Crampton.

His finest year in a superb twenty-year career on the US Tour came in 1973, when Crampton won four tournaments and finished second on the money list with over $US274 000. That same year he became only the fifth player in PGA history to earn more than $US1 million in prize money, adding his name to the exalted list of Arnold Palmer, Billy

Casper, Jack Nicklaus and Lee Trevino.

He was perhaps the best player of his time not to win a major. But he did come close: he was equal second in the 1972 US Masters and twice second in the US PGA (1973 and 1975). In the US Open he had a fifth, a sixth and, in 1972, a second to Nicklaus. So in 1972 he was second in two of the four majors.

Greg Norman's final-round 78 that turned a six-stroke lead into a five-stroke loss at the 1996 US Masters in August provoked 'overwhelming' support from the Australian golfing public. He was 'flooded' with faxes. The Green Jacket winner, Nick Faldo, said, 'I've come out great but I do feel sorry for Greg. I hope people will remember that I shot 67 to come roaring back. But it's going to be remembered for what happened to Greg.'

The US press reacted with sympathy – 'God, but this was painful to watch. A man bled to death on a golf course. Right in front of us. The life leaked right out of Greg Norman. And if you took any pleasure at all in witnessing this, then your heart is as hard as a tombstone' intoned Bill Lyon in Knight-Ridder Newspapers. While Bob Gillespie in the same paper said, 'This was golf's equivalent of watching a five-car pile-up, in four hours of slow motion.' Norman remained philosophical. 'Maybe these hiccups that I have inflicted on myself are meant for another reason. I think there is something waiting down the line that's going to be good for me.'

Karrie Webb hit the US LPGA Tour in 1996 like one of those tornadoes which frequently sweep through America's mid-west.

Having won the British Open for her first tournament win, the twenty-one-year-old decided to try her luck in America. Except that luck never really had to provide any assistance.

After finishing runner-up in her debut tournament, in only her second start she won the Health-South tournament at Lake Buena Vista, one of five championship courses at Disney World.

Co-incidentally, she was just a shy schoolgirl when she first visited Disney World. The winner of a Greg Norman Foundation Scholarship, part of her prize was to spend a week with The Shark and his family at their home in Florida; the visit to the famous theme park was an extra treat. That was nearly four years before.

Webb's extraordinary success continued unabated during the season, with some experts labelling her the finest golfing prospect, male or female, to have appeared for ten years.

Her long-time coach Kel Haller, who has shaped her game for the past thirteen years, says: 'She'll go all the way. And I think she'll get there sooner than anyone expects. We knew this would happen. The only surprise is that she's running well ahead of time.'

Haller, a former greenkeeper and three-marker at Webb's home course in Ayr, Queensland, is a quadriplegic, following a work accident some years ago. Though he cannot be with her at tournaments, his eyes and ears is his nephew Todd Haller, who is both her caddie – and her fiancé.

'She doesn't need to ring home to go over her game,' says Kel. 'Having Todd there is great. He's a pretty good golfer and analyst himself. She has got great trust in him on the course, while he's there for her off it as well.'

BIBLIOGRAPHY

The Complete Book of Australian Golf, Terry Smith, ABC Enterprises, Sydney, 1988.

Discover Australia's Golf Courses, Tom Ramsey, J. M. Dent, Melbourne, 1987.

Great Days of Australian Golf, Phil Tresidder, Ironbark Press, Sydney, 1990.

It's a Sporting Life, Jim Webster, Macmillan, Sydney, 1986.

The Masters of Golf, Dick Aultman and Ken Bowden, Stanley Paul, London, 1975.

Pro Golf, Out of the Rough, Colin De Groot and Jim Webster, Professional Golfers' Association of Australia, Sydney, 1991.

The World of Professional Golf, Mark H McCormack, Hodder and Stoughton, London, 1971.

RUGBY LEAGUE

Alan Clarkson is a long-time sports reporter with the *Sydney Morning Herald* and the *Herald Sun*. In his earlier years he was a soccer writer before becoming involved in rugby league as understudy to one of Australia's great sports writers, Tom Goodman. When Goodman retired in 1967 Alan Clarkson became chief League writer for the *Sydney Morning Herald* and the *Herald Sun*, a position he held for twenty-one years.

He received an Order of Australia Medal for services to sport in journalism in 1990. In 1995 he assisted Mal Meninga, the former Australian and Canberra captain, with his autobiography, *My Life in Football*.

195

RUGBY LEAGUE PAIN IS PART OF THE GAME

If you ever want to start a lively discussion at any rugby league gathering, simply pose the question, who was the toughest player?

After setting the scene, stand back and enjoy some fierce arguments over the merits of those gladiators who regard pain as being part of the game.

In fairly recent times there was John Sattler's incredible effort of playing through most of the 1970 grand final at the Sydney Cricket Ground with a double fracture of the jaw. Sattler, the South Sydney captain and front-row forward, was one of the toughest, most uncompromising players. He gave plenty and received some back but he always accepted it as part of the game.

Sattler's jaw was shattered by a blow from a

Manly forward early in the first half of the grand final.

'Grab me Lurch, don't let me fall,' Sattler mumbled to his front-row partner John O'Neill. Sattler's only desire was to stay on his feet because he did not want to go down and let the Manly players and the crowd know he was hurt. It was an incredible feat of endurance and courage. He remained in the thick of the action, setting an example in defence and taking the ball up time and time again. There was never any question of his going off. He played out the match, led Souths to a 23–12 win and made a gracious acceptance speech when it was all over.

Only the South Sydney players and officials knew the terrible injury Sattler had suffered. The media were kept out of Souths' dressing room for an unusually long time after the match. When they were finally admitted they found Sattler sitting in the bath, a slight trickle of blood coming from the corner of his mouth. The bottom part of his jaw swung around like a gate in heavy wind.

'Don't say anything about it, I might be able to get through the medical in the morning,' Sattler said. He was hoping to be selected in the Australian team for the World Cup series and then convince the League medical officer he was fit enough to play. But it wasn't to be. Hours after the final whistle,

Sattler was admitted to hospital to have his jaw wired.

Then there was the equally incredible feat of courage by the brilliant Clive Churchill in the dramatic 1955 premiership season.

The star-studded South Sydney team had won just three of their first ten matches and it seemed inevitable their run of premiership success was about to end. When they lost the first match of the second round they faced the formidable task of having to win every remaining match to take out the premiership. It was virtually a grand final every weekend and the class and experience of the great Souths team responded to the challenge.

Their real test came early in the match against Manly when Churchill snapped his left forearm. In those days there were no replacements and Churchill did not consider coming off the field. At half-time he refused point-blank the request by the team doctor to stay off the field. Instead he had a pain-killing injection and his left arm encased in a make-shift cardboard cast.

Churchill did not flinch. He tackled as tigerishly as he usually did and his feat of endurance was an inspiration to his team-mates. Five minutes from the end, Souths' great lock Len Cowie held up a pass to winger Ian Moir and crashed over to level the score seven-all. Captain-coach Jack Rayner had to decide who would take the kick which could determine whether or not Souths remained in the running for the premiership. Rayner stopped at Churchill, handed him the ball and the fullback calmly built up a little divot, placed the ball and sent it spinning rather sloppily through the posts for a great victory.

It was blood pressure time in every match from then on. Souths beat Manly 14–12 in the semi-final, and St George 18–14 in the final after trailing 14–9, then a nerve-tingling 12–11 win over Newtown in the grand final, after being down 11–7 only seven minutes from the end, gave them the premiership.

South Sydney's goal-kicking second rower Bernie Purcell was an important factor in their climb back from near the bottom of the table in 1955, not only for his goal kicking but for his outstanding play. Looking back, Purcell is still at a loss to explain just why Souths went off the boil in the first part of the season.

'After losing the first match in the second round, Jack Rayner our captain-coach, called a meeting behind closed doors,' Purcell recalled.

'It was a no-holds barred meeting and everyone

was on the receiving end. Rayner showed himself an outstanding leader and coach.

'To me that was the turning point for the team. I felt it was starting to click into place.

'From then on there was no second chance for us. We had to win every match and with a number of them we just scraped in by a couple of points. In some of those sudden-death matches we trailed with less than ten minutes to go. But we survived. The further we went the more confident we became, although at no stage were we cocky about our chances.

'The loss of Clive after the Manly match was a massive blow but we were lucky we had a great back-up in Don Murdoch who would have been a first grader at any other club.

'The player I felt sorry for was one of our prop forwards, Jim Richards. Jim had played every match during the season but a shoulder injury kept him out of the big one, and there are few things to equal winning a grand final.'

After the initial grand final celebrations at the Sydney Cricket Ground, the entire South Sydney team packed themselves into cars and went out to visit the club's former President, Jack Glasheen, who had stood down from the position because of ill-health.

'When we arrived at Jack's place there he was in

his pyjamas and wearing his premiership blazer from our 1954 win,' Purcell said.

Purcell made the point that five of the South Sydney pack that season, Len Cowie, Ernie Hammerton, Denis Donoghue, Jack Rayner and himself played over 150 first grade games for Souths, something that rarely happens in the 90s.

While discussing Purcell, he was on the receiving end of one of the most ridiculous questions ever posed by a sports journalist, which just happened to be me.

Purcell was injured and was carried off the field in agony, his collarbone badly dislocated. After the match I went into the Souths' dressing room. Purcell was lying on the table, his face white and contorted with the pain.

'How are you Bernie?' I asked.

Purcell looked at me, shook his head and said, 'Just great and thanks for asking!'

One journo back to the drawing board to study appropriate questions.

When you think about the really hard players in the game – not those who drop their knees onto a player who is already on the ground or hit them high from behind – there's an army of granite-tough talent.

Two of the hard men of the game, Sattler and

John O'Neill nominate Kevin Ryan as the hardest player they encountered.

Kevin Ryan was a well-performed rugby union international before making the decision to switch codes in 1960.

I was in Brisbane covering a tennis tournament when a friend said that Ryan was keen to play rugby league. I spoke with Kevin and when I returned to Sydney rang a few clubs, South Sydney, Western Suburbs, Manly and the St George secretary, Frank Facer. He asked if I had a photo of Ryan and when I produced one he looked at the superbly built player and said, 'I like the look of the boy.'

Ryan was not an overnight success at St George. He had potential, there was no doubt about that, but perhaps the best thing that happened to him was being dropped back for a brief spell into reserve grade where the old fox, Harry Bath, was coaching.

As far as playing skills were concerned, Bath and Ryan were like chalk and cheese. Bath was a clever ball-playing forward while Ryan was a rather straight-up-and-down player who could destroy opponents with the sheer ferocity of his defence. It is history that Ryan, after being moved from the second row to the front row, became one of the best props in the game. He was tough and relentless, but to his great credit he never went looking for trouble. However, if it started, he could handle it.

There is a great story about Ryan, supposedly told by the Balmain prop, the late George Piper. Ryan was having a great game against Balmain, destroying their attacks with his defence and creating problems with his driving bursts. A hasty meeting was called and Piper was elected to stop Ryan by any possible means. Piper said that he hit Ryan with the best right-hand he had ever thrown, claiming that the punch would have ripped the head off a bullock. But Ryan merely looked at him and said, 'Not a bad one George ... yours is coming.'

Piper, who had plenty of courage, was later sent off.

Another story testifying to Ryan's strength came from the former Test forward Dennis Manteit. Playing his first Queensland representative match at the Sydney Cricket Ground Manteit faced the seasoned Ryan, and being a brash young kid at the time suggested that Ryan should be elsewhere rather than on the field with the young up-and-comers. Manteit took the ball up and Ryan met him head on. 'All I wanted to do after that was crawl off the ground and go home to my mother,' Manteit said.

In 1965 many believed the St George reign was over, to be replaced by a South Sydney team bristling with future talent.

In the grand final, watched by a record crowd of

78 056, Saints triumphed 12–8 and while there was only a four points' difference at the finish, Saints were never going to lose.

Ryan was great that day. He was a mobile powerhouse, dominating the forward play and, with help from his friends, smacked the tails of the pretenders.

After the match, in the crowded dressing room, secretary Facer came up to me and said, 'Clarkson, if you ever find another Kevin Ryan bring him straight to me.'

I never did find another like big Kevin.

Once you have settled just who was the toughest player you may as well keep the argument on the boil by asking just who was the best Australian player?

There will be strong arguments for Clive Churchill, for Johnny Raper, for Reg Gasnier and Graeme Langlands, for Wally Lewis, Arthur Beetson, Peter Sterling, Bradley Clyde, Laurie Daley and Bobby Fulton.

Try to imagine in the mad market operating in rugby league in the 90s what Churchill, Raper, Gasnier, Langlands and Fulton would be worth.

When you have a group of players like that, just how do you separate them? Each was a footballing genius, a thorough tradesman to back up marvellous talent. Churchill, Gasnier, Langlands, Lewis, Beetson, Sterling, Fulton and Daley could win a match in the blink of an eye while Raper and Clyde could win a match through their defence.

Over the years I watched Raper play, I never saw him play a bad match. There were simply degrees of excellence with him. One of the little known stories about Raper emerged recently from the former St George Chairman of Selectors, Laurie Doust. St George played Newtown and they were beaten mainly because of the incredible work rate of Raper, who was then playing for Newtown. The St George secretary, Frank Facer, turned to Doust and said, 'We would have won except for that kid. We'll have to get him.'

So Saints went after the young second rower. Armed with a contract Facer and Doust set out to talk to Raper at his home but they could not find the house.

'We called into a hotel which was closed but we knew the publican,' Doust recalled. 'He asked what we were doing in the area and we told him we were looking for Johnny Raper's home. There was a policeman there and he said he knew where Raper lived and he would take us there. He was on his police motorcycle so we arrived with a police escort.

'We talked to Raper in the front room of his home

with his brand new twin brothers asleep in their cots. It was Raper's 19th birthday and he agreed to the contract and signed it, using one of the twin's cots as a table. While we were having the discussion in the front of the house, Newtown officials were out in the backyard preparing a barbecue for his 19th birthday.'

For the record, Doust rates Raper the best from his time at St George and that certainly takes in a lot of super footballers.

The late Dave Brown, Australian captain in 1986, never hesitated when asked to name his best player . . . the great Reg Gasnier.

Brown argued that Gasnier could win a match for his team in a split second and no one could argue with that.

Another great in that era was the gifted Graeme Langlands, a dynamic player at either fullback or in the centre. It is a cruel twist of fate that Langlands will be remembered for one match, the 1975 grand final when Eastern Suburbs scored a 38–0 win over St George, led by Langlands. He had been troubled for most of the season by a groin muscle strain, so to make sure everything went right for the big match Langlands had a painkilling injection before the match. But it went horribly wrong. The injection hit the wrong spot and he could not control his right leg. His attempts at clearing the ball and finding touch went astray and at half-time both Frank Facer and Laurie Doust wanted him to stay off. But Langlands refused and no one really expected anything different.

He was a miserable sight at the end of the match as his good friend, Easts' captain Arthur Beetson, tried to console him. But when you are a champion like Langlands and your team gets beaten by a record score to which you were a major contributor, there is no consolation.

Kangaroo tours have been a constant source of anecdotes, some able to be told, others to be forgotten.

My first Kangaroo tour was in 1967 when the team and the small party of media stayed at the Ilkley Moor Hotel in the delightful village of Ilkley on the Yorkshire moors.

A great place to visit but it wasn't the right venue for twenty-six footballers. The hotel was a horror, it made Fawlty Towers look like The Regent. Years after the tour, when fire destroyed the hotel, about a million cockroaches and mice were suddenly homeless!

Imagine the scene. Twenty-six footballers racing back to the hotel after training to get to the bathrooms as quickly as possible. The reason is simple. After about a dozen baths, the hot water always ran out and there is nothing worse than easing into a cold bath in the middle of an English winter.

There were some great players on that tour, Graeme Langlands, Reg Gasnier, Johnny Raper, Noel Kelly, Peter Gallagher, Les Johns, Ron Coote, John McDonald, Johnny Greaves, Johnny Gleeson, Ken Irvine, Johnny King, Billy Smith, Tony Branson and many others.

Three of the hard men of the tour, Kelly, Peter Gallagher and John Sattler were room-mates. Their room, room 4, became known as Boys Town. It was customary to knock before being granted permission to enter.

Winger Les Hanigan was the unfortunate player allocated the task of duty boy on the first morning of the tour. It was the duty boy's task to get the players out of bed and ready for early morning training, and on match days to make sure all the gear was on board the team bus.

Hanigan bowled into Boys Town and came out backwards at breakneck speed with Kelly's bellowed, 'Knock before you enter, Meece' laying the ground rules for entering room 4.

('Meece' was the term used by the forwards to

describe the backs although I doubt if Mal Meninga or Gene Miles could ever be included in that category.)

There were problems on the 1967 tour, axes in a door, some furniture destroyed to keep the fire going, to mention just a few incidents.

On the French leg of the tour there was the very real risk the team would be thrown out of one hotel. Noel Kelly asked team manager Jack Drewes to call a meeting and there, behind closed doors, Kelly laid it on the line to the players who were causing problems. It boiled down to the simple fact – behave or he would take them on one at a time. He had support from Gallagher and Sattler and that strong stand virtually saved the tour from self-destruction.

Kelly was a tough, no-nonsense type of footballer who was equally at home at prop or hooker. The 1967 tour was his last and before the Ashes-deciding third Test I did an interview with him for Channel 7.

Kelly came out with one of the classic sporting predictions about his last hurrah in a Test match against Great Britain.

'If we are well in front and it's close to the final whistle, I reckon I'll have a bit of a go,' Kelly said.

Being a man of his word, Kelly looked at the scoreboard, then at the clock and finally at Tommy Bishop's head. That big right arm went whizzing for the great little halfback's head, Tommy ducked, the crowd roared and the referee added to Kelly's record by sending him off.

It says a lot for the 1967 team that after losing the first Test to Great Britain, they won the next two and overcame incredible hurdles to win the Ashes.

Two of the stars, captain-coach Reg Gasnier and lock Johnny Raper were badly hurt in the first Test and were out of the second Test at White City, London. To make matters worse, halfback Billy Smith had to withdraw from the match which meant that Australia went into the Test without three of their top players.

Early in the match prop Noel Gallagher, playing in his first Test, was badly concussed by a swinging English arm. But he kept going, probably on instinct, and was there at the finish but he took little part in the celebrations back at the team's hotel.

While everyone in that match played magnificently, if there was one incident which could be classified as a turning point it was a brilliant covering tackle by Ron Coote.

Great Britain speedster, Ian Brooke, was put into the clear and raced down the sideline, but Coote cut across field and took him in a glorious tackle which put him metres over the sideline.

It was a classic covering tackle, one of the many memorable moments during Australia's superb 17–11 win after the scores were locked two-all at half time.

The 1967 tour produced one of the really sad moments of the game when the magnificent centre, Reg Gasnier, 'Puff the Magic Dragon', was forced to retire. He'd fractured his leg in the first Test against Great Britain and worked long and hard in a bid to get back on the field. Gasnier made his comeback in the Australian team playing the French Young Hopefuls at Avignon. He started the match in his customary position but when his leg started to hurt switched to lock. Early in the second half the crestfallen Gasnier slowly walked off the ground and his departure was hardly noticed by the tiny crowd of 1100. It was a miserable ending to the career of one of the greatest players the game has produced.

The French Rugby League came up with a couple of great characters in their representative teams in 1967. There was the fullback Pierre Lacaze who wore a wig on the field and the French forward who we were told was completely fearless. He had nothing to fear since he was playing with several bullets in his body after being shot by an irate husband!

But the real highlight of the tour was a conversation with that incredible footballer, Puig Aubert.

Puig Aubert wanted to dwell, rather heavily, on his success in the 1951 Test series against Australia and in particular the great Clive Churchill.

'Churchill there,' Puig Aubert said pointing to the left, 'then I kick it there' with his finger pointing to the right.

'But you didn't like to tackle.'

'Tackle. Me? Very small heart,' Puig Aubert replied, making a tiny circle with his thumb and forefinger and placing it on the left side of his chest.

That surely must go down as one of the games classic quotes.

Puig Aubert became a legend during the French 1951 tour of Australia, not only for his goal kicking, but for his habit of striding downfield and berating his forwards for letting an opposition player through.

His theory was that he was there to kick goals . . . the others were there to defend.

The French team did not set the rugby league world on fire in the first weeks of their tour. They lacked discipline, they squabbled with the referees and there were genuine fears the tour could end in disaster.

Before the first Test the then Chairman of the Australian Rugby League, Harry 'Jersey' Flegg, laid down an ultimatum. He did not mince words. He told them that it was a case of perform or there was every chance they would be sent home.

The Australian players probably wished Flegg had kept quiet because the French were transformed into a magnificent team of tough, brilliant footballers. They played a brand of football rarely seen before, or since, with devastating attacks from both the forwards and the backs.

In those days of unlimited tackle football Edouard Ponsinet and Elie Brousse, the two great second rowers, ripped the Australian defence to shreds.

France destroyed the Australian team 26–15 in the first Test, Australia won the second 23–11, but went down seven tries to two, a massive 35 points to 14, in the Ashes–deciding third Test.

The magnificent Australian second rower, Arthur Clues, who was acknowledged as one of the finest of all-time in his years with the Leeds club in England, had a number of 'confrontations' with French player, Edouard Ponsinet.

Clues was a regular member of the Other Nationalities team which played matches against both Great Britain and France with Harry Bath his regular second-row partner.

Clues tells of one match against France when he went head-hunting for Ponsinet, connected, and then watched him being carried off.

'In the return match France kicked off and incredibly the ball went to me. I went downfield, intent on getting through the clutch of players, and guess who was waiting ... Ponsinet.'

He estimates he was on the field a little over a minute before being carried off.

But forwards being forwards Clues and Ponsinet send each other Christmas cards!

The late South Sydney and international winger Johnny Graves loved to tell a story against himself.

Graves was on the 1948 Kangaroo tour of England and France and was selected to play against Warrington opposed by Brian Bevan the incredible Australian winger. Bevan was a legend with the English fans for his incredible ability to score the 'impossible' try.

In an interview several months before he died of cancer Graves said he had been worried about facing Bevan. 'But when we lined up and I saw this skinny little runt I started to grin. He was bald, he had no teeth and almost every part of him was strapped up.

'We kicked off, the ball went behind the Warrington line, Bevan picked it up and then proceeded to beat nearly all the Australian team and put the ball down between the posts.

'No more laughter ... ' was Graves's final comment on one of the greatest wingers the game has seen.

During his incredible career in English football Bevan scored 796 tries. Coach Harry Bath tells a story that in one match Bevan attempted to tackle an opponent. At half time the coach walked up to him, glared and said; 'Don't you ever do that again ... you are there to score tries ... they will do the tackling,' pointing at the rest of the team.

How things have changed.

Johnny Graves, apart from being one of the great characters of the game, was a superb winger who built up a solid working relationship with Clive Churchill in the South Sydney team.

There was one match played at Brookvale Oval on Anzac Day, 1951, when a record crowd filled the ground and overflowed onto the sideline.

Twice Graves had to clear a path through spectators to attempt kicks from close to the sideline.

'You'll never kick that,' one hopeful Manly fan yelled.

'Check tomorrow's paper,' Graves said as he moved in and booted the ball over the crossbar.

A young English couple, married in 1973, will never forget the few minutes before they went into their reception at the famous St George Hotel in Huddersfield.

The couple and their attendants, smiling at the battery of cameras trained on them, suddenly froze. There was a strange sound coming from the first floor which grew louder and louder. It turned out to be a couple of Australian players involved in a wrestling match. They wrestled their way down the stairs, and ended up at the feet of the startled bride and groom. They were then rounded up by the team manager, Charlie Gibson, and locked in their rooms.

It was a little like a couple of naughty boys being sent to bed without a beer.

The unmarried media representatives who travel with Australian Rugby League teams have been known to have a small amount of success with the North of England ladies.

There was one young buck who got a little greedy. He was courting two young ladies at the same time and such is the arrogance of youth, believed he would get away with it.

One evening Australia's answer to Rudolph Valentino was entertaining one of his young ladies when the other arrived at the hotel. Fortunately for the young media whiz one of Australia's finest sports writers, the late E.E. Christensen, was in the foyer and he made one of the great intercepts of the tour. After making a call to our young hero to alert him of the danger, Christo asked the young lady if she would like a drink. She agreed, and as they walked into the bar their appearance was greeted with thunderous applause from a number of Australian players.

It must be stated categorically that Christo's only vices were lollies and an occasional punt!

Another favourite media anecdote involved one more of the younger brigade with a keen eye for the ladies. On a trip to England he was determined to get some sleep on the plane and took some sleeping tablets just before it landed in Singapore. When he returned to his seat after the stopover he was stunned to find he'd been joined for the leg to London by a particularly beautiful woman. And she was very friendly. Our hero gave thanks and proceeded to enter into meaningful dialogue. Sadly for him any dreams of joining the exclusive Mile High Club faded as the sleeping tablets took their full effect. All converstion ended as his face dropped inelegantly into the trifle.

A businessman staying in the same hotel as an Australian team in Leeds had little to be grateful for. Emerging from the shower he saw his lady companion of the evening slipping out of the room with his wallet. Wrapping a towel around himself, he took off after her intent on getting his wallet back. He managed to prise open the door of the lift and they began to westle. The lift stopped at the ground floor and in stalked a media representative. Trained to make quick assessments, he knocked out the businessman, satisfied he had stopped him attempting to force his intentions on the woman. She then alighted from the lift, offered her profuse thanks to the media hero, and left with the wallet safely in her keeping.

A rugged English forward met an attractive young

lady during a tour of Australia. The pair had dinner several times and the player was invited home. During the evening there was this noise.

'What's that?' said the Englishman.

When told it was likely to be the lady's husband the Englishman asked, 'Where's the back door?'

'We don't have one,' she replied.

'Well, where would you like one,' said the frantic pom.

It sounds far-fetched, but it has become part of English rugby league folklore.

The marvellous English journalist, Jack McNamara, tells the story about one of the English tourists who met a woman from Sydney's eastern suburbs. He kept talking about her home, the magnificent paintings, the silver, the fine ornaments.

'Hang on,' said one of his team-mates after ten minutes or so of this. 'What are you planning, to make love to her or rob her?'

Former Australian and Manly captain, Max Krilich, would reluctantly agree he could not possibly be included in the category of goodlookers. Let's face it, packing down in the middle of a scrum for 334 or more games tends to alter the features.

Krilich made a couple of Kangaroo tours, in 1978 and as captain in 1982 when the team became the first to go through a tour of England and France unbeaten.

During the 1978 tour Krilich trained very hard and on one particular night was so exhausted he fell into a deep sleep. He awoke refreshed in the morning, made the customary trip to the bathroom and glanced at himself in the mirror. Who was that strange fellow in the mirror? Turned out it was Max ... minus one eyebrow.

Someone, during the night, realising Max was in a deep sleep, had slipped into his room and shaved if off. It remains one of the League's great secrets just who wielded the razor, although one rather rangy second rower has had the finger pointed at him. He's not talking!

Australian players, and even some members of the media, have been guilty of presenting a false impression of Australia to some of the north of England inhabitants.

There was a classic example on the 1990 Kangaroo tour when room-mates Bob Lindner and Gary Belcher had a housemaid convinced they had a vinyl farm in Australia.

But among the best was the discussion a few

media people had with some locals during the 1970 World Cup tour. They convinced them that the then *Daily Mirror's* chief League writer, Bill Mordey, was the hunt master of a club which set out from Sydney's Martin Place every Saturday! The mind boggles at the thought of 'Breakeven' Bill leading the hunt ... he'd probably want to get a bet on the fox!

Among the media group that afternoon were former Test forwards Peter Gallagher and Ian Doyle. Gallagher told the locals about driving from Brisbane to Canberra to attend the wedding of his sister. One of them asked Gallagher if it was tough going on those Australian roads.

Gallagher stopped for a second and straight-faced replied, 'The toughest part is when you have to swim your horse across the rivers.'

There have been countless bloody battles in rubgy league over the years but it would be difficult to find a more ferocious clash than the 1970 World Cup final between Australia and Great Britain.

The stage was set for a no-holds barred contest after the Great Britain team won the Ashes in Australia, and in a preliminary round of the cup between the two countries Australian prop John O'Neill was cautioned five times in the first half.

At half time, the Australian coach Harry Bath warned O'Neill that if he received another caution, he would be replaced. O'Neill fumed at the restraint placed on him.

'We were just starting to get on top of them and we had to ease off,' he said later.

Great Britain won the match 11–4 and Australia scrambled into a final which set a new standard in thuggery. From the start, O'Neill was the main target. He was punched in almost every tackle, had his head stomped on, was kicked and had a huge gash on his shin from a well-directed English boot. But this great warhorse kept going.

Ron Coote captained the Australian team in the series and he has very vivid memories of the clash, 'It was without any doubt the toughest game I played in.' Coote recalled. 'All you had to do was to look around the dressing room after the match and see the gashed eyebrows, the wounds on the players' legs and other assorted damage ... The referee just let things go along and there was mayhem. John O'Neill was on the receiving end of some heavy treatment but he wasn't backwards in that area himself. In every scrum he would grab a handful of Dennis Hartley's flesh on his ribs and squeeze as hard as he could. After a couple of scrums Hartley kept calling out to the referee, 'He's nipping me.' By the end of the match there was a large patch of blood on Hartley's jumper from attention 'Big Lurch' (John O'Neill) gave him in the scrums. Those who saw the match on television missed most of the heavy action which was in the background. 'I have a video of the match and every time I watch it I marvel at the dedication of the players. There were many outstanding players that day, particularly Billy Smith, one of the game's great competitors. Billy Smith is right up there with the very best.'

For the record Australia won 12–7 with John Cootes and Lionel Williamson scoring tries and Eric Simms kicking two goals and a field goal.

To add a little bit more to the drama of the afternoon, there was a bomb alert before the match started.

There's an English lady in London probably still wondering what the world is coming to. The cause of her problem, two of Australia's roughest and toughest prop forwards, Glenn Lazarus and Steve 'Blocker' Roach.

Lazarus and Roach were room-mates on the 1990 Kangaroo tour, and before the first Test I spent time with them in a quiet corner of a hotel. We had a couple of beers and after a while 'Blocker' stood up and said, 'Come on darling, let's go to bed!'

The stunned look on the lady's face as those two

man-mountains wandered off would have won first prize in any 'Funniest Home Video'.

In any list of Australia's great players, Arthur Beetson will be there as either a prop forward or a second rower. He was a superb footballer, a scheming ball player who could create opportunities out of nothing. For a while he had to live with the nickname 'half-a-game-Artie' but most would have given their eye-teeth to cram into that half Beetson's flair.

That unwanted title was earned in 1966 when Beetson destroyed the Great Britain team with forty minutes of inspired football, setting up the first try for Ken Irvine and then grubber-kicking through for winger Johnny King to score.

Beetson was the centre of a major selection controversy in the 1977 World Series. He had captained Australia in the first two matches, and at a meeting in Brisbane the selectors had to name the team to play New Zealand in Auckland.

Several members of the Australian Rugby League board had heard rumours that there would be a major change in the team, but few dared to predict that Arthur Beetson would be the centre of the problem.

The newly appointed chairman of the selection panel, John Kelly, presented the team to the ARL chairman Kevin Humphreys for its ratification, but a quick glance was enough. With Beetson's name missing the ARL refused to accept the team which left the selectors with a couple of alternatives – either resign or name Beetson in the team.

They re-instated the talented Beetson, but the drama was not over. The next day Beetson, a man of great principle, withdrew when he discovered that he had been omitted from the original selection. He said he could not play if the selectors orginally did not want him and only the intervention of the ARL had earned him his spot. Beetson's decision had the full support of Kevin Humphreys who publicly applauded the stand taken by the Australian captain.

The one good thing to come out of that piece of selection nonsense was it brought about a change in the selection panel. From then on there were three selectors from NSW and three from Queensland with the ARL chairman the arbiter.

The 1969 Australian tour of New Zealand provided some fireworks hours before the players were due to return home.

The tour had been an outstanding success. It confirmed what everyone knew, that big second row forward Bob McCarthy was star material. For some reason the Australian selectors had left McCarthy out of the 1967 Kangaroo touring team.

The argument was that he scouted too wide. The fact that he took a match-winning intercept in the 1967 grand final when South Sydney toppled Canterbury, and that he outsped Johnny Greaves, who was named as a winger in the touring team, did not influence the selectors.

On the night before leaving New Zealand one of the Australian players caught a few of the 'locals' going through the rooms and taking football jumpers. He tackled them but there were too many so he raced to the lounge section where the Australian players were relaxing and told them what had happened.

Captain John Sattler led the charge and it wasn't a pretty sight as the Australians went about collecting their jumpers. It turned really nasty when one of the players received a flesh wound from a knife.

On a lighter note an Australian player chasing the jumper thieves saw a face in a darkened doorway. Reasoning it was one of the culprits he unleased a big right-hand to the mouth. There was only one problem. It turned out the 'culprit' was actually a trumpet player from the band who had gone for a cigarette and looked out to see what all the commotion was about. Unfortunately he couldn't blow his trumpet for a couple of weeks ...

Rugby League

It was the in-thing during Kangaroo tours for players to club together to buy a car for a few hundred dollars and then re-sell it at the end of the tour.

While the players were taken to their matches in the team coach, in their spare time they toured around looking at the north of England countryside.

On the 1982 Kangaroo tour a couple of players bought a vehicle which had seen much better days. Still, it served the purpose, although it certainly added to pollution problems in Leeds.

At the end of the tour the players tried to sell the car but the salesman took one look and shook his head, muttering something about forty-foot poles!

What to do with the machine? Being tidy young fellows they did not want to just leave it on the street. Brainwave ... they drove the car to the canal which ran behind the hotel and pushed it into the murky depths. But they'd forgotten to turn out the lights and the alarm was raised. The Leeds police arrived and divers checked for bodies. By this time the 'bodies' were safely on the fourth floor of the hotel, watching the activity and mar-velling at the endurance of the diving team as they plunged into the icy canal.

On that same tour the rugby league writer Bill Mordey was loaned a car, a four-seater MG. After

one night-match two policemen, who were in
England to escort a prisoner to Sydney, were
stranded. 'Breakeven' Bill heard of their plight and
offered to drive them to Leeds. On the way Mordey
was pulled over by one of the north of England's
finest. The car was only supposed to carry four but
there were six bodies crammed in. One of the
Sydney policemen said he would settle the problem.
He managed to get out, 'I'm Detective . . .' before his
Yorkshire counterpart said, 'You are a pedestrian on
a motorway, get back in the car.'

Rugby league will never be the same for many of its
followers following thirteen months of bitterness
and wrangling which took the game out of the
playing fields and into the courtrooms.

The bid by News Ltd-backed Super League to
take over the code ended a little after midday on 25
March 1996 when the full bench of the Supreme
Court made a critical decision. The 'no play no pay'
ruling by the court scuttled Super League and
forced players back to the ARL competition.

Rugby league players all have one thing in
common, they love to win and those who had backed
Super League to the hilt suffered a massive case of
wounded pride. The feelings of two of the outspoken
Super League advocates, Canberra chief executive

Kevin Neil and Canberra and former Test halfback Ricky Stuart surfaced just hours after the club decided to return to the ARL competition.

Stuart predicted the attitude by the League towards the Raiders would get worse during the season.

'It's going to be pay-back time now for the Canberra Raiders. The attitude shown towards the Raiders over the years, as far as the judicial system and the representatives season is concerned, is probably going to get worse.'

Neil heaped more coals onto the fire when he predicted the first Canberra player to go before the Judiciary would receive eight to ten weeks' suspension.

'The right thing is not going to be done. The ARL is all about recrimination. They have never listened to the Canberra club previously and there is no reason to think they will start now.

'But that's OK. We've made our bed and we'll cop it.'

Right through the bitter conflict, senior ARL officials had been guarded in their statements and there had been no criticism of the players. Ken Arthurson, the ARL Executive Chairman, stressed time and time again that there would be no recriminations from the League.

But Arthurson and his colleagues had to bite

their lips following Laurie Daley's statement that the ARL 'Treated you like dogs'.

Mr Arthurson confined his response to the simple statement: 'When the Australiam team travelled to England and back for the Kangaroo tour they went business class. They stayed at a five-star hotel and received a very generous allowance. I only wish someone would treat me like a dog that way.'

Daley, the former Australian captain, who stated categorically 'he was 99.9 per cent sure he would sit out the 1996 season', had a change of heart within twenty-four hours of the ruling and agreed to play for the Raiders.

When Super League made its bid to take over the code, some officials likened it to a 'Pearl Harbor attack'.

Fifty-one days of wordy arguments ended in a crushing victory for the ARL with the judgment by federal court judge, Mr Justice Burchett, who did not mince words in his criticism of News Ltd and a number of officials involved in the cloak and dagger manoeuvring. One of the key factors was the fact that the twenty clubs involved in the League competition had signed loyalty agreements with the ARL.

His original judgment was a massive victory for

the ARL, but in later interlocutory orders Mr Justice Burchett went even further. He ordered that the players had to return to the ARL and that Super League could not conduct, organise or promote any competition not authorised by the ARL until 31 December 1999. News Ltd was directed to tell the Super League players to return to the ARL and be paid the money in their News Ltd contracts. If a player refused to comply with the order News Ltd was directed not to pay him.

Bob Ellicott who led the ARL's legal team said, 'As a person, and not a lawyer, what has happened today should lay the foundation for those forces involved in this to co-operate to put the League back together. Those forces include television and newspaper proprietors and they, as well as the League, should think very carefully about further litigation. What is more important than anything else is that the clubs get together and the League continue the best it can in the circumstances, that the players come back and the League, the clubs and the players face up to whatever issues that are around and proceed on the path they were taking before all this business arose. It was Shakespeare who said to kill the lawyers. There is a time to kill them but you can't get rid of them until you put things together.'

The top ARL officials, Executive Chairman Ken Arthurson and Chief Executive John Quayle shouldered most of the pressure during the bitter battle. John Quayle is not a man to pussy-foot around. He says what he thinks, although he kept waving the olive branch. He had no illusions about the reasons for the attempted takeover. 'It was not about football but simply for profit and pay television. What the ARL did basically was to defend itself against an attempted corporate takeover. When you look back to the early days of the sport and appreciate the hard work and sacrifices that were made, you could not let it be handed over. The traditions of the game, important things like loyalty have been destroyed.'

After the March 1996 verdict was handed down Mr Quayle simply stated what the public had been saying for months, get back to playing football.

'The supporters of the game are not interested in what happens in a boardroom. All they want to do is go out and support their teams. It is going to take a long time to repair the damage.'

As this book went to press, News Ltd's appeal against the judgement had been heard and was being considered. A decision was not expected before the end of the 1996 competition.

ATHLETICS

Jim Webster was a senior sports writer with the *Sydney Morning Herald* and the *Herald Sun* for more than thirty years. He covered five Olympic Games, six Commonwealth Games, four Wallaby rugby tours and nearly 200 rugby Test matches and numerous Wimbledon and British Open golf championships. In 1987, he was honoured with the Diploma of the International Amateur Athletic Federation. He officially retired in 1988, but has not been allowed to rest. He is consulting editor of *Golf Australia*, was media attaché for Australia's team at the 1992 Barcelona Olympics and media director for the 1996 Atlanta Olympics. He is the author of seven books on sport.

ATHLETICS
I CAN WIN!
Ralph Doubell

The men's marathon at the 1984 Los Angeles Olympics was talent-filled with seven different runners who had clocked times under 2 hours 9 minutes.

They included Robert de Castella, who had won the famous Fukuoka Invitational in 1981 in 2:08:18, a tantalising five seconds short of the world record, in the following year had triumphed over Tanzania's Juma Ikangaa in a fantastic battle at the 1982 Brisbane Commonwealth Games and had then added the world championship in Helsinki in 1983. Yet Deek was beaten. The gold medal went to thirty-seven-year-old Carlos Lopes, of Portugal, who had completed only one of the three previous marathons he had attempted, from Ireland's John Treacy, who had never run one before, and Britain's Charles Spedding.

Marathons can play dreadful tricks on one's mind and body and that day Deek didn't function as he would have wished and finished in fifth position. When he talked with the media shortly afterwards, his eyes were not moving in tandem and he matter-of-factly observed that when he removed one of his shoes after the race two toenails fell out.

It seemed certain that the women's 4x100 metres relay team – Marjorie Jackson, Shirley Strickland, Winsome Cripps and Verna Johnston – would win gold for Australia at the 1952 Helsinki Olympic Games. They won their heat easily, breaking the world record with 46:1, and looked to have the final won as Cripps made a clean pass to Jackson at the last changeover with a lead of one metre. Then came an incident that has passed into both Australian and Olympic folklore, for after the change had been made the baton suddenly flew into the air, bounced on the track and was caught on the rebound by Jackson. What had happened was that Jackson was striding away when Cripps' knee collided with her arm, knocking the baton from her grasp.

At these Games Jackson, the 'Lithgow Flyer', won two gold medals, breaking world records in the 100 and 200 metres.

Bill Emmerton never competed at an Olympic

Games, yet his solo runs were of Olympian magnitude. At the age of forty-nine, the Tasmanian gained attention throughout America by running from Houston, Texas, to Cape Kennedy, Florida, a distance of more than 1600 kilometres. In accomplishing this astounding feat he averaged 64 kilometres daily.

Emmerton is probably even better known for his successful attempts to cross California's torturous Death Valley. In 1968 he tried to find others to challenge him in the 200 kilometre run, but no one else wished to conquer the desert that had taken so many lives.

Bill, therefore, ran the whole way alone, with his wife Norma following in a jeep stocked with first-aid supplies. At one point he inhaled noxious sulphur fumes, reeled and collapsed. His wife, sensing it was all over, bathed his temples, massaged his muscles and drenched him with water. A few minutes later, though, he jumped up and resumed running. Eventually, Emmerton finished with holes cut in his shoes to aid the circulation in his swollen, blistered feet.

Instead of resting on his laurels, he decided this run wasn't long enough and so four months later he crossed Death Valley again, this time covering 340 kilometres. The day he began the temperature touched a searing 57°C!

He later moaned that this crossing was comparable to 'running through Hell'.

John Cann, who finished tenth in the decathlon at the 1956 Melbourne Olympics with 6278 points, was a marvellous character as well as a versatile sportsman. He was Australian hurdles champion, won six state athletic titles, represented New South Wales at rugby league and narrowly missed selection as a boxer at the 1958 Cardiff Empire Games when beaten by future Olympic bronze medallist Tony Madigan.

His occupation? A snake handler from La Perouse.

Four years after competing in the Olympic decathlon he broke his neck playing in a country rugby league match.

It remains one of those unexplainable happenings – Raelene Boyle's sensational disqualification from the 200 metres semi-finals at the 1976 Montreal Olympics.

She had been in five Olympic sprint finals, winning three silver medals. In this particular semi-final, the electronic starting device had registered a clean start the first time but the recall judge claimed Raelene had rolled her head and shoulders while waiting on the blocks for the start.

Unaware she had been credited with a false start, rather than the customary warning, she false-started again and was therefore automatically disqualified. There have been many reasons given as to why Raelene would break a second time, when she was fast enough to have given the whole field a start and still qualified among the four who would progress to the final.

After walking from the stadium in disbelief, Raelene came upon a throng of waiting Australian media. Overcome by the emotion of missing the chance of another Olympic medal and feeling she had let down so many people, especially herself, she burst into tears upon the shoulder of an old friend – this writer.

On 16 January 1932 on the Sydney Cricket Ground, Jimmy Carlton (born 1908 in Lismore) won the Australian 220 yards title in a sensational 20:6 secs – a world record. The shape of the track made it difficult to assess wind assistance – there being no wind gauges in those days – and so the referee, shocked at Carlton's time, disallowed the record.

It was the perfectly executed plan; one that had been carefully and concisely conceived by Debbie Flintoff-King and her coach-husband Phil King at their home at Moorooduc on Victoria's Mornington Peninsula.

Debbie had shown that she had the talent in the 400 metres hurdles, if not the execution, when she went out far too fast then faded into sixth placing in the event's introduction to the Olympic program in Los Angeles in 1984.

If she was going to win gold at what would obviously be her final attempt four years later in Seoul, then the couple reasoned that she would have to develop not only more speed but a technique which allowed that speed to flow across the hurdles with a minimum of interruption.

Hers was perhaps the most technically demanding of all track and field events, for it poses problems of exacting technique as well as extreme athleticism. While the distance between the hurdles remains constant, runners' strides shorten as they tire. She would normally take fifteen strong paces between hurdles, her left leg leading over them, until about hurdle six when her stride would have shortened to where she would be forced to take seventeen strides and upset her rhythm.

The Kings knew this had to change. So session

after session they worked on Debbie taking off with alternate legs, a practice which gave her sixteen strides and a smooth progression over the obstacles.

In the between years, Debbie won the 400 metres flat and 400 metres hurdles at the Edinburgh Commonwealth Games in 1986, the Grand Prix championship in Europe in 1987 and recorded the world's fastest time of 54:02 in Berne in 1988. She was as ready for Seoul as she possibly could be.

Then, in Melbourne three days before she was due to depart for the Games, Phil informed Debbie that her older sister Noeline had died suddenly of a heart attack on the Gold Coast. She went ahead with a planned time trial the following day, flew to Queensland for the funeral and the next day left Sydney for Seoul.

By the eighth hurdle in the final, Debbie was still in fifth position. The Soviet runner Tatyana Ledovskaya moved decisively into the lead over the ninth hurdle. As they cleared the tenth and final barrier, Flintoff-King caught the world champion Sabine Busch but still trailed the other East German Ellen Fiedler and Ledovskaya. She sprinted past Fiedler then, right on the finish line, Ledovskaya failed to dip into the tape and Flintoff-King nipped her by just one-hundredth-of-a-second. Her time was 53:17 seconds, an Olympic record.

Noeline would have gained so much enjoyment from it.

Ron Clarke broke more official world records for running than any other athlete in history.

Altogether Clarke broke a total of eighteen world records ranging from two miles to the one-hour run. He trimmed 13.4 seconds off the 5000m run and 35.8 seconds off the 10000m run.

In 1965, during a forty-four day tour of Europe, Clarke competed eighteen times in eight countries and set twelve world records.

Marathon runner Claude Smeal was one of the more remarkable athletes to compete in the Helsinki Olympics in the summer of 1952. More than most, he exemplified the spirit of Baron Pierre de Coubertin's adage about the important thing being not to win, but to take part.

Smeal, an army captain, was signals officer with an Australian infantry battalion in Korea. The previous year, before being shipped off for active service, he had been New South Wales marathon champion.

He was not even considered when the national athletics selectors made their recommendations to

the Australian Olympic Federation; but he continued to train, running at first light each morning
along a supply route just behind the front line, in
an area prone to land mines and infiltration by
enemy Chinese and North Korean troops.

Despite warnings, Smeal continued to run and
finally completed a full, measured marathon course
outside Seoul, under supervision and with time-
keepers. In makeshift shoes and on a rough track,
he covered the 26 miles and 385 yards in 2 hours
44 minutes 5 seconds – 6 minutes 8 seconds outside
the Australian Olympic standard.

Two war correspondents who watched this effort,
Noel Monks and Norman Macswan, sent back
praiseworthy reports, and the Sydney *Daily Telegraph* took up Smeal's cause. Within days the
national selectors nominated him to the AOF for
inclusion in the team, the selectors said yes, and the
army undertook to give him leave and pay his
return fare from Tokyo to Helsinki.

Smeal hitched a ride from Seoul to Tokyo in a
United States transport plane, and was still in bat-
tledress when he caught up with the team in
London. He travelled to Helsinki in an Australian
tracksuit.

At the Olympics, Smeal showed the kind of
unbending determination that had got him there in
the first place. Although way behind Czech legend

and gold medal winner Emil Zatopek, he nevertheless completed the marathon, finishing in 45th
position.

Ralph Doubell and his renowned coach Franz
Stampfl believed he could win the gold medal in the
800 metres at the 1968 Mexico City Olympics – even
if no one else did. He was comparatively unknown,
but with great winning potential: the kind of com-
petitor Stampfl considered the most dangerous of
all.

Favourite for the gold medal was Kenya's Wilson
Kiprugut. Even though the 800 metres was not considered one of the events which would be affected
by the high altitude, the Kenyan's high-level preparation was seen as an advantage. He had also won
the bronze medal in Tokyo after tripping forty-five
metres from the finish.

When the Aussie nipped Kiprugut in the second
semi-final, everyone suddenly sat up and took notice
of Doubell. The unheralded Australian really did
have some talent.

Stampfl's race plan for the final was for Doubell
to stay back in the field, while remaining in touch,
and to let someone like Kiprugut set the pace in
front. Sticking to the plan, Doubell settled in fifth
or sixth position where he watched Kiprugut set up

a five-metre lead after 600 metres.

Then he sprang. 'I came up to him with eighty metres to go and for the first thirty he was still with me. I thought I had him about there, though for those first thirty metres up the straight I wasn't so sure,' he recalled. 'As I finally passed him, I was screaming to myself, "Christ, I can win it! I can win!"'

Doubell's time of 1:44:3 equalled Peter Snell's world record.

'I don't know how you beat this guy, unless you tie his legs,' said Ireland's 1956 Olympic 1500m champion Ron Delaney as the incomparable Herb Elliott approached his peak.

Stan Rowley holds a rather unique place among Australia's Olympic athletes, as he won three bronze medals for Australia and a gold medal for Britain – all at the same Games.

Rowley had won the sprint double, over 100 and 220 yards, at the 1897 and 1899 Australasian championships, and held New South Wales records at 10 seconds and 22.4 seconds. A strong move began to send Rowley to England and Paris, with designs upon the English championships and the 1900 Paris

Olympics. While funds were hard to come by, he eventually left Sydney by train for Melbourne where he caught the P&O liner *Australia* for England.

Rowley performed extremely well at the Olympics, finishing third in the 60 metres, 100 metres and the 200 metres.

Then the British found themselves short of a fifth runner in the 5000 metres cross-country team event and they approached Rowley, even though he was a sprinter. He agreed to compete for them. The Americans withdrew on religious grounds because the event was being contested on a Sunday (22 July) and so only the combined Britain/Australia team and France competed.

In this event (discontinued after 1900), each finishing place represented a point and the team with the lower total of points was judged the winner. After British runners had finished first, second, sixth and seventh, it was clear that they would win – even if Rowley came last, which he did. He ran for a lap, then started to walk and eventually was told to stop and awarded last position, although several laps remained. Britain's total was 26 points, and the French (3, 4, 5, 8 and 9) was 29.

Even though Rowley treated the whole thing as something of a joke, historians argued for many years as to whether or not this qualified him as an Australian Olympic gold medallist. The matter was not fully clarified until the Australian Olympic Committee's historian Harry Gordon, researching Australia and the Olympic Games, received an acknowledgment from the International Olympic Committee in 1992, advising that 'Mr Rowley qualifies for the status of a gold medallist.'

No athlete, male or female, has ever touched the hearts of Australians more than the remarkable Betty Cuthbert.

At the 1956 Melbourne Olympics this warm, unassuming eighteen-year-old won the 100 metres, 200 metres and earned another gold medal as part of Australia's 4x100 metres relay team. At those Games the now defunct Melbourne newspaper the *Argus* tagged her the Golden Girl, a pseudonym which has stuck throughout her lifetime.

At the Rome Olympics in 1960 she was suffering from a hamstring tear and was eliminated early from the 100 metres before having to scratch from the 200 metres.

By the time of the Tokyo Olympics four years later she had switched to the 400 metres and, in the inaugural final in this event, she ran what she later described as 'the only perfect race I have ever run' to win her fourth gold medal. There and then the Golden Girl retired, ending one of the greatest running careers in the history of Olympic competition.

Years later Betty developed multiple sclerosis. But her unbending Christian beliefs and a move to Perth have seen her continue to fight the crippling disease just as courageously as she did opponents on the running track.

Ian Campbell may have been robbed of a gold medal in the triple jump at the 1980 Moscow Olympics. Officially he finished fifth, but in the third round he received a most unusual no-jump after allegedly dragging his trail leg during the step stage. It would have put him ahead of the two Russians, Jaak Uudmae and Viktor Saneyev, who were holding first and second place at the time.

Campbell later appealed, but it was claimed that he should have lodged the complaint thirty minutes after the event finished.

'The takeoff in the centre of the arena for the hop, step and jump was in shocking condition through a rodeo having been held there only a week previously. Only for that, I am certain that (Jack) Metcalfe would have established new world figures.'

A report by Australian team manager Mr

H.K. Maxwell after the Second Empire Games in London in 1934. As it was Metcalfe set a Games record which stood until 1958.

The greatest miler in history? Herb Elliott, according to a survey by the sport's Bible, *Track & Field News*.

It's hard to go past someone who, between 1954 and 1960, won forty-four consecutive races over a mile and 1500 metres and won the 1500 metres final at the 1960 Rome Olympics by the extraordinary margin of eighteen metres in a world record 3:35:6.

Elliott has shown similar success in business, for these days he heads the Puma footwear company in the United States.

When Bobby McDonald, of Bourke, went down on his hands and knees to start in a Sydney sprint race in 1884, the surprised starter ordered him to stand up. McDonald persisted and finally was permitted to start his own way, though the starter clearly believed he was at a disadvantage.

McDonald's technique was eventually followed by sprinters elsewhere in the world and a slightly modified version of his start is now used universally by all sprinters.

The 10 000 metres at the 1964 Tokyo Olympics produced one of the most astonishing upsets in Games history.

Predictions centred around it becoming a battle between 1960 5000 metres champion Murray Halberg (NZ), defending champion Pyotr Bolotnikov of the Soviet Union, and Australia's multiple world record-holder Ron Clarke.

With two laps to go, Clarke had dropped everyone but Tunisia's Mohamed Gammoudi and American Billy Mills, who had finished second at the US Olympic trials. He seemed assured of victory, as neither of the others had ever broken twenty-nine minutes.

Clarke passed Gammoudi at the beginning of the homestretch, Gammoudi came again to draw level and then, out of the blue, Mills shot passed both of them and into history, winning by three metres in 28:24:4.

A part-Sioux Indian, born in South Dakota and orphaned at twelve, Mills had been sent to a school for Native Americans in Kansas. He had taken up running as training to become a boxer, but after losing a couple of fights had decided to stick to running.

That day in Tokyo he delivered the cruellest blow possible to Ron Clarke's chances of ever winning an Olympic gold medal.

Edwin Flack was Australia's first Olympic champion. Twelve months old when his family migrated from England in 1878, the Flacks settled in Melbourne and his father opened a small accountancy practice in Collins Street the same year.

When Edwin (generally called Ted or Teddy) finished school, he joined the company and in due course his father arranged that he should return to England for further experience. He arranged a job for the youngster with his old firm, Price Waterhouse.

Flack joined three running clubs in London, showing reasonable ability, and it was from London that the youngster decided to travel in 1896 to the Olympic Games in Athens. His idea was that if he could compete, well and good; if not, then he would enjoy being a spectator. Such were the loose competitive standards then.

After a six-day journey getting to Athens, he was at once intrigued by the Olympic city and its preparations, and not very taken with the standard of other athletes who had come to try their luck, other than the Americans. He decided to unpack the club competition vest he had brought along and have a go.

Flack's first race was on the opening day, the heats of the 800 metres, and he finished well ahead of Hungary's Nandor Dani, who had been credited with some fast times before the Games. The event favourite, Frenchman Albin Lermusiaux, won the other heat.

Before that final, Flack lined up on the second day against seven opponents in the 1500 metres and it proved a battle between himself and the American Arthur Blake. Finally, Flack broke away to win by five metres in 4:33:2 – the first non-American to win any track and field event.

The third day of the Games should have been the chance for him to rest. Instead, he teamed up with his English friend George (later Sir George) Robertson and entered the doubles at lawn tennis, in which they won the bronze medal behind teams from Ireland/Germany and Egypt/Greece. He was also bundled out of the singles in the first round.

The tennis diversion did not seem to have any undue affect on Flack and he lined up in the 800 metres final against three others (the fourth qualifier having withdrawn). He cleared out early and won easily from Dani in 2:11:0.

As soon as that was over he immediately dressed and drove off in a carriage for the four-hour journey to Marathon, where he was intent on running the first Olympic marathon the next day, although he had never before run a race of more than 10 miles.

He did marvellously well, taking the lead for a spell towards the finish. Then he began to weave and sway and while a companion, V.W. Delves-Broughton, ran off to fetch a blanket to drape around Flack he asked a Greek bystander to support him. The fellow hugged Flack, who took exception to such close attention and punched the helpful Greek with his fist. He was then loaded into a carriage and driven to the dressing room at the stadium.

He returned to London and eventually to Australia to join his father and brother in an accountancy partnership. Upon his father's retirement he became the senior partner and died in Melbourne on 10 January 1935, aged 62.

Only trivia buffs might recall that an Australian once held the world record for the women's javelin. The Hungarian-born Anna Pazera (née Bocson), broke the world record in Cardiff on 24 July 1958 with a throw of 57.40 metres.

Her record lasted only until October that year when Birute Zalogaitite, of the Soviet Union, threw nine centimetres further.

Two years later at her only Olympic appearance in Rome she finished sixth in the final with 51.15m.

While her deeds are sometimes obscured by those of

Marjorie Jackson and Betty Cuthbert, Shirley Strickland won more Olympic track and field medals than any other Australian woman.

She finished with seven medals – three gold, one silver and three bronze – and should have had eight.

Shirley went to the 1948 London Olympics as the nation's best sprinter, but like everyone else was overshadowed by the remarkable Dutch athlete Fanny Blankers-Koen, who won four gold medals. Shirley won a silver in the 4x100 metres relay (Blankers-Koen coming from fourth on the final changeover to catch the Australians on the line) and bronze medals in both the 100 metres and 80 metres hurdles.

At the 1952 Olympics in Helsinki she again came up against Blankers-Koen, but in the hurdles final the Dutch champion hit the first two hurdles and stopped running while Shirley streaked to the gold medal in a world record 10:9 seconds. Her other medal was a bronze in the 100 metres behind team-mate Marjorie Jackson.

By the Melbourne Olympics in 1956 she had become a wife and mother. Her three-year-old son Phillip was among the crowd who saw her easily win the hurdles gold medal again and collect her third gold in the victorious 4x100 metres relay team.

While she continued running for a while, her

magnificent Olympic career was over.

In 1975 it was discovered that Shirley should have won another bronze medal in the 200 metres at her initial Olympics in London. The photo finish of the final was turned up by an athletics official in London after all those years and it revealed unequivocally that she had actually finished third ahead of America's Audrey Patterson, and not fourth.

The mistake occurred because the judges believed that the American was third and did not call for the photo-finish.

Victorian 100-metre hurdler Max Binnington wasn't injured or sick, nor did he fall, yet he failed to clear a single hurdle in his heat at the 1976 Montreal Olympics.

Binnington stopped in his tracks after hearing what he thought was the recall gun, while the other runners continued.

Ted Best, who won bronze medals in the 100 yards, 220 yards and 4x110 yards relay at the Third Empire Games in Sydney in 1938, became Lord Mayor of Melbourne from 1969–71. In the same athletics team were brother and sister Henry (Harry)

and Nell Gould, who both competed in the broad (now long) jump.

'I had a few wines last night, maybe I should do that more often'.

Cathy Freeman after setting an unofficial 400m grass track world record at the Stawell Gift in April 1996.

BIBLIOGRAPHY

Ampol Australian Sporting Records, John Blanch, Budget Books, 1968.

Australia and the Olympic Games, Harry Gordon, University of Queensland, 1994.

Australians at the Olympics, Gary Lester, Lester-Townsend, 1984.

The Complete Book of the Olympics, David Wallechinsky, Aurum Press, 1992.

Marathon. The World of the Long-Distance Athlete, Gail Campbell, Sterling Publishing, 1977.

HORSE RACING

Bill Whittaker was a racing and trotting writer for over forty years writing mainly for the *Daily Telegraph* and the *Sydney Morning Herald*. He retired in 1988 and now contributes a weekly column to the Saturday edition of the *Sydney Morning Herald*. He was Australian Sports Writer of the Year in 1984, and the Australian Racing Writer of the Year in 1987. These awards followed the Joseph Coulter Award (trotting) in 1979. He regularly attends race meetings in Sydney.

HORSE RACING THE SPORT OF KINGS AND THE KING OF SPORTS

Anon.

The Melbourne Cup will never be the same following the success of Vintage Crop, more of an Irish hurdler than a classic horse. Trainer Dermot Weld quotes Banjo Paterson like a bushie with an Irish twang and he made winning our most famous race look easy. Vintage Crop arrived in Australia looking, as one wit observed, like he had spent a long stop-off in Biafra. But he walked into the parade ring before the cup with a grace and power of a topline stayer.

Max Presnell, *Sydney Morning Herald*, November 1993.

Horse Racing

You have to think and think quickly during the run in the Melbourne Cup but usually you are gone unless you can start improving at the half-mile when the leaders are tired.

Harry White, retired champion jockey, who rode four Melbourne Cup winners, Think Big (twice), Arwon and Hyperno.

In fact, I would rather win the Snake Gully Cup than another media award!

Larry Pickering in conversation with Bill Whittaker. The Walkley Award winning cartoonist was preparing Rising Fear for the 1986 Melbourne Cup. The fine stayer finished second to At Talaq. The neck defeat cost Pickering a minimum $1 million betting win for a small outlay at odds of up to 250–1.

Yes, I bought Kiwi for $1000 as a yearling. Just a woman's whim. I liked the sire Blarney Kiss and I like chestnut horses.

Anne Lupton, part-owner of Kiwi with her husband Snowy, *Sydney Morning Herald*, November, 1985. Although Kiwi didn't win the 1985 Cup he had won in 1983 – last to first in the straight.

'When did you think Subzero had it won, Lee?'
'For about the last ten days!'

Trainer Lee Freedman's reply to the *Age's* Les Carlyon immediately after Subzero's 1992 Melbourne Cup win.

Whenever foreigners coming here ask me where to find Australia, I tell them to go to the racecourse. There you find the rich, the poor and all those in between.

What other organisation in our nation and around our nation so regularly brings together such a broad and representative spectrum of our people? The answer I suggest is none!

Racing has no rival.

Bob Hawke, former Prime Minister, from the foreword of Stephen Brassel's 1990 book, *A Portrait of Racing*. Bob Hawke was a keen and knowledgeable follower of racing during all of his years in politics. He remains so.

Men of the turf are not equal – only those below it.

This old quote, emanating from the UK, sums up the wide range of people who patronise the racing game.

Horse Racing

There is no place like a racecourse where one can hear so many whispers, where so few of the whispers are true and where so many believe them!

Bill Whittaker, the *Sydney Morning Herald*, 1986. Rumours fly quicker at the track than at the stock exchange, though it's a photo finish!

Gai Waterhouse is the best thing to happen to racing since Phar Lap.

Bob Charley, Chairman Australian Jockey Club, speaking to the public at the presentation ceremony after the Gai Waterhouse trained colt Nothin' Leica Dane had won the Hobartville Stakes at Warwick Farm on 24 February, 1996.

Having a horse like that is like living in a dream.

Helen Dalton, part-owner Nothin' Leica Dane, in an interview with Kerry Buckeridge, radio station 2KY the day after the Hobartville stakes.

Robbie Waterhouse is an itch the AJC can't scratch.

Max Presnell, *Sydney Morning Herald*, December 1995.

Presnell was reporting on Robbie Waterhouse's appeal to have his warning-off lifted.

Jockeys especially will send you broke. They ring you up and say this will win and they haven't even ridden it to work. But such tips influence your own judgment. Next minute their horse wins and you feel like you've got to bet more and more.

I think the less you have to do with jockeys and trainers the better; especially in this day and age when 99 per cent of horses are trying anyway.

From *George Freeman: An autobiography*, 1988. The late George Freeman was accused many times of being a 'race fixer'. He always denied the accusations. However, Freeman admitted freely to being an illegal starting price bookmaker. He was a big punter on Sydney trotting meetings during the 1970s and on galloping events.

Next Saturday at the races you will find successful politicians and businessmen and bankers, the elite of society, and some of Sydney's best prostitutes and pimps and gangsters, and best and worst journalists, all rubbing shoulders – all on a level footing.

There would be plenty of poor judges, having a bad trot, among all of them.

Horse Racing

John Schreck, *Sydney Morning Herald*, 14 April, 1994.

On John Schreck's last day as chief steward at Randwick races, the AJC's chairman Bob Charley said, 'I would liken thirteen years as AJC chief steward to being given a twenty-five year sentence on Devil's Island.'

John Schreck spent thirteen years as chief stipe from 1982 to 1995.

Discussing his professional relationship with John Schreck, Pat Lalor noted, 'We didn't always agree on issues, but John was about promoting John. I promote racing, the interests of racing overall.'

Pat Lalor, *Australian*, 15 May, 1995. Pat Lalor is the long-time chairman of stewards at the Victoria Racing Club.

We are seeing a possible saturation in Australia's stallion market – saturation that down the track will see the spilling of breeders' blood in sales rings around the country.

John Messara writing in Arrowfield (NSW) Stud's spring

Newsletter, 1995. He is one of Australia's most successful and authoritative thoroughbred breeders.

As you slide down the bannister of life, you are bound to pick up a splinter or two in your arse!

Vic Rail speaking after Vo Rouge, whom he trained, lost the 1990 St George Stakes on protest to King's High at Caulfield.

We copy too many ideas from overseas including South Africa where they have had the infernal cutaway rail for a long time. Our racing is the best in the world, why copy anyone?

Ken Callander is a critic, along with many others, of the cutaway rail used by the Australian Jockey Club at Randwick and Warwick Farm. He was speaking on radio station 2KY, 3 March, 1996.

This property is for horses, not cows. Why, I don't even drink milk.

George Hanlon, veteran Melbourne trainer of three Melbourne Cup winners was talking about his lush horse training establishment at Leopold near Geelong.

Two nude streakers – a male and a female – jumped the fence and ran down the straight towards the winning post during the running of Tontonan's 1974 Doncaster Handicap at Randwick.

When the streakers reached the gate leading into the enclosure where the horses return to the weigh-in scales, the gate was securely latched.

Male streaker to the veteran green-coated AJC employee in charge of the gate: 'Open it up, we have to get in, the horses are coming.'

Green-coat: 'No! You can't come in here.'

Male streaker: 'Why?'

Green-coat: 'Because you haven't got a ticket!'

I suppose the greyhound that tested positive for cocaine (*Herald* 6 December, 1995) didn't win by a nose.

From Letters to the Editor, *Sydney Morning Herald*, Andrew Anderson, Frenchs Forest.

South Australian jumps jockey Les Boots was so accident-prone his wife would pack his pyjamas when he went to the track because he was odds-on to finish up in hospital.

It is said nurses would read the form guide every Saturday morning to see if he was riding so they would know to prepare a bed. But it was as the man who had thirty-nine rides and forty falls that Boots won immortality. Forty falls from thirty-nine rides?

Legend has it he fell from a stretcher when being put into an ambulance!

Mike Colman, Sydney *Sunday Telegraph*,

It isn't who wins or who loses, it's who winds up with the money.

Anonymous. Anyone can pick a winner, it is finishing with the cash that counts on a racecourse.

It's the one criticism I have of racing, it's a very jealous industry.

Robert Sangster, leading breeder and owner.

Who blew my racetrack money on the rent!

Anonymous. Setting aside a 'bank' for betting is a definite priority for all keen horseplayers.

I'll always be happy to lay 3–1 on or 4–1 on, as long as I think the correct price is 100–1 on.

Eddie Birchley – 'The Fireman'. Birchley's career as a big punter was shortlived. 'Odds-on, look-on' is a well-worn piece of racing advice that many punters accept without question.

I'd like to remember how I made my money and got where I am today. It all came from mugs backing horses.

Sol Green, a wealthy Melbourne bookmaker during the first thirty years of this century. Green was an owner, breeder and bookmaker. His best horses were the 1910 Melbourne Cup winner, Comedy King and Strephon, winner of the 1928 Victoria Derby.

Money lost – nothing lost; courage lost – everything lost.

Eric Connolly, punter, owner and trainer in Sydney and

Melbourne. Connolly won a fortune, said to be £180 000, in November 1929 when Nightmarch won the Melbourne Cup beating Phar Lap into third place.

A few years ago racegoers laughed at a story of a Randwick bookmaker's clerk who made a mistake in his betting sheets. His boss turned to him testily and growled, 'Wake up to yourself muggins. You've got no more sense than a punter.'

James Holledge, *The Great Australian Gamble*. Hollege's book details the exploits of some of Australia's most successful punters including Eric Connolly, Rufe Naylor, Fred Angels, Bob Skelton and Bill Tindall.

I will never ride for Sunny Yam again. I will never speak to him until the day I die!

Jockey Shane Dye speaking to interviewer Keith Hillier on Channel 7 (26 November, 1995) two months after Mr Yam, of Hong Kong, sacked him as the rider of Danewin after the horse was beaten in the George Main Stakes at Randwick.

Thank you Sunny Yam for sacking me from Danewin.

Horse Racing

Shane Dye talking at the presentation ceremony after his win on Octagonal in the 1995 Cox Plate on 28 October.

We all bask in his reflected glory – some horse!

Mrs H.J. Dalton, Nothin' Leica Dane's part-owner, talking to the crowd after Nothin' Leica Dane had won the 1995 Victoria Derby from Octagonal.

On Tuesday he was walking on water, today he was drowned.

Lee Freedman after his stable jockey, Damien Oliver, fractured his collarbone in a race fall at the start on Chiricahua two days after winning the 1995 Melbourne Cup on Doriemus.

'It's the classical lunacy of the English Race!'

Mr Herbert of *Punch* magazine after a visit to Epsom for the 1930 English Derby. Just as well Mr Herbert has not been to a modern day Melbourne Cup.

The Derby is a little like your first experience of

sex – hectic, strenuous, memorable, pleasant and over before you know it.

USA writer Bill Bryson, 1990.

Every man has three secret wishes: To outsmart racehorses, women and fish!

Anonymous.

I don't want to be told what he's by or what he's done or how many watches he's broke. All I want is to see the owner go in and put his own money on and wink at me.

A.B. (Banjo) Paterson, 1864–1941.

1. Never back a horse that the owner does not fancy
2. Never back a horse with a bad rider on board
3. Never back a horse out of condition
4. Never back a horse running out of his distance
5. Never back a horse running out of his class
6. Never back a bad beginner in a short race in the hope he may for once get away well or a finisher in a long race in the hope he may get up

Horse Racing

Banjo Paterson's golden rules of betting.

They know just as well their success
As the man on their back;
As they walk through a dense human lane
That sways to and fro,
And cheers them again and again;
Do you think they don't know?

A.B. (Banjo) Paterson.

I don't know which is the hardest, the human race
or the horse race. You can tell pretty well what a
horse will do but when a man starts backing horses
you never know what he'll do.

A.B. (Banjo) Paterson.

There's some that ride the Robbo style, and bump
   at every stride;
While others sit a long way back, to get a longer
   ride.
There's some that ride like sailors do, with legs, and
   arms, and teeth;

And some ride on the horse's neck, and some ride
   underneath ...

The rule holds good in everything in life's uncertain
   fight:
You'll find the winner can't go wrong, the loser can't
   go right.
You ride a slashing race, and lose – by one and all
   you're banned!
Ride like a bag of flour, and win – they'll cheer you
   in the stand.

A.B. (Banjo) Paterson, the Sydney *Evening News* 12
August, 1903.

Flogging horses is counter productive.
If you trained a dog that way it wouldn't work. It is
almost Pavlovian in concept.

Lee Freedman, Melbourne trainer, *Racetrack* magazine,
1994.

I named him (Crying Game) after racing in general.

Angela Johnson, owner-trainer of the 1995 West Australian Derby winner, Crying Game, after her horse's win in

the Perth classic on 26 December, 1995. Crying Game
went on to win the Perth Cup a week later. And she was
laughing.

There's nothing wrong with racing that money won't
fix.

Noel Simpson, a 90-year-old New Zealander who has raced
many horses – thoroughbreds and standardbreds –
including the topliners Up And Coming, So And So, Spray-
man, Smoke Cloud and Karamea Duplicity, the last three
horses being pacers. He has been going to the races for
more than 75 years.

You put your hand up and there's no sky hooks!

John Letts, a former crack jockey and rider of two Melbourne Cup winners, discussing race accidents.

In the more than sixty years in which I have had
an association one way or another with the sport of
kings, I can claim to have put countless bowls of
fruit upon the sideboards of many bookmakers, provided the funds to educate many of their children –
some to tertiary level – and even, on some rare

occasions, come away from the track winning.

I claim, however, that the race callers, that body of men who can pick up a racebook five minutes before a race, glance at the horses and their jockeys' colours, commit them to memory and then call eighteen or so horses in a sprint race and get them accurate, are geniuses.

Ellis Glover, retired Sydney journalist and public relations executive is a regular, small better on Sydney's racecourses.

The favourite is a heck of a long way back and seeing more tales than Hoffman.

Bert Bryant, one of Australia's most vibrant race callers during the 1950s, 60s and 70s. Bryant was a master at entertaining his listeners in pre-TV days when viewers and listeners were not subjected to the immediacy and drawing power of a television picture of the race.

A South Australian health inspector, on visiting Cummings' stables in Adelaide, complained, 'Mr Cummings, you've got too many flies at these yards!'

Cummings replied, 'Yes, well how many am I allowed?'

Horse Racing

J.B. (Bart) Cummings.

A television interviewer asked, 'Do you think Veandercross can run the 3200m of the Melbourne Cup, Bart?

Cummings, 'He ran it all right the other day in the Caulfield Cup.'

Bart Cummings. This was a criticism of jockey Shane Dye's tactics on Veandercross in the 1992 Caulfield Cup in which the New Zealand gelding was steered very wide before finishing a close second to Mannerism on a heavy track. Veandercross ran the 3200m strongly in the Melbourne Cup but was beaten by Subzero, again on a wet track.

When the going got tough, they bolted and left me holding the bridle.

Bart Cummings speaking in the federal court. The 'bridle' was $17.9 million worth of unpaid yearlings which Cummings had bought as a joint venture with KPMG Peat Marwick and Coopers and Lybrand. Cummings lost the case.

His system is based on a real liking for horses, and key words including an eye for a horse; an eye for a pedigree; an eye for a horse's style; and eye for detail, no matter how minor; an eye for a jockey; an eye for staff; an eye for what is best for his horses ('he is the best feeder in Australia,' said his foreman, Leon Corstens. 'Nothing is too good for his horses.'); and an eye for the future.

Glenn Lester in the *Age*. A story during the Cummings' court case.

Nature is that way a little bit. You do try a bit harder; it's like when I have a bad day at the track on a Saturday. I am always first up on Sunday morning trying to figure out what went wrong.

Bart Cummings discussing his financial problems after winning the 1991 Caulfield Cup with Let's Elope.

I'm on cloud nine. I've been on it for the past two weeks and I'm going to stay on cloud nine until I fall right off!

Dennis Marks, owner of Let's Elope which won the 1991 Caulfield-Melbourne Cups double.

Horse Racing

You've got to get them thinking right.

Bart Cummings chatting about his extraordinary training achievements.

I suppose you must have to think like a horse, become one. My knowledge of bloodlines which I gained from my father must have something to do with it.

Bart Cummings.

There is an art to training animals. Thoroughbred horses can become stressed very quickly. The skill is in keeping them relaxed with their reserves of strength saved for the last 300 metres of a race. There is such a thing as having an eye for a good horse. I can look at a horse and say whether it might win or not. A blood test by the vet might confirm these things. But you still need that horseman's eye. I'm not sure many of the young trainers have it. They rely too much on science.

Bart Cummings.

On the announcement, in the mid 1980s, of the running of the first $1 million Melbourne Cup, Bart Cummings said he wished it could be made retrospective. Bart Cummings at that time had won seven previous Cups.

Cummings' application for leave to appeal to the High Court over the failed, tax-driven bloodstock venture of 1989, was denied in the High Court.

Justices Dawson, Toohey and Gaudron agreed almost immediately after a thirty-five minute address by Cummings' counsel, David Jackson, QC, that leave to appeal 'was not waranted'.

On exiting the court to the outer foyer, Cummings turned to Mr Jackson's assistant, Francis Douglas, QC, and said, 'I couldn't hear all that was being said, but what I did hear didn't sound good.'

'No, I'm afraid we did not succeed,' Mr Douglas said.

'That's that, then,' said Cummings shrugging.

'But,' Mr Douglas shot back, looking skywards, 'there is a higher court.'

'Well I'm darn sure I won't be turning up there for a while yet!' replied Cummings, once again demonstrating his celebrated sense of humour.

Tony Arrold, *Australian* 18 September, 1993.

Horse Racing

There are two sides to training, the physiological and the psychological. We don't like leaders. Being in front too early can cause adrenalin exhaustion. We train them to come from behind so they produce their best finish. A horse gains confidence as it passes other runners and finds a better final thrust that way. Horses that lead all the time don't win many races.

Bart Cummings.

Never run up steps, never fish from rocks, never lay odds-on.

It's God's own day out here at Randwick.

Heads are up and heads are down – PHOTO – but it's London to a brick on that Dark Marne has won.

Ken Howard, race broadcaster, 2UE and 2GB, gained renown for his 'London to a brick on' predictions in close photo finishes. He was right ninety-nine times out of a hundred and the racetrack wits used to call him 'old magic-eye'.

There's one fly in the Warwick Farm broadcast box.

Guess where it ended up? That's right. Straight down ole KH's throat!

Ken Howard had momentarily lost his voice while calling a race to an Australia-wide audience.

I've called the wrong horse the winner. The winner, incidentally, is by an unidentified sire from an unidentified mare ... and don't I know the feeling!

Des Hoysted, a brilliant race broadcaster, had made one of his rare mistakes.

Driver Ken Belford crouches low in the sulky, breaking wind!

Terry Spargo calling the Redcliffe trots during the 1980s. He was referring to Belford seeking to minimise wind resistance.

Horse sense is what keeps horses from betting on what people will do.

Anonymous.

Horse Racing

The smart gambler manages his money. The foolish gambler lets his money manage him.

Anonymous.

The only difference between a top trainer and a battler is a good horse.

Jack O'Brien was a Sydney racing writer on the *Daily Telegraph* before he turned to racehorse betting as his first priority in the mid 1950s. And he was highly successful but died at age 45 in 1958.

In December 1974 I realised that I had achieved all I wanted from racing – namely financial independence for life. I announced my retirement from professional punting and took four years off to relax and write. The Legal Eagles disbanded, and Clive Evatt and Bob Charley went their separate ways.

Don Scott, writing in his book *Winning More*, 1988. Bob Charley, Clive Evatt and Don Scott were a betting team known as the Legal Eagles on Sydney racecourses during the 1960s and 70s. They enjoyed considerable success. Bob Charley became chairman of the Australian Jockey Club, Clive Evatt is a barrister and art dealer. Don Scott wrote several books dealing largely with the complexities of betting. He died suddenly at his Sydney home in January, 1996.

Only fools and horses work.

Jim 'Grafter' Kingsley's place in Australia's 'Hall Of Racing Notoriety' became firmly established on 20 April, 1903 when he rigged the scales at Broadmeadow Racecourse in Newcastle. His horse, Gentleman Jim, handicapped at 10st 9lbs (67.5 kgs), landed a fortune in bets, said to be £20 000 for Kingsley. The ingenious Kingsley had constructed a tunnel under the timber floor at Broadmeadow and in a dug-out directly under the scales sat a small boy. The boy's job was to attach a 29lb (12.5 kgs) lead weight to a wire which ran through a hole in the floor. Thus Gentleman Jim carried 55kgs (not 67.5) and won. Kingsley collected his winning bets because the tunnel was not discovered until long after correct weight had been declared. He was disqualified for life. However, he was eventually allowed back on racecourses and became a reasonably successful owner winning the 1931 Villiers Stakes with a good horse, High Disdain.

He grabbed my leg sir, it was as though I was being bitten by a snake.

Tommy Hill, jockey, giving evidence before the stewards at

Horse Racing

Randwick on AJC Derby day, 1961, when he successfully protested against Mel Schumacher who rode the first-past-the-post, Blue Era. Stewards upheld Hill's protest and awarded the Derby to Summer Fair.

That's preposterous, sir!

Jockey Mel Schumacher's reply to Tommy Hill's evidence. Race film showed that Schumacher had indeed grabbed Hill's leg during most of the last one hundred metres. Schumacher was disqualified for life but resumed riding after five-and-a-half years. He later joked, 'I couldn't help it if Tommy put his leg in my hand, could I?'

I should like to be a horse.

HRH Queen Elizabeth II, when asked about her ambitions as a child. Her Majesty has bred and raced many good racehorses. She maintains a keen interest in horses and racing.

You cannot work out a race riding plan on a blue-print. You are bound to fail by using a stereotype method of riding in sprint races or in distance events.

An interview with George Moore by Max Gray in *Turf Monthly*, December, 1953. Moore was probably the first jockey in Australia to study race films on a regular basis. He employed a professional movie photographer to film races for him in Sydney more than forty years ago.

The Melbourne Cup is the Australasian National Day. It would be difficult to overstate its importance. It overshadows all other holidays and specialised days of whatever sort. Overshadows them? I might almost say it blots them out. Each of them gets attention, but not everybody's; each of them evokes interest, but not everybody's; each of them rouses enthusiasm, but not everybody's. In each case a part of the attention, interest, and enthusiasm is a matter of habit and custom, and another part of it is official and perfunctory. Cup Day, and Cup Day only, commands an attention, and interest, and an enthusiasm which are universal and spontaneous, not perfunctory. Cup Day is supreme – it has no rival. I can call to mind no specialised annual day, in any country, which can be named by that large name – Supreme. I can call to mind no specialised annual day, in any country, whose approach fires the whole land with a conflagration of conversation, and preparation, and anticipation, and jubilation. No day save this one; but this one does it.

Horse Racing

Mark Twain's observations 100 years ago on a speaking tour of the 'colony'. They hold true to the present time.

A difference of opinion is what makes horse racing.

Mark Twain.

That horse is further back than my car payments.

'Clarence the Clocker', Arthur Davies, who hosted a TCN Channel 9 Saturday morning racing program for twenty-two years.

Betty Le Roy was about to mount a horse at Taree one day when the trainer warned her the animal was a ferocious puller. To Betty's surprise the horse was never on the bit and finished a long last. 'Did he pull?' enquired the trainer. Came the reply, 'He wouldn't pull the skin off a custard!'

Betty Le Roy, jockey.

The punter got his mate to back a horse for him at Randwick. When the mate said he had secured 9–2

for his money, the punter said, 'You're kidding; they tell me a bloke on crutches got 5–1!'

Anonymous.

That finish was as close as a boarding house scrape of butter, and ...That finish was as close as a housing commission coat of paint!

John Tapp, Sky Channel race broadcaster.

A dry-witted bush trainer had a horse for sale and got the animal out to parade it for a potential buyer. The buyer took ten minutes to inspect the horse's legs and conformation before asking, 'Is the horse quiet?'

'Let's put it this way,' said the trainer. 'I've had him for twelve months and he hasn't said a bloody word!'

Country trainer, anonymous.

In no part of the world can be found more enthusiastic followers of the turf than in Australia, and I may also add New Zealand and that tight little island, Tasmania.

Horse Racing

Racing, in my humble opinion, is the most absorbing and interesting of sports. To love horses is an inherent characteristic of Britishers, and the bulk of the colonial people come from good old British stock.

Nat Gould who lived for more than ten years in Australia from 1884 to 1895. Interestingly, he detached Tasmania from Australia and seemed to regard it as another small country such as New Zealand. Multi-culturalism was an unknown word when Nat Gould wrote his classic, *On And Off The Turf in Australia* in 1895.

Always keep your racing information to yourself, then you will be the only sufferer.

Nat Gould, *On And Off The Turf.*

When the temptation to bet became too strong I always recalled an expression my master Fred Hood often repeated – 'three cheers are better than three years.'

From *Born to Ride* – the Kevin Langby story by Mick Contos. Kevin Langby was emphasising that it is better to abide by the rules than risk a disqualification, of say, three years.

Cocky, boastful, outspoken and with a reputation for cunning, toughness and ruthlessness, TJ was nonetheless admired internationally for his unequalled ability.

He was the first trainer in Australia, and probably the world, to treat the training of horses strictly as a business. He employed a secretary, accountant and all the backup facilities that any large business would need and laid down a policy to maximise results.

From T.J. Smith's biography, *The Midas Man TJ* by Kevin Perkins, 1993. The above is a concise summation of Tommy Smith's amazing success as trainer of racehorses in Sydney.

I have never been approached by anyone and offered money to pull a horse.

Tommy Smith. He remains adamant on this ticklish subject.

Jockeys don't know anything about training racehorses.

I will never retire. You won't be getting rid of me that easily.

Horse Racing

Tommy Smith.

If you've got first use of the track (in the mornings) it's even, like carpet. Get out here (Randwick) late and there are holes everywhere.

Tommy Smith, Sydney *Telegraph Mirror*, 21 June, 1991. The main reason why Smith always works his horses exceptionally early.

Redcraze, Gunsynd and Analie came to me as good horses and I made them great.

Tommy Smith talking about three of the best horses he ever trained.

I've known some great trainers and I've beaten them all. I just happen to be like Don Bradman, a bit better than the rest.

Tommy Smith may rightly brag about his achievements. Thirty-four times premier trainer in Sydney, a record unlikely ever to be broken. Additionally, the trainer of the champions Tulloch, Kingston Town, Redcraze and Gunsynd.

I won a hat full of money out of Bragger and knocked it all off.

The high life and bad punting took care of the cash – I couldn't win betting on horses, dogs or the two-up.

Smith was a fearless gambler during his early days as a trainer.

They used to teach the kids how to box at the AJC apprentices' school. What a load of bullshit!

You should be trying to teach them to be jockeys, not fighters.

Tommy Smith. For many years the Australian Jockey Club's apprentice school's 'chief', Major E.N. (Norman) Larkin, encouraged his students to box. He considered the boxing matches to be character building and an important part of the aspiring jockeys' education.

Without Bragger I would never have been heard of. He taught me so much because he was so good and honest, he overcame the many mistakes I made with him early and was still able to win.

I learned to train by constantly experimenting with him, he was such a tough old horse but was always suffering from bad legs and bleeding attacks. He bled dozens of times. Under our current rules he would not have been allowed on a racetrack, but he certainly started me off on the right leg. I owe Bragger a lot, he is one horse, apart from Tulloch that I ever feel sentimental about.

Tommy Smith would surely have made it without Bragger but the old horse, nicknamed 'Dadda' by Smith, certainly hastened his young trainer's rise to racing fame in the 1940s.

He is sixty-six, and his sun is supposed to be going down. He has set records in racing as Bradman did in cricket. He has changed the way horses are trained as surely as Ali changed the way men moved around the boxing ring. He has even contrived to ruin a stereotype: because of the way he is, he has made racing seem wholesome.

Les Carlyon, distinguished Melbourne journalist, on trainer Colin Hayes at the time of his retirement, *Age*, 1990.

It's the sensitivity to the animal, that's what it's about. It's everything. It doesn't matter whether it's dogs or cats or horses. You've got to be sensitive to them. You spot little things in the eye or the gait. They tell you what the animal's thinking, how it's feeling. The eye contact – it's so important.

From Les Carlyon's interview with Colin Hayes before his retirement.

Once you take the initiative from a good jockey, he's not a good jockey.

Colin Hayes, who trained more than 4000 winners from stables in Adelaide and later at Lindsay Park in the Barossa Valley.

The only way they're going to beat him is if they breed a horse with wings and get Kingsford-Smith to ride him.

Jim Pike, champion jockey, discussing Phar Lap in a Cinesound newsreel interview in 1931 after it was announced the big chestnut was going to the USA to race. Pike did not make the trip to America to ride Phar Lap. He stayed at home while Bill Elliot took the mount on the champion to win the Agua Caliente Handicap on 20 March, 1932. Phar Lap died suddenly sixteen days later at Menlo Park, California and the accolades flowed.

What is the use of winning a High Court decision and losing Phar Lap, the death of this wonderful horse is a great sporting tragedy.

Prime Minister Joe Lyons, April 1932.

Every follower of racing is shocked at the sudden death of Phar Lap, one of the greatest racehorses that ever set hoof on American soil.

Los Angeles Times, April 1932.

Phar Lap was the most remarkable horse I have ever seen – in fact the best horse ever to race in America; including Man O' War.

George W. Schilling, senior American racing steward, 1932.

Those Australian handlers and his trainer were the real reason Phar Lap died. They made two foolish mistakes. They let him eat green alfalfa and fed him grain brought from New Zealand that had become musty and damp. He was given a bucket a day of this poison.

Ed Perry, American Ranch owner, 1932.

Phar Lap was NOT given green or damp feed. I suspect someone 'got' at that last bag of feed.

Tommy Woodcock, Phar Lap's devoted attendant, Melbourne 1945.

It will be a dark day for racing if there are untouchables in the industry and if stewards have to approach matters on the basis of personalities.

Ray Murrihy, AJC Chairman of Stewards.

These are big animals that can shift ground quickly. There has to be a fairer way of dealing with this. Most jockeys feel the same as I do. We have to earn a living. You can expect a united push for a fairer deal.

Mick Dittman, champion jockey, in the Sydney *Sun-Herald*, 4 February, 1996. Dittman was speaking several days after being given the benefit of the doubt by Queensland stewards over his riding of Count Gaffa at Eagle Farm, Brisbane, on 1 January. Count Gaffa finished a close second.

It (the stewards' inquiry) has been bad enough on me. But there has been a lot more stress on my wife. She has had a long illness and this has been terribly hard on her. This is the last thing she needs in her circumstances.

I have a little boy to worry about as well. I don't think I have a long time left riding. This certainly has brought my retirement plans forward.

Mick Dittman, speaking immediately after the stewards' decision, 30 January, 1996.

Don't come here to ride like that. We want the best horse winning, not the last man standing.

Ray Murrihy, Sydney *Sun-Herald* 17 March, 1996. Mr Murrihy was addressing the New Zealand jockey Peter Tims whose mount, Batavian, had caused a scrimmage in the Todman Slipper Trial Stakes at Rosehill.

When I saw Mr Bell it soon became obvious what the real trouble was. He was convinced that I was a heavy-betting jockey. This was simply not true then or at any other time, but Alan Bell took a lot of convincing. In fact, I'm not sure even now that I ever did convince him but it clearly did no harm to put all my cards on the table. Mr Bell could produce no evidence of my alleged betting activities, simply telling me that he and some other stewards had heard a lot of gossip.

Scobie Breasley from his book *Scobie: A Lifetime in Racing* by Breasley and Christopher Poole, 1984. Scobie Breasley was harking back to 1942 when he was suspended three times in quick succession in Melbourne. Alan Bell was a widely respected and long-running chairman of stewards to the Victoria Racing Club. Breasley left Melbourne for England in 1950.

Of all my rivals – either in Australia or in England – Lester Piggott was the hardest man to beat.

Scobie Breasley, *Scobie.*

I can assure you the three words for 1996 in the racing industry are Tax, tax and tax!

We need relief quickly or we will continue to fall further behind Victoria.

Horse Racing

Bob Charley, *Sporting Globe*, 2 January, 1996. Bob Charley is Chairman of the Australian Jockey Club. His admission that NSW racing was lagging behind Victoria startled many racing observers.

I don't want any more bad horses to train. It's a different game now. All mass production. These blokes have got hundreds in work and if thirty break down there's another fifty to get through. I've only got a handful, so the ones I've got have to be good.

George Hanlon, *Sporting Globe*, 2 January, 1996. George, a veteran trainer, with an outstanding ratio of success, was replying to a question about his New Year's resolution.

The Derby's ours and Blue Eagle wins the Derby – God bless you!

Brian Markovic, Melbourne harness racing broadcaster on 2KY describing the 1995 Victoria Pacing Derby. Markovic had a vested interest – he is part-owner of the horse.

I never wanted to be a big fish in a small pond. I'm happy to be a small fish in a big pond.

Lisa Cropp in a 2KY radio interview, December 1995. Lisa is a New Zealander who has enjoyed considerable success as a jockey in New Zealand, Australia and Japan.

Every great handicap offers a premium for fraud, for horses are constantly started without any intention of winning merely to hoodwink the handicapper.

Suppress betting by legal enactment and the game is up. Thoroughbred stock would depreciate 60 per cent and our racecourses would be ploughed up. Racing has always been and always will be a gambling speculation.

Keep yourself in the best company and your racehorses in the worst.

Admiral Henry Rous, in his book *The Laws And Practice of Horse Racing, circa* 1866. Admiral Rous, 1795–1877, was one of the early 'dictators' of the English turf. He devised the widely used weight-for-age scale and was handicapper to The Jockey Club, England, until shortly before his death. Rous disliked heavy betting and hated the idea of generous presents to jockeys whom he considered should be kept in their place. At Newmarket races he usually sat on his horse at a position opposite the track in close proximity to the straight and within hearing distance of the jockeys. He would shout at them if he thought they weren't trying. His ideas on betting hold good today. He knew 140 years ago that the betting public is racing's lifeblood.

I train the same as my father but maybe with a few subtle changes at times. There are a lot of gimmicky things being tried in racing these days and it pays to keep an open mind.

In the past thirty or forty years Tommy Smith, Bart Cummings and Dad have been the most successful and I think honours have panned out fairly equal in that time. But I believe my father has been the dominant force in the last ten years.

David Hayes, *Age*, Melbourne, April 1991 speaking a few months after taking over Lindsay Park Training Stables, South Australia, from his father Colin. He switched to training in Hong Kong in 1995.

Sydney newspaper proprietor John Norton stood trial in Sydney in September, 1896 for sedition. He'd described the Prince of Wales (later King Edward VII) as a 'turf-swindling, card sharping, wife-debauching rascal' and his mother (Queen Victoria) as 'flabby, fat and flatulent.'

Norton conducted his own defence. The jury failed

to agree and the charges were eventually dropped.

Norton immediately became the hero of every radical, republican and working-class person in Australia.

Michael Cannon, author of *That Damned Democrat – John Norton, an Australian Popularist.* King Edward VII was the most successful owner-breeder of all the British monarchs, including Queen Elizabeth II who is Edward VII's great granddaughter. King Edward VII won three English Derbys with Persimmon (1896), Diamond Jubilee (1900) and Minoru (1909). (He was Prince of Wales in 1896 and 1900 and King in 1909.) He remains the only monarch to have won the English Derby. His mistress at the time was Alice Keppel, the great-grandmother of Camilla Parker-Bowles, the now much-publicised mistress of the present Prince of Wales who is King Edward VII's great, great grandson.

King Edward VII was popular with British racegoers during the Victoria-Edwardian eras. His influence on world racing was far-reaching because he strengthened the belief that racing is the Sport of Kings.

John Norton's son Ezra, who followed his father as proprietor of the *Truth* and *Sportsman* newspapers, was a successful Sydney owner, his best horse being Straight Draw, winner of the 1957 Melbourne Cup. He founded the now defunct Sydney *Daily Mirror.*

Horse Racing

It will be Eclipse first, the rest nowhere.

Dennis O'Kelly, Epsom, England, 3 May, 1769. Eclipse, regarded by many as the greatest thoroughbred ever was foaled in England in 1764. He was never beaten and in fact was never fully extended whilst winning prize money of £25 000 during his unbeaten career, an enormous sum in that period. Major Dennis O'Kelly eventually owned Eclipse outright.

Eclipse was bred by William, Duke of Cumberland. He was sold after his breeder's death for seventy-five guineas to Mr Wildman, a meat purveyor. In 1770 Major O'Kelly bought a half share in him for 650 gns and later paid another 1750 gns to buy him outright. O'Kelly was an Irishman who had been a billiards room marker.

Eclipse remains the most revered thoroughbred sire, more than 90 per cent of modern-day racehorses carrying his blood.

He sired three English Derby winners: Y. Eclipse (1781), Saltram (1783) and Sergeant (1784).

When he died aged twenty-five he had sired 335 winners of £160 000, again a fortune.

Major O'Kelly's 'the rest nowhere' has been copied thousands of time by generations of owners/punters around the world, especially Sydney's greatest racehorse trainer Tommy Smith who always has high confidence in his horses.

I think someone up above was looking after me, telling me where to go!

Darren Beadman, jockey, after winning the 1991 Epsom Handicap on the champion, Super Impose. Beadman weaved Super Impose between horses, eventually getting right along the rails at a critical point as he went from last to first.

Beadman's devotion to God and religion strengthened three years later when he resumed riding after disqualification imposed on him by stewards of the Hong Kong Jockey Club.

It can, I believe, be fairly stated that Star Kingdom was the most successful thoroughbred stallion ever to set foot on Australian soil.

Peter Pring, a renowned researcher and historian in racing matters, expressed this view in the first paragraph of his book *The Star Kingdom Story*.

I used to rave and rant at my staff. That was all part of learning. You can't expect people to do it as well as yourself – they are only working for wages.

And, I don't have owners worrying me as I contact them before they contact me.

Horse Racing

Brian Mayfield-Smith after winning his third successive
Sydney Trainer's Premiership, July 1988.

Of the works of His hand,
by sea or by land,
the horse may at least rank second.

No game was ever yet worth a rap
For a rational man to play,
Into which no accident, no mishap,
Could possibly find its way.

There's danger even where fish are caught
To those who a-wetting fear;
For what's worth having must aye be bought,
And sport's like life and life's like sport,
It ain't all skittles and beer.

She passed like an arrow Kildare and Cock
    Sparrow,
And Mantrap and Mermaid refused the stone wall;
And Giles on The Greyling came down at the paling,
And I was left sailing in front of them all . . .

Adam Lindsay Gordon, poet cum politician cum jumps
jockey in Victoria was born in England in 1833. He saw
hurdle racing at its very best at Cheltenham. He never

lost his love of the horse and one memorable day at the 1869 Melbourne steeplechase meeting rode three winners, Babbler, Viking and Cadger. A month later he won the VRC Steeplechase on Viking. This tall, slim jockey/poet wrote beautiful words on many subjects that illustrate his compassionate nature.

In June 1870, aged only thirty-six, Adam Lindsay Gordon took his own life by gunshot at the Melbourne seaside suburb of Brighton. There is a small memorial to him in Gordon Park near Parliament House, Melbourne.

The whole set-up was stupid from the word go. It was ridiculous.

It had an effect on my career all right. I seemed to go quiet from then on. I think a bit of the mud stuck, but I suppose you couldn't blame people for being a bit sceptical.

Gus Philpot was an innocent victim as Fine Cotton's jockey at Eagle Farm. *Courier Mail*, Brisbane, 24 July, 1989.

I find it difficult to reconcile the clean-cut GPS educated, ethical young millionaire, with the sort of people with whom he is pleased to associate.

Judge Alf Goran gave that view on Robbie Waterhouse in

his 1995 108-page judgment on Waterhouse's failed appeal to the NSW Racing Appeals Tribunal against his warning-off by the Australian Jockey Club in 1984.

This must be a ring-in.

Bookmaker Mark Read, speaking loudly on his 'stand' at Warwick Farm during the Fine Cotton betting plunge, 18 August, 1984. He continued cheerfully to invite more bets. He was fortunate that the discovery by the Queensland stewards was made and the horse disqualified so that he retained the money so wagered.

It was greed that wrecked their rort; it would have come off had they gone for little fish.

Mark Read, *Sydney Morning Herald* 20 August, 1984.

On form, it would indicate that Fine Cotton was a picnic horse with a right price of 50–1, or 100–1.

Bruce McHugh, Sydney Turf Club director and retired bookmaker, talking before the AJC committee during the Fine Cotton hearing, 14 November, 1984.

The banning hasn't worried me one ounce. In fact I've done more out of it now than I ever did before. I've got clients all over the place.

Hayden Haitana reflecting on his life disqualification over the Fine Cotton affair, *Courier Mail*, Brisbane 24 July, 1989.

Haitana was Fine Cotton's trainer on the fateful day in August 1984. He became an overnight celebrity.

Brisbane racing is as clean as anywhere else. Sydney bookmakers are responsible.

Russ Hinze, Queensland's former Minister for Racing in the State Parliament, speaking at a press conference the day after the ring-in.

His summation of the situation was partly correct due to Sydney bookmaker Robbie Waterhouse's involvement. However, it is generally agreed that the Fine Cotton ring-in mastermind was John Patrick Gillespie. He was to plead guilty to fraud and conspiracy charges over Fine Cotton and was sentenced to four years' jail in February, 1986.

Before his trial on the fraud and conspiracy charges Gillespie spent almost twelve months on the run before police found him hiding in a cupboard at his sister's house in Victoria in November, 1985.

I don't need money. Somebody will always buy me a beer. You see I'm the bloke that did something everybody dreams of doing but never gets around to it.

Hayden Haitana reflecting on Fine Cotton after serving six months of a twelve months' jail sentence for his part in the ring-in.

It's like cutting off your arms and legs and telling you to swim!

Gai Waterhouse after her husband Robbie's appeal to the NSW Racing Appeals Tribunal was dismissed.

When will this nightmare end. I've taken courses to try to help find a decent job, but the stigma and notoriety of that bloody scandal follows me.

All I want to do is get back to the track. I miss the horses and the lifestyle and so does Glenis.

Gary and Glenis Clarke *New Idea*, 25 September, 1994. They were warned off by the AJC over their betting involvement in the Fine Cotton affair.

David Waterhouse has come here with extremely

damaging claims against his brother and his father. I'm seeking to show that this man is a liar.

Frank McAlary, QC was counsel for Robbie Waterhouse at his December 1995-January 1996 appeal before the Australian Jockey Club committee to have his warning-off from all race tracks lifted.

I'm not here to help Robbie. I think it would be terrible for racing if he gets back.

David Waterhouse speaking to the AJC committee at his brother Robbie's appeal against his warning-off.

I am terribly sad that my brother is taking this action against me.

Robbie Waterhouse after his younger brother David lodged an unfriendly document with the AJC solicitors a few days before his appeal against his warning-off from all racetracks.

I know police who were told to go out and get the Waterhouses.

Why is he forbidden access to racecourses when murderers are allowed on them?

Horse Racing

Alan Jones, radio station 2UE's talkback host, speaking as witness for Robbie and Bill Waterhouse before the AJC committee in December 1995.

There have been great racehorses and great trainers but there has been nothing to compare with Dad. (Tommy Smith.) And if he says run Nothin' Leica Dane in the Cup, who am I to disagree?

Trainer Gai Waterhouse immediately after Nothin' Leica Dane's victory in the Victoria Derby at Flemington on 4 November, 1995. The decision had to be made whether or not to start the colt in the Melbourne Cup three days later.

Run the bugger!

Tommy Smith's no beating-about-the-bush remark on a Cup start for Nothin' Leica Dane. He lined up in the big race and finished a fine second to Doriemus on a rain-soaked track. Three-year-olds, such as Nothin' Leica Dane, rarely contest the Melbourne Cup.

Today was a perfect example of what type of trainer Gai Waterhouse is. She is the best trainer we have seen since her father.

Jockey Shane Dye after Nothin' Leica Dane's win in the 1995 Victoria Derby.

Sellwood and I were given our licences by the QTC (Queensland Turf Club) on the same day in 1938. But Sellwood was six months older than I. He quickly started riding winners and became a glamour boy. He never gave me a look-in. It was no piece of cake getting started in those days.

George Moore, talking to Peter Cameron, Brisbane *Courier Mail*, 4 February, 1986. George Moore and Neville Sellwood became two of the greatest jockeys in world racing. Sellwood was killed riding a horse called Lucky Seven at Maison Lafitte, Paris, on 7 November, 1962 aged thirty-nine, at the zenith of his career.

Tommy was a super optimist. Yet he hated 'yes men' and 'bulldust'. We had plenty of arguments over the years, but only about six fair dinkum ones. A week was the longest a feud lasted. Tommy never sacked me. We were good mates. He'd just say 'buzz off'.

This strapper Tommy Smith got on the train at Albury or Wagga with the horses Dollar and Fearless. He never had a zac. We were stabled next to each other at Caulfield when we reached Melbourne and used to play cricket in the afternoon.

He used to skite, 'One day I'll train the Derby winner and you'll be leading jockey.' I thought he was soft in the head. He didn't even have a trainer's licence.

George Moore discussing Tommy Smith with Peter Cameron.

At the time, October 1940, Smith was a strapper working for the Riverina racing identity Mack Sawyer, a wealthy pastoralist, owner-trainer and breeder of thoroughbreds.

Moore was a teenage apprentice indentured to the Brisbane trainer W.J. (Jim) Shean who was preparing a good galloper, Gold Salute, for races in Melbourne. Gold Salute was owned by the mercurial owner-punter of the time, A.E. (Alan) Cooper.

I was nearly always innocent when I was disqualified or warned off. But then jockeys in my day could get away with a lot more than they can now.

I was once given two disqualifications in four years. When Schumacher was given life a bloke asked me what I thought. I said, 'There, but for the grace of God, go I!'

I never had a greater thrill than winning those

two Doomben races and the VRC Newmarket at Flemington on Bernborough.

Athol (George) Mulley, talking to Peter Cameron, Brisbane *Courier Mail*, 7 July, 1986.

Mulley rode the mighty Bernborough to victory in the 1946 Newmarket then three months later the Doomben 10 000-Doomben Cup double, humping the huge weights of 10st 5lbs (65.75kgs) and 10st 11lbs (68.5kgs) in the two races.

Once I had a double going for £90,000 ($180 000) but, of course, the second leg got rolled. I never seemed to have much luck with doubles.

Mulley, after his retirement from racing, freely admitted that he broke the rules of the turf by betting heavily at times.

Jockeys are banned from betting in Australia.

People make threats. Never worry about the ones who ring you; it's the ones that don't ring you, they're the ones to worry about.

John Schreck, AJC Chairman of Stewards, the *Australian* magazine, 25 May, 1992.

Horse Racing

I have been doing this job a long time now.

I was looking at the records the other day and there has been no one else that has had to punish as many people that I have.

There will be more problems in the future but racing will weather them as it has before.

John Schreck speaking on 8 June, 1995, his last day as AJC Chairman of Stewards.

One white foot, ride him for your life.
Two white feet, give him to your wife.
Three white feet, give him to your man.
Four white feet, sell him – if you can!

Anonymous. In olden days when horses were used largely for transport, white-hooved horses were not popular as their hooves could prove softer than dark-hooved steeds. White hooves were also soft in many cases with racehorses. For example, the great Carbine's white hind hoof, caused him problems for the last two years of his wonderful career.

They are only races. No one dies, though I nearly have myself once or twice.

Peter Chapple-Hyam, Robert Sangster's trainer.

Nothing improves a horse's form more than ownership.

Bruce McHugh, former leading Sydney bookmaker, is now a prominent owner-breeder and a director of the Sydney Turf Club.

When a Sydney newspaper described him as a 'gambler pure and simple', his indignant reply was, 'I might be pure but I'm damned if I'm simple!'

Humphrey Oxenham, Sydney bookmaker *circa* 1895. Oxenham was Sydney's most colourful bookmaker in the late 19th and early 20th centuries.

Gambling is a massive business, the biggest industry in the world. People don't take it seriously: I do. I take my gambling very seriously.

Bill Waterhouse from *The Bookie Book* by Harry Robinson and written before former leading Sydney bookmaker Bill Waterhouse was warned off all racecourses after the Australian Jockey Club's investigation into the Fine Cotton 'ring-in' in 1984.

BIBLIOGRAPHY

The Bookie Book, Harry Robinson, John Fairfax, 1985.

Born to Ride – the Kevin Langby Story, Nick Contos, Lester-Townsend, 1988.

George Freeman: An Autobiography, George Freeman, 1988.

The Great Australian Gamble, James Holledge, Horwitz, 1966.

The Laws and Practice of Horse Racing, Henry Rous, A.H. Bailey & Co, 1866.

The Midas Man TJ, Kevin Perkins, Macmillan, 1993,

On and Off the Turf in Australia, Nat Gould, 1895, Libra Books edition, 1973.

A Portrait of Racing, Stephen Brassel, Simon & Schuster, 1990.

Scobie: a Lifetime in Racing, Scobie Breasley and Christopher Poole, Queen Anne Press, 1984.

The Star Kingdom Story, Peter Pring, Thoroughbred Press, 1983.

That Damned Democrat – John Norton, an Australian Popularist, Michael Cannon, Melbourne University Press, 1981.

Winning More, Don Scott, Horwitz-Grahame, 1988.

Jim Main is a Melbourne sports writer with more than thirty books to his credit. After graduating from La Trobe University (majoring in history) he began covering the VFL/AFL scene and with over 25 years' experience is now regarded as one of the code's foremost historians. His books include *The Encylopedia of League Footballers*, and *This Football Century* (both with Russell Holmesby), and *EJ – The Ted Whitten Story*.

AFL
UP THERE CAZALY!
South Melbourne supporters

If he'd lost the first few they (Magpie supporters) would have been ready to shoot him.

Bob Rose on Collingwood coach Leigh Matthews, after the former Hawthorn champion had taken the Magpies to the 1990 premiership – the club's first in 32 years. Rose stood down as Collingwood coach in favour of Matthews early in the 1986 season.

I'll never play for South Melbourne again. Not this year, not next year, or the year after, or the year after that. Never!

John Pitura, the South Melbourne star, who was involved in a bitter struggle to leave the Swans for Richmond in 1974. Pitura eventually returned to South and played out the 1974 season with the Swans before joining Richmond the following year. However, his move was a dismal failure as he played just 40 games in three seasons with the Tigers. The deal provided the Swans with Brian Roberts, who finished equal fourth in the 1975 Brownlow Medal, Graham Teasdale who won the 1977 Brownlow and Francis Jackson, who became a Swan stalwart at centre half-back.

I don't think I will ever play again. I was prepared to take my punishment, but when it was shown that I was the retaliator I expected to get half the sentence of (Harry) Caspar.

John Coleman, the champion Essendon full-forward, after being suspended for four matches on the eve of the 1951 finals. Carlton's Caspar and Coleman threw punches at each other in a final round match and Coleman's suspension almost certainly cost Essendon the flag that year as the Bombers, without their match-winner, lost the grand final to Geelong by just 11 points. Coleman did play again, but was forced to retire in 1954 because of a chronic knee injury.

The only thing that beat us was the final siren.

Malcolm Blight, the Geelong coach, after Hawthorn had defeated the Cats by 6 points in the 1989 grand final.

Handball, handball, handball ... handball at all cost.

Ron Barassi, as Carlton coach, at half-time in the 1970 grand final against Collingwood. Barassi's tactics helped Carlton turn a 44-point half-time deficit into a 10-point premiership victory.

God bless Mummy, God bless Daddy and God Bless Peter Burns.

When the brilliant Peter Burns was South's great champion for the pre-VFL era, local children were taught this prayer. Burns later was cleared to Geelong and played 89 games for the Pivotonians from 1897–1902.

Dealing the White Australia policy a death blow.

An anonymous writer, when Carlton selected Chinese footballer Wally Koo-Chew for his first senior VFL game in 1908, an unsigned letter from the Ancient Order of the Druids warned Carlton.

Koo-Chew was the first of several Asian VFL/AFL footballers. Others have included the Singapore-born Danny Seow (Collingwood and Melbourne) and the Korean-born Peter Bell (Fremantle and North Melbourne).

As long as they (Aborigines) conduct themselves like white people, well, off the field, everyone will admire them and respect them.

Allan McAlister, the Collingwood president said this in 1993 following the disclosure that St Kilda's Aboriginal footballer Nicky Winmar had been subjected to racist taunts at the Magpies' Victoria Park.

This remark, of course, only fuelled the fires of the racism-in-football furore and McAlister later travelled to the Northern Territory to apologise to the Aboriginal community.

There are two things you can be certain of: dying and getting the arse as a football coach.

Norm Dare, after being replaced as Brisbane coach at the end of the 1990 season.

If there had been trial-by-video in those days they would have rubbed out every bloody player.

Jack 'Basher' Williams, the tough South star, on the infamous 1945 'Bloodbath' grand final.
The 'Bloodbath' grand final (won by Carlton) was reputedly the toughest and dirtiest game in VFL/AFL history, with 10 players reported for various offences.

I suppose we are both very lucky we were given some sort of gift by God.

Phil Krakouer describing the incredible on-field bond he had with brother Jimmy during their years with North Melbourne (1982–89).

How the ---- did you do that Cazaly?

Norm Beckton. Beckton is the player seen alongside the legendary Roy Cazaly in the famous photograph of the South Melbourne champion taking a one-handed mark in 1922. Beckton asked Cazaly: How the ---- did you do that? Cazaly modestly suggested that it was not a remarkable mark. However, the photograph of that mark is possibly the most reproduced in the code's history.

The players who go out there and do it on the day –
they're the heroes.

Leigh Matthews, the Collingwood coach, after the Magpies'
1990 grand final win, the club's first in 32 years.

No, I wasn't surprised, just heartened.

Graham Cornes, the Adelaide coach, after the Crows' 86-
point demolition of Hawthorn in their inaugural AFL premiership match, on 22 March, 1991.

Poor kid, he's got a bit of a name to live up to. But
he uses handball intelligently and kicks to position.

Ted Whitten, the Footscray legend, in 1968 of his 11-year-
old son Ted Jnr. Ted Jnr. eventually played 144 senior games
for Footscray from 1974–82 and represented Victoria.

I say a prayer every night . . . 'please God, keep me
out of the papers'.

Allan McAlister, the controversial Collingwood president.

You were spectacular, Bob. But not very effective.

South Melbourne official when the legendary Bob Pratt failed to win South's 1934 best and fairest award (it was won by Terry Brain) despite kicking a league record of 150 goals for the season.

There's only one thing worse than having a South Australian in your team, and that's having 20 of them.

Jack Dyer, the former Richmond great, on the introduction of the Adelaide Crows to the AFL competition in 1991.

That was just rubbish. It was no different to thousands of other incidents, but was just one of those fluke things that happen.

Jim O'Dea. The St Kilda defender was involved in one of football's most sensational incidents when, in 1972, he collided with Collingwood star John Greening, who was knocked unconscious and never again recaptured top form. O'Dea scoffed at suggestions that he collected Greening with a karate blow.

AFL

I don't care what the critics say. The critics' team is never selected. It never plays, it never wins and it never loses.

Denis Pagan, the North Melbourne coach on football critics.

I only came here (to the count at Melbourne's Southern Cross Hotel) for the free meal.

Robert DiPierdomenico, the champion Hawthorn winger, a rank outsider, after sharing the 1986 Brownlow Medal honours with Sydney's Greg Williams.

I decided not to have a drink after the win as I wanted to keep everything fresh in my memory. Unfortunately, I cracked just before midnight and I now have a thumping headache. But it is a good headache.

Tony Jewell, the day after coaching Richmond to the 1980 premiership.

We're sorry you're going, boy.

Alf Foley, the VFL Tribunal chairman, after clearing

Melbourne's Carl Ditterich of a striking charge in his final league match, in 1980. Ditterich averaged one tribunal a season in his 18 years as a league footballer with Melbourne and St Kilda.

In the past, Geelong has been branded as the weakies, but I couldn't say that about any of our players, and no one else could either.

Billy Goggin, after coaching Geelong to a four-point loss to Collingwood in the 1980 preliminary final.

Fair dinkum, I am in more places than Elvis Presley, if you listen to the Geelong rumours.

Mark Bairstow, before returning to Geelong in 1991 after a season playing country football in Western Australia.

Football clubs are full of pretenders, hangers-on and people telling you they are doing you a good turn when they are really kicking you in the arse.

Tony Lockett, the St Kilda (now Sydney) full-forward in 1990.

I get embarassed when people say 'you have won the Brownlow Medal' because I can't believe I won the bloody thing. I'm not sure whether I'm that good a footballer.

Paul Couch, the Geelong centreman after winning the 1989 Brownlow Medal.

These guys are bloody mad. You wouldn't get me to play that game for quids.

Ray Stewart, the West Ham United and Scotland soccer star, after watching the 1989 Hawthorn-Geelong grand final (won by the Hawks).

He's only played the one game and already they're taking the piss out of the Irish.

Jim Stynes, after fellow Irishman Dermott McNichol was drug-tested following his 1990 debut with St Kilda.

We don't want him replaced by a fresh young player.

Brighton Diggins, the Carlton captain-coach saw Colling-wood's Albert Collier limping in the 1938 grand final and instructed his players not to harm the Magpie champion. Carlton won by 15 points.

Keep moving, so that the blood you have forced into circulation does not get cold again. A cold body is subject to cramps, takes the knocks and feels them, thus losing energy, and a slow muscle does not respond as quickly as a warm one. A warm man is 50 per cent more efficient than a cold man.

Roy Cazaly, the legendary South Melbourne and St Kilda champion in 1946, giving advice to young footballers.

You were allowed to push a man from behind without a penalty. Think of the golden opportunities presented! There was the opposition high mark just settling under the dropping ball when you gave him all you carried right plumb in the small of the back. The busters were indescribable.

Peter Burns, the early VFA and VFL South Melbourne and Geelong champion describing turn-of-the-century football.

Among many fine things, we (Collingwood) had the

gamest man football ever produced. His fortitude stands as the embodiment of the Magpie spirit.

Harry Curtis, the Collingwood president, of champion Dick Lee (230 games from 1906 to 1922).

Well boys, have you heard the news? The other fellows are holding a meeting at Buxton's Art Gallery. They are going to break away and form another body to be called the Victorian Football League.

Donald McDonald, *Argus* football writer. He burst into a VFA meeting late in 1896 and told the delegates. The news of the formation of the VFL (now AFL) was made public the next day.

The number of head-high tackles in the past couple of weeks is a worry. We just can't have players marking the ball and then being crunched and the only thing that happens is to give away a 15-metre (now 50) penalty – or kicking the ball and being crunched and another kick being given down the ground.

David Parkin to reporters in 1982.

If any boy given to me for coaching lacks courage
he is just wasting my time and his own trying to
break into senior football. A boy without courage
will let you down when the pressure is on, and
will fail to measure up to League football
requirements.

Perc Bentley, Carlton coach (1941–55).

What Len did was to put down on paper a modus
operandi of how to play a game of football. He put
things in the most simple way, making them easy
to understand and easy to teach. It was Len's simplicity which was so important.

Ron Barassi, on the coaching techniques of the late Len
Smith who coached both Fitzroy (1958–62) and Richmond
(1964–5) and is regarded as the 'father' of modern tactical
thinking.

Some of you seem to think that all I ever see are
your faults. They're not all I see, but they're what I
comment on, because that's a coach's job – to correct
faults. The good things I take for granted.

Ron Barassi apologising to his Carlton players for being so

tough on them as coach in the Blues' premiership sesason of 1968.

You have a spendid team. It is better than the one I captained when I was down here for about two years.

H.C.A. Harrison, the man regarded as the 'father' of Australian football at a Geelong-Melbourne match at the Corio Oval in 1924. Someone in the crowd called out: 'When?' and Harrison replied: 'Oh, about 50 or 60 years ago.'

I won't, at this stage, speak publicly about premierships, but there is no doubt on every occasion we take the field we will have the best team available.

Graham Cornes, the inaugural Adelaide coach, before the Crows' first season, in 1991. Adelaide made only one finals series – in 1993 – before Cornes was sacked at the end of the 1994 season.

Winners can laugh. Losers can please themselves.

Mike Patterson, the St Kilda coach, following a complaint by an Essendon official that the Saints played like 'animals' in a 1977 match at Moorabbin.

North Melbourne came down to St Kilda,
They were confident of a win.
Colin Watson was injured at practice,
St Kilda put young Matt Cave in.

The ball was bounced in the centre,
Downie hit the leather towards the sky;
Matt Cave went into accept it
And caught four stitches in the eye.

The game went on, the air was thick.
The supporters jumped the fence.
They had not found their footing,
When off came 'Tiger' Bence.

The forwards, they were going great,
They would have kicked a score.
But North Melbourne put the dirt in
And broke the ribs of Billy Mohr.

Doctor Jones said: 'Oh, my word,
I think this game is rotten;
If any more stitches went in
I'll run right out of cotton.

Jack McLeod, the St Kilda player following a remarkable
Saints' win over North Melbourne at the Junction Oval in
1933 in which St Kilda finished with only 15 fit men. The

win prompted St Kilda officials to present the players with medallions with a special commemorative shield. That shield now is part of the St Kilda guernsey. This is part of McLeod's long poem about that historic 1933 victory.

They're like sausages. You can boil them, grill them or curry them. But in the end. They're still sausages.

Allan Jeans, the St Kilda and Hawthorn premiership coach on coaching tactics.

I look at him in the morning every time I shave.

Laurie Nash when asked to nominate the greatest-ever footballer. Nash, who played 99 games for South Melbourne from 1933–7 and in 1945, once kicked 18 goals for Victoria against South Australia after being shifted from defence.

I would do anything for the club – I always would since I joined it in 1903 (as a player). I am a sad man today, but I will be delighted if this grand side goes on to big things.

Jock McHale, the legendary Collingwood coach to the

Collingwood players soon after the announcement of his retirement in 1950 after 38 years as coach.

There is no need for a player to wash himself in it, but a taste now and again is the best thing going.

Jock McHale, who worked at the Carlton and United Breweries.

Look, I've just got off Devil's Island; I'm not going to live on Alcatraz.

Jack Hamilton, the VFL boss on his retirement in 1986 when asked if he would take up a position with the club he represented as a player, Collingwood.

A man who jumps out of telephone boxes and has a big S on his chest.

Jack Hamilton, when asked who would be the best replacement for him in his VFL job.

It wasn't until my kids were 15 that they found out my first name was Jack. They thought it was Bloody.

Jack Hamilton, after announcing his retirement.

I can't really see what the fuss is all about. I mean, how many times have you seen players kick goals in the last few seconds of a game or after the siren?

Ross 'Twiggy" Dunne, on his last-minute goal to level scores in Collingwood's drawn 1977 grand final against North Melbourne. North won the replay the following week.

You're girl's a bloody whore!

Dick Condon, the early Collingwood champion (1894–1906) was suspended for life in 1900 for this remark to umpire Ivo Crapp after having a free kick awarded against him. The suspension was lifted two years later.

Today I want you to bleed for Collingwood ... bleed for me. I will be out there every second of the game. I'll be feeling every bump, every mark, every kick ... I want you to go in harder than any Collingwood player before you.

Phonse Kyne addressing his players before the 1958 grand final against Melbourne. Collingwood defeated Melbourne to prevent the Demons equalling the Magpies' record of four consecutive premierships (1927–30).

They are just the kind of men to make ideal fighters for the Empire. They have played the game of ball magnificently and when they get going against the murdering Kaiser's mob they will make their presence felt.

The *Football Record*, the official VFL publication, in a 1915 edition, paid tribute to Collingwood's Malcolm Seddon, Paddy Rowan and Jim Jackson, who had just enlisted in the AIF. Tragically, Rowan was killed in World War I, but Seddon returned to the Magpies in 1919 and Jackson became Hawthorn's first VFL captain, in 1925.

A Victorian club in normal times is strong to 30 or more places, whereas in the other states club teams tail off after about 14 places and there is a dearth of reserves.

Hayd Bunton, the Fitzroy triple Brownlow Medallist, who also won three Sandover Medals with Subiaco, comparing the standard of football played in Victoria and other states in 1946.

Everyone thought I was stuffed. I went back to training for the first time and got halfway around the oval, but my leg wouldn't go.

Peter Box, the Footscray star who made a remarkable comeback after shocking leg injuries in a 1953 motorcycle accident to win the 1956 Brownlow Medal.

Why grouch? You could have been in the cut-up too.

An unnamed Essendon player, after being defeated by VFA premier club Footscray in an end-of-season charity match in 1924. There were rumours that some Essendon footballers had 'played dead'. Skipper Tom Fitzmaurice had taken one of the players to task. Fitzmaurice joined Geelong the following year. Footscray was admitted to the VFL the same season.

My brother and I got sunburnt one day and someone suggested my brother was as red as a lobster. Dad said: 'What about the little bloke?' and my father replied 'Oh, he's just a little yabby'.

Allan 'Yabby' Jeans, the St Kilda and Hawthorn coach.

They'll die. The club was all they had in life. They get up each day and all it meant to them was they're one day closer to watching their team.

Ted Whitten on supporters of his beloved Footscray (he had played 321 games for the Bulldogs) at the mooted amalgamation with Fitzroy in 1989.

As a kid I barracked for the club and I always wanted to play for Footscray. Last year I had three offers to leave the club; much better than what Footscray offered me. The only reason I stayed was loyalty. When this happens you wonder – you wonder what life really is all about.

Bran Royal, the Footscray rover on the suggested merger. Footscray members and fans blocked the proposal.

They (the fans) had paid their money; they can do what they like. What did they do at the end of the game?

Malcolm Blight, the Geelong coach, after he had been booed before the Cats had pulled a game out of the fire against St Kilda in 1994.

It's a pretty select group of people I'm with now, those who have coached three losing grand final sides, and we all know where they ended up.

Malcolm Blight, the Geelong coach, after losing the 1994 grand final to West Coast.

Coming down the race I lost it for about two minutes. I had tears running down. I said 'Super' (Footscray teammate Steve 'Supermac' Macpherson), I'm in trouble here.' He just grabbed me really tight, we banged heads a couple of times and said, 'Mate, just get it together, you'll be right.'

Doug Hawkins, in 1994, on his 322nd game for Footscray, breaking the 321-game record of the legendary Ted Whitten (1951–70).

I know the painters and dockers haven't attracted good publicity in recent times, but the name Docker refers to the wharf workers of the 1800s, when Fremantle was mainly a port town.

David Hatt, the Fremantle Docker's chief executive at the launch of the club in 1994 for its AFL debut in 1995.

You see, footballers of today are young men, and for the most part, not receiving big wages. Well, in the case of apprentices, and those not blessed with much of this world's wealth, it comes pretty hard on them to buy their own uniforms and boots. Therefore, I think in such cases claims of the kind should be met by the clubs, who are pretty well all in a sound financial state.

C.S. Cock, the Fitzroy football club's first secretary, advocating professionalism in 1889.

Moriarty, with the goog, goog, googly eyes,
Moriarty who Fitzroy idolise.
Who's the chap who kicks the goals
Send them through the poles –
Moriarty, with the goog goog, googly eyes.

Norm Byron, regarded as Fitzroy's poet laureate in the years between the two world wars. Bryon (who played two games for Fitzroy in 1918), wrote this tribute to goalkicking ace Jack Moriarty in 1924 (to the tune of 'Barney Google').

To me football is more than a mere game. It is not only a wonderful recreation, but an inspiration and a mental and physical tonic. How I look forward to each Saturday's play.

Doug Nicholls, (later Pastor Sir Douglas Nicholls). Nicholls, an Aboriginal who later was Governor of South Australia, told the *Sporting Globe* in 1935 of his love for football. Nicholls played 55 games with Fitzroy from 1932–7 and was knighted in 1972.

It was made clear to me by the president and secretary of the club that as the money was not coming from the club, I was not breaking the Coulter Law. I asked about that.

Haydn Bunton, regarded as one of the greatest players the game has seen. Bunton had to stand out of football for the entire 1930 season after Fitzroy recruited him from Albury in 1929. The VFL claimed Bunton had breached the Coulter Law banning the payment of inducements to sign with a particular club. Bunton had received expenses of £158 from a Fitzroy supporter. Bunton eventually started his career with Fitzroy in 1931 and won three Brownlow Medals.

The amazing deeds of this great player are still green in the memory of all those who were fortunate enough to have seen him play, and his manliness both on and off the field endeared him to those privileged to know him. During his association with Fitzroy he held pride of place as a great clubman, and his many kindly acts to those less gifted than himself earned for him the love and affection of a legion of friends and admirers.

From the Fitzroy Annual Report. The great Haydn Bunton was killed in a motor accident outside Adelaide on 5 September, 1955.

When I found that World War II started, I found the call.

Wilfred 'Chicken' Smallhorn, the Fitzroy winger won the 1933 Brownlow Medal but left the Maroons in 1940 to join the army. He was captured by the Japanese and was a prisoner of war at the infamous Changi camp.

I don't find the game as interesting as Australian Rules, but tackling and playing in the scrums is priming me for another season with Carlton.

Mike Fitzpatrick, the Carlton ruckman stunned the football world in 1976 when he announced that he would be studying, as a Rhodes Scholar, at Oxford University and would have to put his football career on hold. Fitzpatrick played rugby to maintain fitness. He returned and captained the 1981–2 Carlton premiership sides.

It was a good day for footy, not just in Queensland, but for the national competition, that we were able to come down here, eighth against first, 20 wins against 10, and give them a fight they they were pretty happy to get out of.

Robert Walls after the Brisbane Bears' first finals appearance, in the 1995 fourth qualifying final against Carlton. Carlton won by just 13 points but went on to win the premiership.

AFL clubs are role models in our society. Kids follow us. It's all very well for people to say it's been going on all the time and you will never wipe it out, but that's no reason why we should not take action. We have a responsibility and obligation to not only the club and football, but to society in general, to try and do our part to try and get rid of racism in our society.

David Shaw, the Essendon president on the 1995 racism-in-football controversy.

Gary Ablett has got to take responsibility for his own actions on the ground. When he's leading for the ball and in certain situations he's got to be careful in terms of the way he makes physical contact with players.

Neil Busse, after the AFL Tribunal cleared Geelong superstar Gary Ablett of charging West Coast's Mitchell White in Round 13, 1995. Ablett was suspended for two matches on an almost identical charge later in the season.

I have been knifed.

Bernie Quinlan on being sacked as Fitzroy coach late in the 1995 season.

It was just frustration I suppose. I am allowed to do that. Sometimes silence is the best word of all.

Kevin Sheedy. At half-time in a 1993 Essendon-Hawthorn match at the MCG, the Bomber coach waited near the umpires' dressing rooms and glared at the men in white. Umpires John Russo and Darren Goldspink wrote to the AFL about this incident. The AFL informed Sheedy that such action would not be tolerated in future.

I cried a little. I feel extra good. I haven't been here as long as these other guys. They're really crying.

Ron Barassi after he coached the Sydney Swans to a 40-point win over Melbourne in Round 20, 1993, for the Swan's first win in 27 matches.

It is the worst job in football.

Ron Barassi after taking over the Sydney coaching position from the axed Gary Buckenara three months earlier. The Swans won just one game in 1993, but four in 1994 and eight in 1995 before Barassi stepped down.

I kicked a goal early in one game; it was a bit of a fluke. The next thing, I found myself on the ground. Chitty had nearly knocked my teeth out. He stood over me and said, 'Kick another goal and we'll see how you get on then.'

Jim Thoms, the Footscray rover (1937–46) on Carlton tough man Bob Chitty.

I broke my nose a few times, but I never counted injuries like that.

Bob Chitty, the 1945 Carlton premiership captain.

Chitty never needed armour.

Jack Dyer when told that Bob Chitty would star as Ned Kelly in a film just after World War II.

When I entered the dressing rooms at the Melbourne ground on the Saturday afternoon, bag in hand, I went up as usual, to have a look at the list of players and I noticed, as I walked through the room, the fellows all looking up at me without saying a word.

I nodded to them but they still looked at me without speaking. I thought this was curious but did not take much notice of their looks until I glanced at the list. I looked at the rover's name and then at the ruck, and saw that my name was not there.

I was surprised, but I was amazed when my name was not among the half-forwards. 'So that's the team!' I exclaimed and walked away. I spoke to the president and then to Mr Ford (the Carlton secretary) and asked them what was the matter.

'You have been bribed,' said Mr Ford. McGregor (Carlton star Rod McGregor) came up to me and said he would not play. I told him the facts and he then consented to play. As I told Mr Ford and Mr McGregor, I was approached in the street by a man who asked me: 'Will you run a bye?' I refused and then I thought that as he was trying to play a game on me, I would turn the tables.

He wanted me to 'run a bye' as he called it, and pay up afterwards, but I demanded the money. After some argument he handed me £10. I had not the money in my possession ten minutes. I gave it to a friend to back Carlton with and he got £12 for £10. I never intended for a moment not to push myself in the match.

I would not know how to do it. I must play the game when I am on the field. Mr Ford and Mr McGregor asked me why I did not tell them. I told them I wished I had but, as they knew I had been off colour somewhat for several weeks past, and I thought if I did not happen to give a good account of myself, my mentioning the fact I had been given the money would be regarded as an excuse to cover up my play and they would be suspicious of me. I would not for the world take my comrades down and I had no intention of not playing the game. I did not even promise to do so.

Alex 'Bongo' Lang in an interview with the *Argus* newspaper. Lang, one of Carlton's earliest VFL stars, was the centre of football's greatest controversy. He was charged with 'playing dead' – along with three other Carlton players – in a match against South Melbourne in 1910.

The VFL subsequently suspended Lang and teammate Doug Fraser for five years, but cleared two other Carlton players. Fraser never played with Carlton again, but Lang returned in 1916 to play two more seasons with the Blues.

If I never had the grit I would be of no use to the Collingwood side. The Magpies have no use for any player that lacks determination.

Ernie Wilson. Wilson, who played with Collingwood from 1919–28, was regarded as the toughest player of his era and, in a 1925 interview with the *Sporting Globe*, defended his vigorous play.

A place that looks more like a lady's boudoir than a football secretary's office. The walls have been done in a beautiful shade of blue, there is a blue carpet on the floor, a suite of Jacobean chairs and a table.

In 1929, the *Truth* newspaper's criticism of Hawthorn's headquarters.

It doesn't take much to confuse him.

Dennis Carroll, the Sydney captain of goalkicking team-
mate Warwick Capper in 1991.

I don't care if you are the last man in defence and
you've got Peter Hudson, Tony Lockett and Doug
Wade sitting on the full-forward line – that pressure
doesn't compare with the pressure on a coach.

Michael Malthouse, the West Coast Eagle coach in 1991 on
the pressures of the job.

People might think it's like Stalag 13 down here at
the moment, but it's not.

Tony Shaw. The Collingwood coach demanded discipline at
Victoria Park right from the start of his tenure in 1996.

The game was just as tough in my day as it ever looks
like being now, but it was never bitter. We would not
have tolerated in those days things I have seen done
many times in finals games before big crowds at the
Melbourne Cricket Ground. I think the players of
today are spoon-fed – too much so. They want everything done for them. They squabble over money. They
won't buy a bootlace for themselves.

Peter Burns, a South Melbourne legend when the club played in the VFA and than a VFL star with Geelong in the league's earliest years. He wrote in 1940 of the changes he had seen in football since his retirement in 1902.

There is no hiding from it; the expectations on the players are unrealistically high and we have to live in that environment.

Graham Cornes, the Adelaide coach in 1993.

No, I'm not bitter. In hindsight, I was on a hiding to nothing.

Bernie Quinlan, the former Fitzroy coach, six months after being sacked late in the 1995 season. Fitzroy won only two games under Quinlan in 1995.

He was strong, tough, fearless ... I admired the bloke for his ability to lift his team. It shits me how people have read only the bad things about Darren Millane because Darren was down to earth, one of the best. He was an all-round champion bloke. He was a man's man, and that's how people should remember him.

Doug Hawkins, in a *Herald Sun* tribute to Collingwood's Darren Millane, who was killed in a motor accident on 7 October, 1991.

I feel sorry for what I have done. It's been about seven years since I was suspended and I've let myself down and everybody connected with me.

Peter 'Crackers' Keenan at the VFL Tribunal on a charge of allegedly striking Hawthorn's Don Scott in the 1978 VFL second semi-final. Keenan was suspended and missed the 1978 grand final against Hawthorn. The Hawks won by 18 points.

It's not easy to understand a game in which you get in front by kicking a few behinds. But coming from the Liberal Party I take great heart in that, I can tell you.

John Hewson, then federal opposition leader and a New South Welshman, in 1990.

We are just not in business to keep funding mediocrity.

Geoff Slade, the Sydney director, on a Swans' pay cut during the 1990 season.

Before the game, GR sidled up to Jimmy (Jess) and with a look only he could give hissed, 'If you see his head, kick it over the grandstand.'

Dale Weightman, the Richmond rover, describing the influence of the late Tiger powerbroker Graeme Richmond in one 1979 game.

Family club! You call yourselves a family club!

Richmond coach Kevin Bartlett during one match against Hawthorn in 1990.

They (Richmond) have fired the first shot; now we'll round up a few cannons.

Lindsay Fox during a tug-of-war with Richmond for defender Doug Cox in 1981, after the Tigers had complained that the Saints had played Cox without a permit and the VFL had stripped the Saints of eight match points. The Saints went to the Victorian Supreme Court, enabling St Kilda to play

Cox in the next round – against Richmond. The VFL later restored the match points.

When I joined Richmond (in 1967) I couldn't get a kick, mark or run, but they gave me a game because I could get the ball. Now, 253 games later, I can kick, mark and run – but I can't get the ball.

Kevin Sheedy, in 1981, on what he suggested was his limited playing ability.

Even Frank Sinatra singing won't help you play good football.

Royce Hart, the Footscray coach after being asked if the playing of a Mike Brady song before the Bulldogs first win of 1981 had helped lift his team.

We really had something to prove. The character of the side was on trial today.

Alex Jesaulenko, the Carlton captain-coach after the Blues' 1979 grand final win over Collingwood. Carlton was regarded as physically 'soft' and unable to absorb pressure.

How do you think I feel when my heart's in my throat?

Peter Moore, the 1979 Brownlow Medallist, immediately after the count when asked how he felt.

He has been made the biggest scapegoat since Lee Harvey Oswald – the sacrificial lamb.

Peter Jess, players' agent, after the AFL had deregistered client Greg Williams over contract irregularities with the Sydney Swans before joining Carlton in 1992.

He'd be better off and could do more good with a Sherrin under his arm instead of a Bible.

Peter Jess on the premature, and temporary, retirement of client, Geelong superstar Gary Ablett in 1991 for religious reasons.

I felt there was a lot of us in a rowboat bailing out water for a good many years and then all of a sudden there was only one left to bail out the water and I sank.

Kevin Bartlett after being sacked as Richmond coach in 1991.

If I was a horse I would be pets' meat by now.

Mark Harvey, the injury-prone Essendon star in 1991.

Phonse Kyne (the Collingwood coach) told me to come back in a few years after I had put on more weight.

Ted Whitten on why he did not join Collingwood after being recommended to the Magpies before he made his debut with Footscray in 1951.

I had played three years under Tommy at Geelong and he knew my style. Greg, David and I got our heads together with our wives and girlfriends and decided to have a go in Sydney.

Bernard Toohey on why he and Geelong teammates Greg Williams and David Bolton defected to join dumped Geelong coach Tom Hafey in Sydney in 1986.

If you put it in plaster I'll be out for the year.

Darrel Baldock, the 1966 St Kilda premiership captain. He almost missed that year's finals series because of a knee injury. The medical advice was that the knee be placed in plaster. He played on.

If you want to know when a man is washed up, look at his feet. If he can't lift his feet, how can he lift his game?

Roy Cazaly, who was a fitness fanatic.

Any contact around the face had me in trouble. These blows affected my vision and the only solution was to wear a helmet. I think the only times I did not wear a helmet in my final years was when it was too hot for comfort.

Rod Ashman, the Carlton rover (1972–86) on why he wore a helmet in matches.

All of my best pals in the club are dissatisfied with the present management. The club will sink because they have kicked out the man (Worrall)

that brought it up. The club will do no good without him.

Frank 'Silver' Caine, the early Carlton star on the Blues' sacking of legendary coach John Worrall over the summer of 1909–10. Worrall had coached Carlton to the 1906–7–8 flags but Caine's warning did not hold as Carlton had further premierships successes in 1914–5 under the coaching of Norman Clark.

I met Reg Hunt (Carlton's secretary) in the railways office and he got me to go across to Carlton.

Newton Chandler, the oldest living VFL footballer, born on 19 September, 1893 and still going strong in July 1996. Chandler played 69 games for Carlton from 1919–24 and then spent more than half a century at Carlton in one capacity or another.

I noticed that he (Coventry) was holding the ball at a funny angle and it was no fluke that he kicked several goals with these kicks.

Ansell Clarke. The star Carlton rover (1929–37) claimed that Collingwood's Gordon 'Nuts' Coventry had invented the 'banana' kick.

I have lost interest, mainly because of my foot injury. It may well be all right now, but I don't want to test it at training.

Gordon Collis. The 1964 Carlton Brownlow Medallist shocked the Blues when he walked out on the club before the start of the 1966 season, citing a foot injury. Collis returned to the Blues for one more season in 1967.

Stay out of it, son.

Ron Clegg. The South Melbourne star saw that Carlton opponent Bert Deacon was about to jump into the fray during the 1945 'Bloodbath' grand final – the most vicious game in VFL/AFL history and grabbed the youngster. Deacon went on to win the 1947 Brownlow Medal and Clegg the 1949 medal.

Basically, I'm a bit sad about losing the record, but if anyone was going to break it, I'm pleased it's Bruce. I probably respect him more than anyone at Carlton and I'm tickled pink he's going to do it.

John Nicholls on Bruce Doull breaking his record of 331 senior games for Carlton, in 1985. Doull eventually played 359 games for the Blues, from 1969–86.

Who's the dashing sheik who runs around it's Keith
  Shea, I declare.

Have you ever smelt the axle-grease he uses on his
  hair?

Ronnie Cooper feels so proud when he hears everyone cheer,

Till a squeeky little voice yells: 'Pull up your socks,
  Ronnie dear.'

Frank Anderson, with his long socks, now they say
  that he's a peach;

He once kicked the ball at Carlton; it landed on St
  Kilda beach.

If Charley Davey goes much higher when he goes
  up for a mark;

He'll be going up in the afternoon, and coming down
  after dark.

A Carlton song of the 1930s.

I could not say what happened after that (Caspar
striking him) as I was surprised. I put up my hands
in an attitude of self-defence.

John Coleman to the VFL Tribunal on the eve of the 1951
finals series, after being reported for striking Carlton Harry
Caspar in the final round. Coleman, in probably the greatest
Tribunal sensation in League history, was suspended for

four matches and old-time Bomber fans still insist this cost Essendon the 1951 flag.

I'm probably disappointed that the whole thing came up. I've played in three or four grand finals and every grand final you see these sort of things. It's not something you can put your finger on. How do you control this sort of thing? I thought the whole thing was very poorly controlled at the time. The umpires didn't seem to have a hell of a lot of control over the situation.

Terry Daniher, the Essendon star, to the AFL Tribunal after being reported for striking Collingwood's Gavin Brown in an ugly mêlée during the 1990 grand final. Daniher was suspended a total of 11 matches on various charges arising from this infamous final.

Terry Daniher will play on, don't worry about that, because he's got a heart as big as the moon.

Kevin Sheedy, the Essendon coach after the hearing. Daniher resumed his career late in the 1991 season and played with the Bombers until the end of the following season.

I put myself in front, stood my ground and held onto the mark. They said I grabbed Barry by the shorts, but if you look at the camera shots of the incident you'll see it would have been extremely difficult from where I was. Perhaps I might have knocked him slightly by holding my ground – but that's different. When Peter Barry was awarded the free I couldn't believe it – I was stunned. I remember Barry did not act as if he expected the kick.

Doug Wade. Wade was involved in a sensational incident in the last minute of the drawn 1962 Geelong-Carlton preliminary final. The Geelong full-forward took a mark only 30 metres from goal, but impire Jack Irving disallowed it, ruling that Wade had held onto opponent Peter Barry's shorts. Carlton won the replay, but went down to Essendon in the grand final.

I recruited Wade (for the start of the 1961 season) and as I looked him over I said – 'you're a bit puddeny, aren't you?'

Bob Davis, the Geelong coach, on how he nicknamed star Cat full-forward Doug Wade 'Pudden'.

Thank goodness it's all been settled once and for all.

Now we can get on with playing football.

Ricky Quade, the first Sydney coach (1982) said when it finally was decided, on Christmas Eve, 1981, that South Melbourne would relocate.

The place was a shambles. They were recruiting blokes who thought they would come up here for a holiday and, to make matters worse, they were on big bucks. All we wanted was a proper club with good facilities. There was a time when we were training at Randwick army barracks and, fair dinkum, the club rooms were the size of my lounge room. Honestly, Noble Park (Bayes' junior club in Melbourne) had better facilities.

Mark Bayes, the current Sydney star, who started with the Swans in 1985, on the club's early struggles in the Harbour City.

From a player's point of view, all you want is something that resembles a good footy club. We've got that now ... there's a new gym, new changerooms. It feels like a real league club and it is certainly the most professionally run since I have been here.

Mark Bayes on the current Sydney set-up.

Today I want to see blood. I don't want to see anyone not prepared to take physical risks. I want to see blood.

Ron Barassi, in 1977, addressing the North Melbourne players before a game.

I don't know that I really wanted to create League history. Obviously, it's a bigger thing than I really expected. Now I see there is a fair bit of involvement in what we have created. I suppose it will go down as a memory.

Paul van der Haar, the fiery and brilliant Essendon key forward created football history when he successfully appealed against a Tribunal suspension in 1989.

The city of Footscray has changed with the Vietnamese and drug addicts moving there. The club's supporter base has changed.

Ron Barassi stirred enormous controversy in 1989 with this comment.

I was referring to Footscray moving to a new ground and my comments were certainly not intended to be racist.

Ron Barassi in his defence.

I am still very envious of premiership sides.

Bob Skilton, the South Melbourne triple Brownlow Medallist on his disappointment at playing only one finals match, in a losing first semi-final side against St Kilda in 1970.

Between us, we have won three Brownlow Medals.

Ted Whitten on his triple Brownlow Medallist mate Bob Skilton.

It's great to have got there, it's 200! There are a few more left in the old pins.

Terry Daniher, the star Essendon forward, on his 200th League game, in 1986. Daniher eventually played a total of 313 games.

I'll admit it was a shock as I enjoyed playing with
South Melbourne.

Terry Daniher, in 1978, the season after being traded to the
Bombers from South Melbourne as a 19-year-old. Daniher
went on to captain the 1984–5 Essendon premiership sides.

I'm confident that it's not going to be a major
setback. I've just got to give it 12 months to make
sure the knee is 100 per cent. I'm only 19 and
there's no reason why I should rush things.

Paul Salmon. The giant Essendon forward-ruckman had
knee reconstruction surgery in 1984, just when making a
name for himself in League football. Salmon did return to
play in Essendon's 1985 premiership side and, for good
measure, also played in the 1993 Bomber premiership
side.

Tell that big f ... leprechaun that he'll be on the
first plane back to Ireland if he does that again.

Ray Jordan, Melbourne's Under 19s coach about Irish
recruit Jim Stynes, who had just missed a 'sitter' for goal in
the Dubliner's first game of Australian football, in 1985.
Stynes went on to win the 1991 Brownlow Medal.

Don't you ever f. . . . . . do that again.

John Northey, the Melbourne coach, to Jim Stynes after the Melbourne ruckman had cost the Demons a 15-metre penalty through running over the mark, resulting in the winning goal by Hawthorn's Gary Buckenara, in the 1987 preliminary final.

Oh, so that's why no one is talking to me.

Brian Stynes after his son's mistake was explained to him. Jim Stynes' father and mother had flown out from Dublin for the match.

Excuse me, but aren't you the guy who ran across the mark?

An unknown fan met Stynes weeks after this incident on a train in Paris.

Collingwood thought the time and place opportune to try a new man named Gordon Coventry, from Diamond Creek.

The 1920 Collingwood Annual Report. Coventry went on to

become the greatest goalkicker in league history. He still holds the record of most league goals – 1299 – in a career spanning 1920–37.

I have never, on any occasion, said anything to Syd about his race or colour. So far as race is concerned it is the same as mine, pure Australian, and so far as his colour is concerned I could not care less. I feel a grave injustice has been done to me, in that I was alleged to have made remarks about Syd Jackson's race and colour, and I was not given the opportunity of giving my version.

Lee Adamson's statement (in part) to the Tribunal. Star Carlton Aboriginal forward Syd Jackson created enormous controversy when he accused Collingwood defender Adamson of a racist remark during the 1970 second semi-final. Jackson was reported for striking Adamson and said 'yes' at the Tribunal when asked if Adamson had made a racist comment. Jackson was cleared of the charge and played in Carlton's premiership side less than two weeks later. Many years later he confessed that the 'racist remark' had been a ruse to beat the charge.

For the first time in the last few years I have been able to concentrate on football – and I've finally pulled it off. My head is in a whirl and I haven't come down to earth yet.

John James, the star Carlton defender, on his 1961 Brownlow Medal win.

Get out of here, you f...... vulture!

Tony Jewell, the Richmond coach, to a photographer taking snaps of him after a 1981 defeat by Geelong at Kardinia Park.

We believe he's got more potential than Royce Hart when he signed with Richmond as an untried schoolboy.

Jim Allison, the Carlton secretary, in 1980 after signing South Australian youngster Stephen Kernahan. Kernahan went on to captain the 1987 and 1995 Carlton premiership sides and is regarded by many as the greatest footballer to play for the Blues.

His Dad wouldn't let him play for St Kilda at 14 because he thought he was too young to play against men.

Des Eicke, the son of St Kilda legend Wellesley 'Wels' Eicke (1909–26), of his father's 'delayed' VFL debut at 15 years of age. No 14-year-old has played League football. Eicke was aged 15 years and 315 days on debut. The youngest to play League football was Collingwood's Keith Bromage – 15 years and 287 days – in 1953.

Tell him we're still mates.

Bob Skilton soon after being concussed by a crushing hip and shoulder bump by St Kilda iron-man Eric Guy at the Junction Oval in 1961.

They bounced the ball and it went straight down to Todd who jumped over our full-back Arthur Robertson to take a huge mark. I remember thinking that he was a lair and if this bloke kicks it I'll go home. Not only did he kick it, but it landed in the convent behind the goals.

Alan Killigrew, the St Kilda rover (1938–45), on a goal by Collingwood's Ron Todd at Victoria Park on his senior debut.

Getting him was like making a statement. We had

never had anybody like that before. At last Hawthorn was getting headlines in the papers.

Jack Hale, the Hawthorn coach on the signing of giant South Australian ruckman Clayton 'Candles' Thompson – then easily the tallest man in VFL football – in 1954. Clayton played just 51 games with Hawthorn to 1957.

We chose the lion because we wanted supporters to believe that like the heraldic lion we used as our original emblem, we also were climbing up the ladder.

Ward Stuchberry, the Fitzroy secretary, on why Fitzroy changed its club emblem from Gorillas to the Lions in 1957. Stuchberry described the Gorilla tag as 'dreadful'.

We are certainly considered a glamour team of the VFL. During the year your committee proceeded with the incorporation of the club, which became effective from 1 November, 1981. We can look forward to the next year with real enthusiasm and confidence.

Keith Wiegard, the Fitzroy president to members in 1981. Fitzroy has been struggling for survival almost ever since.

Who wants to play with Fitzroy? There's no suburban ties, no success on the field ... sadly, I feel its days are numbered.

Tony Ongarello, the former Fitzroy goalkicking hero (1952–62), in 1991 of the plight of his old club.

They're like a homeless child now – they don't belong anywhere. They're nowhere. Nothing.

Duncan Reilly, the Fitzroy city council mayor, at the same time. Fitzroy vacated its Brunswick Street Oval in 1964 and has since played its home games at Princes Park, Victoria Park, the Junction Oval and the Whitten Oval.

Football is my recreation. Boxing is hard work and a grind day after day.

Ambrose Palmer, the star Footscray player (1933–43) also held three Australian boxing titles. Ironically, Palmer suffered critical head and facial injuries in an accidental football collision in 1943 and was forced to retire.

Toorak and South Yarra are not my go. I don't drive their cars; I don't speak their language. We in the western suburbs know the value of a dollar – and we're proud of it.

Ted Whitten. The Footscray legend lived all his life in Melbourne's western suburbs.

When I was a kid I wanted to be comfortable and I wanted to play in premierships . . . by the time I was 24 I'd done all those things.

Dermott Brereton, the recently retired former Hawthorn, Sydney and Collingwood star, at the height of his career.

When I got back to Adelaide, actually, it was pretty funny. One kid said that it doesn't matter what I say on television; we all love you and all the rest of it, and that helped a fair bit.

Tony Modra, the star Adelaide footballer on dropping the magic word during a television interview in Melbourne.

It surprises a lot of people inside Victoria that football can be played outside Victoria in a fashion that will bring success at a top-class level.

Graham Cornes, the Adelaide coach, in 1991.

The committee gave us no assistance, bar admitting us to the grandstand. The majority of the public were averse to us speaking and hurled personal interjections at us. We continued the meeting until the match again started and, when coming down the stairs of the grandstand, we were attacked by many men and women, which necessitated our leaving the ground. I am not keen on again being called to attend these matches. My staff also request that they should not be sent.

An unnamed army officer. The 1917 VFL season was almost abandoned because of World War I and one army recruiting officer, after attending a Fitzroy match during this season, wrote to the newspapers of his concerns about crowd behaviour following his appeal for volunteers.

I tried for so long I came to the conclusion that it is so nearly impossible it doesn't matter.

Dave McNamara, the St Kilda champion (1905–24) unsuccessfully attempting to boot a ball 100 yards. McNamara's best recorded kick was 93 yards.

He is the greatest find of the decade.

Frank Reid, the Essendon secretary, in 1934 of second-year Dons' player Dick Reynolds. Reynolds went on to win three Brownlow Medals.

Go ahead, there's so many of us you won't remember all our names.

Maurie Sankey, the Carlton ruckman warned an umpire not to make reports during a brawl in a 1959 finals match.

Football is in danger of changing its image to the detriment of the sport, caused by so much pressure that it's got to be cleaned up, and cleaned up and cleaned up. Those who don't wish to play should go and play tennis or golf or some other non-contact sport.

Allan McAlister, the Collingwood president, in 1990.

It's a challenge being this height.

Tony Liberatore, the current Footscray star on his diminutive stature – he stands just 164cm.

It's a game of young guys in tight shorts and no sleeves running around a field and jumping in the air a lot.

Elle McPherson, the Australian super-model on football, after being made the number one female member at St Kilda.

Do those clubs in Victoria really want a national competition, and it to be a success? Or do they simply want interstate clubs to come in, pay large licence fees and bail them out of financial trouble without winning?

Michael Malthouse, the West Coast coach, in 1991 of complaints from Victorian clubs that their interstate cousins were being given too much assistance.

They are the greatest bunch of misfits and renegades in the history of the game.

Bob Davis, the former Geelong coach on the Brisbane Bears in 1991.

Fair dinkum, you feel like ripping their earrings out sometimes.

Norm Dare, the Brisbane coach at that time.

I was starting to cramp fairly badly during the third quarter and missed two or three simple shots. There were discussions about whether I'd stay on the field in the last quarter. It was decided that we'd see how far it went in the first five or 10 minutes. My cramping phase disappeared as mysteriously as it had come and I remember being absolutely certain every shot at goal would go through. I was just into such a groove, I wasn't going to miss.

Kelvin Templeton, the star Footscray forward on the day, in 1978, when he kicked 15 goals in a match against St Kilda at the Western Oval. Templeton's 15-goal swag was a ground record until Sydney's Tony Lockett booted 16 goals there against Fitzroy in 1995.

Would you mind having a talk to him and see if he's at all interested in playing League football again?

Bill McMaster, the Geelong talent scout to Myrtleford coach and former Geelong player Greg Nicholls in 1983 on the possibility of talking former Hawthorn winger Gary Ablett into leaving the country club and try his luck again in the big time. Ablett, of course, is now regarded as the game's superstar.

It was like a death in the family. We were so used to having Gary there. We all were pretty shaken. We knew he had a lot of football left in him.

Neville Bruns, the Geelong veteran on the sudden decision by Cat champion Gary Ablett to quit football for religious reasons in 1991.

Bugger Ford, Bugger Pyramid. Save Ablett. Save Geelong.

A Geelong bumper sticker in 1991.

It was the best phone call I've had for a long, long time. He (Ablett) had the urge to play again. He had appreciated that we had kept in close contact with him, but we had not pressured him.

Ron Hovey, the Geelong president after a telephone call from Ablett to say he would play again in 1991.

I was about to leave work and put in the draft forms when I got a call from Wheels (coach Terry Wheeler). He told me I was in the senior side to play Collingwood (in a practice match).

Tony Liberatore on how he almost quit Footscray before the start of the 1990 season. Liberatore stayed and went on to win the Brownlow Medal that year.

I don't look at who we're going to play next bloody week.

Michael Malthouse, the West Coast coach in 1995 on the upcoming first West Coast-Fremantle derby match.

It's an education thing, especially for kids. AFL players are role models and if they are allowed to get away with it then it sets a bad example. They'll just keep doing it.

Michael McLean, the star Brisbane midfielder in 1995 on football racists.

As long as the present situation (11 teams in Victoria) remains, we are vulnerable to a Super League-type takeover.

Ross Oakley, the AFL boss in 1995.

I was lucky enough to have a good start. It was just one of those days and you could play 300 games and not be able to do it again.

Tony Lockett, the champion Sydney goalkicker, after kicking a club record 16 goals against Fitzroy at the Whitten Oval in 1995.

Yea, I knew he needed one more for the record and I was only too happy for him to have a shot for goal.

Derek Kickett, Lockett's Sydney teammate on passing the ball to the big fellow for his sixteenth goal.

I'm not out there for looks.

Peter Everitt, the tatooed, dreadlocked St Kilda ruckman on his image.

The funny thing is that when I made my senior debut I had never been in the Collingwood dressing rooms at Victoria Park. The reserves in those days had separate rooms.

Bruce Andrew, the former Collingwood star (1928–34) on his debut with the Magpies.

This is a fight I have to win, and I am giving it everything I have, just like I did in football, coaching, in broadcasting, in everything.

Ted Whitten, the football legend, in March 1995, on his battle with prostrate cancer. Tragically, Whitten died on 17 August 1995.

I am on tablets normally given to ease the nausea suffered by pregnant women. But you can tell all my friends that I most definitely am not pregnant.

Ted Whitten.

The highs and lows of AFL coaching; there is no other exhilaration or experience like it.

Denis Pagan, the North Melbourne coach, in 1995.

For God's sake, Bucky, kick the goal!

Russell Greene to Hawthorn team-mate Gary Buckenara who was lining up a shot for goal after the siren in the 1987 preliminary final against Melbourne. Buckenara did kick the goal and Hawthorn defeated Melbourne by two points.

After the siren went, Libba (Footscray's Tony Liberatore) was saying a few things to me along the lines of 'you're going to miss', with a few adjectives thrown in. I just thought, I've gotta kick this, and the sooner the better. It was drifting towards the post but then swung and went straight through the middle. After that I just took off till Barnsey (John Barnes) grabbed me and kissed me, and they then came all over the top. Great moment, that.

Billy Brownless, the Geelong forward on kicking the winning goal against Footscray in the 1994 first qualifying final.

How can anyone contemplate working for an organisation like that?

Graham Cornes, the former Adelaide coach, when asked if he would like to take over as Fitzroy coach following the sacking of Bernie Quinlan late in the 1995 season.

When do I start?

Michael Nunan, the former Adelaide premiership coach, when asked the same question. Nunan was offered the job and accepted for the start of the 1996 AFL season.

How many of them have seen us train this year?

Michael Nunan just days before the start of the 1996 AFL season, after almost every critic had tipped Fitzroy for the wooden spoon.

He (an unnamed senior player) started to chip away and he had the ear of a couple of younger players. I just hope he finds a coach that he can coach.

Bernie Quinlan on his sacking as Fitzroy coach.

On the whole, the approach of the football season may be heartily welcomed. The game is manly and vigorous in the highest degree, and can only be played under conditions which imply the highest state of physical health. It is not the sport of the lazy, or of the effeminate, or of the self-indulgent. The character of a nation is reflected in its sports;

and a race which finds such passionate delight in the conflicts of the football field must have a very robust strain of manliness runing through it.

The *Argus* newspaper in a report before the opening of the 1892 VFA season.

What happened was that one of the administrations got into a fight with Collingwood over Geoff Raines and David Cloke going to Collingwood and it finished up costing the club a fortune, almost $1 million. And Bryan Wood also went to Essendon. It was basically because we wouldn't pay the players concerned more money.

Tony Jewell, the 1980 Richmond premiership coach on the demise of the Tigers just a couple of years later.

When I started out, I never envisaged that I would be still here at 35 years of age, let alone in a team in Brisbane. It's just incredible how the game has changed.

Roger Merrett, the Brisbane captain, in 1995 on his lengthy career (he started with Essendon in 1978).

When I first walked into the place, especially after having barracked for the club all my life, and still being just a kid in the development squad it was a bit like a dream. To be walking around the dressing room with players I'd always idolised ... it wasn't so much scary, but certainly breathtaking.

Gavin Brown, the 1996 Collingwood captain on entering Victoria Park as a Collingwood junior in 1984.

Every time we play Carlton, even in a normal game, it's big – you'll sometimes get 70–80 000 there ... it's like a final, with people estimating crowds of up to 100 000 and the players love playing in front of big crowds. That's what it's all about.

Gavin Brown on the Collingwood-Carlton rivalry.

The young guys now see it as a business. You just have to watch how they approach their football and the summer training to know how serious it is to them.

Tim Watson, the Essendon veteran, in 1994, on modern footballers.

We'd won the premiership in 1983 and went overseas on an end-of-season trip. When we came back we found Carlton had put Platten on a contract. We had drafted him in 1981 and so started the tug of war for John Platten. We went to the Supreme Court and after all the evidence was given we settled out of court.

John Lauritz, the Hawthorn chief executive on how the Hawks won the race for brilliant rover John Platten. Platten won a Brownlow Medal in 1987.

To offer a bloke a game, sight unseen, just didn't ring true.

John Schultz on being offered a senior game with Footscray immediately after being recruited from country club Boort in 1958. Schultz went on to win the 1960 Brownlow Medal.

For us sex is just a memory due to our fatigued state.

Brian Taylor, the Collingwood full-forward on the Magpies' tough 1990 training program.

To continue to allow a club like the Eagles to have an advantage going into the next year's draft is entirely wrong.

John Elliott, the Carlton president, on a proposed draft concession to the West Coast Eagles in 1991. The Eagles did not get their concession, but won the 1992 flag.

I heard the siren. I didn't see it (the ball) go through. I just saw it going straight. There was a big roar and then I had all the players come all over me.

Rod Jameson, the Adelaide player, after kicking the winning goal in a 1991 match against Fitzroy at Football Park, after a string of controversial free kicks to the Crows.

I think I was always outspoken as a player, both on and off the field.

Ted Whitten on why he never won a Brownlow Medal.

This is the absolute best outcome for the competition and certainly fits into our strategic plan.

Ross Oakley, the AFL chief executive, on the Brisbane–Fitzroy merger after it originally appeared that Fitzroy would merge with North Melbourne.

I assure you that the 113-year-old history of Fitzroy will be reflected as a combined team with Brisbane.

Noel Gordon, the Brisbane chairman, said of the merger.

If we still have the jumper then maybe they (Fitzroy fans) can see this as another chapter in our history.

Brad Boyd, the Fitzroy captain, also on the merger.

I don't see why women should be excluded from the Tribunal. I don't see why it should continue to be secret men's business, as it has been up until now.

Elaine Canty following her appointment, in March 1996, as the first female member of the AFL Tribunal.

BIBLIOGRAPHY

Carlton – The 100 Greatest, Jim Main and Russell Holmesby, Crossbow Publishing, 1994.

The Carlton Story, Hugh Buggy, Eric White Associates, 1958.

Cats' Tales, Col Hutchinson, The Geelong Advertiser, 1984.

A Century of the Best, Michael Roberts, Collingwood Football Club, 1991.

Collingwood Football Club, Percy Taylor, The National Press Pty Ltd, 1949.

Diesel, Greg Williams, Ironbark, 1995.

EJ – The Ted Whitten Story, Jim Main, Wilkinson Books, 1995.

The Encyclopedia of League Footballers, Jim Main and Russell Holmesby, Wilkinson Books, 1994.

The First 100 Years, Rod Nicholson, Fitzroy Football Club, 1983.

The Gary Ablett Story, Ken Piesse, Wilkinson Books, 1994.

The Hard Way, Harry Gordon, Lester-Townsend, 1990.

Heroes and Haloes, Russell Holmesby, Playright Press, 1995.

Pants – the Darren Millane Story, Eddie McGuire and Jim Main, Modern Publishing, 1994.

The Point Of It All, Russell Holmesby, Playright Press, 1991.

Sons of the 'Scray, Mark Butler and Steven Milne, Butler and Milne, 1994.

Too Tough To Die, Kerrie Gordon and Alan Dalton, Footscray Football Club, 1990.

Whatever It Takes, Jim Stynes, Modern Publishing, 1995.

The 1946–7 *Sporting Globe* Annuals.

Numerous football annuals, including the *Gaumont Football Yearbooks*.

Newspaper clippings – from the *Age, Australian, Argus, Herald, Herald Sun, Sun Pictorial*, the *Australasian*, the *Sporting Globe* and other publications; *Inside Football*; the VFL/AFL Records; Club annual reports.

SWIMMING

Jim Webster was a senior sports writer with the *Sydney Morning Herald* and the *Herald Sun* for more than thirty years. He covered five Olympic Games, six Commonwealth Games, four Wallaby rugby tours and nearly 200 rugby Test matches and numerous Wimbledon and British Open golf championships. In 1987, he was honoured with the Diploma of the International Amateur Athletic Federation. He officially retired in 1988, but has not been allowed to rest. He is consulting editor of *Golf Australia*, was media attaché for Australia's team at the 1992 Barcelona Olympics and media director for the 1996 Atlanta Olympics. He is the author of seven books on sport.

SWIMMING MUM, THIS IS FOR YOU

Dawn Fraser

Andrew (Boy) Charlton was among the most cele-brated of Australia's long list of swimming cham-pions and he, perhaps more than any other, first identified our nation as a home to these champions.

His races against the great Swede Arne Borg in the 1924 New South Wales championships at the Domain Baths caused unprecedented excitement and had the Baths jammed with people. In the 440 yards, Charlton, still only sixteen years old, swept past Borg to win by twenty yards in 5:11:8, equall-ing the world record. It was the greatest defeat ever suffered by Borg who set 32 world records in his career.

While Borg offered abundant praise to his conqueror, he promised that he'd beat him in the Paris Olympics later that year.

On the *Ormonde* on his way to the Olympics with the rest of the Australian team, Charlton was accompanied by his coach and trainer Tom Adrian. Unfortunately, Adrian suffered a nervous breakdown and, while watching deck games, suddenly turned and threw himself overboard into shark-infested waters.

The steamer turned around and rescued him, but he was never the same again, and there was apprehension that Charlton's performances would be affected by the strange mishap.

Fortunately, they weren't. In the mile, Borg broke his own world record in the heats with 21:11:4, but Charlton prevailed in the final beating Borg and breaking his two-day-old record in 20:06:6. He also won a bronze medal in the 440 yards, behind the original Tarzan, Johnny Weismuller, and Borg, and a relay silver medal.

At the next Olympics in Amsterdam, Charlton won two more silver medals over the same distances, losing the mile this time to Borg, but on limited preparation at his third Olympics in Los Angeles in 1932 he came home empty-handed.

It is a curious fact that Charlton never swam in an Australian championship.

The first Australian to swim the English Channel was Olympian Linda McGill, who took 11 hours 12 minutes on 7 August, 1965 to swim from France to

England. She was only 11 minutes outside Greta Andersen's record for the crossing. On 3 January, 1968, swimming in a specially constructed cage to protect her from sharks, she also became the first person to swim the forty kilometres across Port Phillip Bay.

When Kieren Perkins won the gold medal in the 1500 metres freestyle final at the 1992 Barcelona Olympics, he went through the 800 metres in 7:48:27 – the third fastest time in history.

Perkins continued to churn on relentlessly, eventually hitting the finish wall in 14:43:48. The nineteen-year-old Queensland University student had swum 4.90 seconds under his own world record in what was the distance swim to end them all.

An Australasian team of ten athletes was sent to the 1911 Festival of Empire at Crystal Palace, London, staged to commemorate the coronation of King George V. The sporting program included athletics, boxing, wrestling and swimming.

Harold Hardwick won the only two championships for the team.

He won the 100 yards freestyle in 60.6 seconds.

On leaving the water, he was approached by the

Australasian team manager Richard Coombes who asked would he compete the following night in the heavyweight boxing championship. He was no novice in the ring, having been beaten in eight rounds by the legendary Les Darcy for the Australian heavyweight championship and knocking out some of Darcy's teeth in the process.

After some quick sparring practice, he stepped in against English policeman William Hazell, holder of the English and Scottish amateur titles, and gave him such a hiding that the referee stopped the bout after only two minutes thirty-three seconds. An hour later, Hardwick fought Canadian Julius Thompson in the final and similarly whipped him, with the referee stopping the bout after just two minutes thirty seconds.

The following year at the Stockholm Olympics, Hardwick gave boxing a miss and concentrated on swimming, in which he won a gold medal in the 4x200 yards freestyle and bronze medals in the 440 yards and mile freestyle.

The finest brother and sister combination in Australian swimming was Latvian-born Ilsa and John Konrads.

The family fled Latvia in 1944 during World War II; their father, Janis, a dental surgeon, took his wife and three children, John, Ilsa and their elder sister, Eve, to Australia five years later.

The kids learned to swim at a migrant camp at Uranquinty. When she was thirteen, Ilsa held two world records. At fifteen, John held six.

John's Olympic career spanned three Games – Melbourne (1956), Rome (1960) and Tokyo (1964). In Rome he won gold in the 1500m freestyle beating Murray Rose and bronze medals in the 400m freestyle and 4x200m freestyle relay.

Ilsa made just one Olympics, winning a silver medal in the 4x100m freestyle relay in Rome.

No swimming pool in the world has had as many world records broken in it as North Sydney Olympic Pool.

Built as the venue for the 1938 Empire Games on the site of the construction workshops for the Harbour Bridge, the first world record fell in 1953, when Manly swimmer Frank O'Neill swam 5:48:5 for the 440 yards individual medley.

A total of eighty-two world records have been set in the pool by some of the all-time greats including Dawn Fraser, Murray Rose, Lorraine Crapp, Kevin Berry, Shane Gould and John and Ilsa Konrads. The sheer volume of water in the pool is thought by many to be the reason.

Swimming

'Yesterday I gave him two raw steaks and three pints of blood.' – Eccentric swim coach Laurie Lawrence responded outrageously to questions about Duncan Armstrong's diet after he had won the 200 metres freestyle gold medal at the 1988 Seoul Olympics. Then Lawrence dived fully clad into the warm-up pool.

Brad Cooper was silver medallist in the 400 metres freestyle at the 1972 Munich Olympics – well, for several days.

He had been defeated by American Rick DeMont by one-hundredths of a second, the smallest possible margin.

DeMont was defeated in turn by Marax, a medication he had taken for asthma the night before the event which contained the banned drug ephedrine. After the final, DeMont, along with the other two medallists, was drug-tested.

Two days later, DeMont, the world record-holder over 1500m, swam the preliminary rounds of that event. The next morning, however, he was told he had failed the drug test from the 400m, could not swim the 1500m final, and was forced to return his gold medal. The Australian subsequently was elevated to first placing.

In three Olympic Games, Australian swimmer Frank Beaurepaire went very close without ever quite winning an Olympic gold medal.

He won silver and bronze medals at each of his Olympics in London (1908), Antwerp (1920) and Paris (1924).

Yet he was a repeated winner in private life, for he later created an empire in manufacturing car tyres, became Lord Mayor of Melbourne and was awarded a knighthood.

'I blew it.'

– Stephen Holland, who led after 1300 metres of the 1500 metres freestyle final at the 1976 Montreal Olympics and finished third behind Americans Brian Goodell and Bobby Hackett in which all three broke Goodell's world record.

Seventeen-year-old Ian O'Brien won the 200m breaststroke gold medal at the 1964 Tokyo Olympic Games in world record time, beating the Soviet Union's Gregory Prokopenko and the American world record-holder Chester (Chet) Jastremski.

But this 'bushie' from Wellington, New South Wales, then lost the will to train hard and three years later, when called up for National Service, was rejected by the Army because he was over-weight and had flat feet.

Although he got himself back into sufficient shape to be chosen for the Mexico City Olympics in 1968, he finished well out of the placings in both breaststroke events.

When Australia's great Olympic running champion Betty Cuthbert announced to the world that she had multiple sclerosis, the first of countless telephone calls she received was from Dawn Fraser, our equally great swimming champion.

'I don't have any money, Bet, but I have my car and all the time in the world,' she said. 'You only have to ask and I'll be there to help whatever way I can.'

They remain tied by the respect for the four Olympic gold medals which each of them won.

Susan Miller, born 18 June, 1968, at Gunnedah, was only twelve years seven months when chosen for the 1981 Pacific Conference Games in Christ-church, New Zealand, making her the youngest to represent Australia in any sport in open competition.

Australian John Davies came fourth in the 220 yards breaststroke final at the 1948 London Olympics and later accepted a scholarship at the University of Michigan, making him one of the first Australian swimmers to attend an American university.

At the next Olympics four years later in Helsinki, he achieved the ultimate success by winning the gold medal, pushing world record-holder Herbert Klein, of Germany, into third place.

Davies remained in America, where he became a lawyer. Eventually he was elevated to the federal bench, capturing world attention as the presiding judge in the famous Rodney King assault trial.

For fifty years a three-mile swim along the Yarra River attracted huge fields. The novelist George Johnston once came 264th in an entry of almost 600.

Dawn Fraser is Australia's finest ever swimmer and perhaps its best-known sportswoman. She was loved for her gritty, down-to-earth attitude, her scallywag antics and her climb from humble beginnings to the peak of Olympic success.

Born to working-class parents in Balmain, Dawn was the youngest of eight children. Her father worked at the Cockatoo Docks, near their home. He suffered from poor health and was forced into long periods of unemployment.

Dawn first learned to swim at the Balmain Baths when she was four. She left school at fourteen to work in a factory, helping the family meet its weekly financial commitments.

She emerged as an Olympic prospect early in 1956 when she beat the favourite Lorraine Crapp in the 110 yards at the Australian championships. Her timing was perfect, with the Games coming to Melbourne later that year.

The Olympic 100 metres freestyle final was seen as being an intense fight between Dawn and Crapp, the world record-holder. That's exactly what it turned out to be, with the two Australian teenagers fighting each other to the line, with Dawn winning by a touch in a world record 1:02:0. Starting that day, she was the world record-holder over 100 metres for the next fifteen years. Gold medal number two came forty-eight hours later when the Australians smashed the world record in winning the 4x100m freestyle relay.

At the Rome Olympics in 1960, not having been defeated since Melbourne, she became the first woman to defend an Olympic swimming title clearly beating American Chris Von Saltza.

On 27 October, 1962, swimming in Melbourne,

Dawn became the first woman to break the one-minute barrier for 110 yards when she covered the longer distance of 110 yards in 59.9 seconds. By 29 February, 1964, she had reduced the time to 58.9 seconds. But in March that year, tragedy struck when she was involved in a car accident in which her mother was killed, her sister was knocked unconscious and Dawn herself spent six weeks with her neck in a surgical brace.

Seven months later Dawn was at the Tokyo Olympics, seeking her third gold medal. At twenty-seven years of age, she was an old-timer by swimming standards and known to her team-mates as 'Granny'. But she had lost none of her speed or determination.

In the 100m final, the young American Sharon Stouder stayed with the champion to the turn and went stroke for stroke with her down the final lap, until twenty-five metres from the finish. Then the champion's qualities took over. Dawn called on everything she had to pull away and win again in 59.5 seconds. Stouder's time of 59.9 seconds made her the first woman other than Dawn to break one minute.

Dawn had become the first Olympic swimmer of either gender to win the same event three times.

When she returned home, Dawn faced enormous controversy when it emerged that she had been arrested in Tokyo after taking an Olympic flag from the grounds of the Japanese Imperial Palace. She was suspended by the Australian Swimming Union for ten years but, after a prolonged public outcry, it was eventually lifted in May 1968 after three-and-a-half years. Dawn had shown, once more, that records and rules were there to be broken, or at least tampered with slightly.

There might never be another Australian sporting figure like Dawn Fraser. She was in Atlanta in 1996 recovering from angina when her 32-year-old record of three consecutive Olympic gold medals was equalled by Hungarian Krisztina Egerszegi.

At the third Empire Games in Sydney in 1938, Margaret Dovey (NSW) came sixth in the final of the 220 yards breaststroke, immediately behind her team-mates Valerie George and Joan Thomas.

While she might not have gained much media attention from this performance, she did later in life as the wife of Australian Prime Minister Gough Whitlam.

Freddy Lane was Australia's first Olympic swimming champion. He won the 220 yards freestyle gold medal in Paris in 1900 in the time of 2:25:2. It was unusually fast due to the fact that the swimming races were held in the River Seine and swum with the current.

For his victory, he was awarded a 23-kilogram bronze statue of a horse and an equally large bronze of Jean Francois Millet's 'The Gleaners'.

Lane's second gold medal came in the 220 yards obstacle race, a quaint event which required the contestants to struggle past three sets of obstacles.

First they had to climb over a pole, then swim to a row of boats, scramble onto one, dive from it, then swim under another row of punts and continue accordingly. Lane's boyhood experiences had taught him that it was easier to go over a boat at the stern than to clamber over the sides and so he won reasonably easily, although he will always be better known for his victory in the unimpeded freestyle event.

The obstacle race had a shortlived history – just one Olympics.

It's inconceivable that an Olympic swimming record could last for 68 years, yet one did.

When Michael Wenden won his second gold medal in the 200 metres freestyle in 1968 in Mexico City, he swam 1:55:2, thus breaking fellow

Swimming

Australian Freddy Lane's Olympic record of 2:25:2 which he had swum in the River Seine at the 1900 Paris Games.

Maroubra lifesaver Des Renford is Australia's most successful conqueror of the English Channel and was dubbed 'King of the Channel' after crossing it for a record 19th time in 1980. His fastest time was 11 hours 42 minutes in 1979 and his slowest was 14 hours and 54 minutes the next year, both times from England to France.

At one stage in her career, Shane Gould held every world freestyle record from 100 metres to 1500 metres.

At the 1972 Munich Olympics she came through a back-breaking program with three gold medals in the 200m freestyle, 400m freestyle and 200m individual medley, silver in the 800m freestyle and bronze in the 100m freestyle.

While the fifteen-year-old schoolgirl had identified herself as one of the greatest swimmers of all time, she had also shown in her losses that she was vulnerable. She admitted after returning to Australia, 'At Munich, I learnt how to lose.'

She was named Australian of the Year in 1972.

Six months after the Games, she became the first woman to shatter seventeen minutes for 1500 metres. But by the end of 1973 she decided that enough was enough. In December that year she retired and signed a contract to work for the Adidas sportswear company.

However, Shane was searching for more out of life than a retailing career could offer. She found it in the Christian faith with West Australian, Neil Innes, whom she married on 15 June, 1975. She disappeared from public life, moving with her husband to a property in the Margaret River area of Western Australia.

Freestyler John Marshall broke twenty-nine world and thirty-eight US records. At the 1947 Australian championships, the young Victorian won the 220 yards, 440 yards, 880 yards and mile finals. Next year at the London Olympics he was raw and inexperienced, yet came second in the mile behind American Jimmy McLane and third in the 440 yards behind Americans Bill Smith and McLane.

These swims impressed US coach Bob Kipputh so much that he persuaded Marshall to accept a scholarship to Yale University, where Kipputh ran a production line of world-beaters. It was there that he began his procession of world records.

Swimming

At 26 years of age, Marshall was killed in a car crash.

Apart from following a seaweed diet, Murray Rose was also one of the greatest of Australia's Olympic swimming champions.

At the 1956 Melbourne Olympics the young Australian hero won the 400 metres freestyle, 1500 metres freestyle and added a third gold medal as part of the 4x200 metres freestyle relay team.

Four years later in Rome he again won the 400 metres freestyle (beating Japan's Tsuyoshi Yamanaka as he had in Melbourne and by exactly the same margin), suffered his first Olympic loss to teammate John Konrads in the 1500 metres freestyle and collected a bronze from the same relay event.

Rose wanted to represent Australia again in Tokyo in 1964 but did not return from America, where he was living, for the Australian championships and was not picked. He subsequently attended the Games as a television commentator for an American network.

His Olympic collection remained at four gold medals, one silver and one bronze, the most gold medals won by an Australian male and equal to Dawn Fraser's and Betty Cuthbert's as the most won by Australians.

He also made a lot of people think about their diet.

'This is it baby, let's go.'

– Bev Whitfield, trailing three others including the Soviet's multiple medallist Galina Stepanova at the end of the third lap in the 200 metres breaststroke final at the 1972 Munich Olympics. She did, and won.

John Devitt's victory in the 100 metres freestyle final at the Rome Olympics in 1960 was among the most controversial in Olympic swimming history.

Brazil's Manuel Dos Santos led through the turn, but Devitt and the American Lance Larson passed him at seventy metres and finished in a flurry of water in what looked like a dead-heat. When Devitt touched he glanced across to Larson's lane and saw him finishing, convincing him that he had won. Then an American friend of Larson walked over and told him he had won. He reacted by throwing his arms in the air, which acted as a victory signal the crowd.

For ten minutes they waited. Larson swam two gentle laps of the pool. Devitt spent the time with team-mates.

Swimming

Finally came the announcement: 'Devitt ... Australia ...'

The American team protested. Confusion developed when the judges met to discuss their verdict. Two of the three judges had voted for Devitt and one for Larson. However, the second-place judges also voted 2–1 for Devitt. In other words, three thought Devitt had won and three thought Larson had won.

To add to the mess, the stopwatches (which started automatically and were stopped manually) showed Larson had registered 55.1 seconds and Devitt 55.2 seconds.

Despite this evidence, the chief judge ordered Larson's time changed to 55.2 seconds and gave the decision to Devitt.

As American anger continued to boil, one US official branded the judges 'a bunch of timid, unemployed pussyfooters ...'

On 21–22 April 1995, marathon swimmer Susie Maroney set a new twenty-four-hour distance record in a fifty-metre pool when she swam 93.6 kilometres (1872) laps, eclipsing the previous record of 93 kilometres held by Melissa Cunningham, with sixteen minutes to spare.

Then in June 1996, in trying to become the first

person to swim unassisted from Cuba to the USA, she swam 142.4 kilometres in thirty-nine hours before being pulled from the water twenty kilometres short of the Florida coast.

Australia has produced few more unexpected winners in Olympic competition than the untried seventeen-year-old Jon Sieben in the 200 metres butterfly at the Los Angeles Games in 1984.

Going into the event, he was overshadowed both literally and figuratively by the world record-holder Michael Gross, of West Germany. He stood 200 centimetres tall and had exceptionally long arms that, when outstretched, measured 225 centimetres from fingertip to fingertip; they called him 'The Albatross'.

Gross had already won two gold medals and was favourite to make it three in his best event.

At the halfway mark, Sieben was well back in seventh place, as he wanted to be. He turned in fourth place at the 150-metre mark behind Gross, Pablo Morales, of the United States, and Venezuela's Rafael Vidal Castro and then appeared to almost climb over the water as he drew level and passed them one after another. He won in a world record 1:57:04.

In winning the gold medal, he had improved his

pre-Olympic best over several hours by 4.13 seconds. In the morning's heats, Sieben brought his previous best time down by 1.54 seconds and in the night's final chopped another 2.59 seconds off his record.

The 1916 Olympic Games awarded to Berlin were cancelled because of World War I. A number of athletes who would have gone to those Games went instead into active service, among them Harold Hardwick, Frank Beaurepaire, Cecil Healy, Billy Longworth and Ivan Stedman.

Healy who, along with Hardwick, had been part of the winning 4x200 metres freestyle relay team at the 1912 Stockholm Games and had also won a silver medal in the 100 metres freestyle, became the only gold medallist in Australian Olympic history to be killed on the battlefield. He died while serving as an infantry officer with the AIF 19th (Sportsmen's) battalion on the Somme.

BIBLIOGRAPHY

Ampol Australian Sporting Records, John Blanch, Budget Books, Cheltenham, Victoria, 1968.

Australia and the Olympic Games, Harry Gordon, University of Queensland, Brisbane, 1994.

Australians at the Olympics, Gary Lester, Lester-Townsend, Sydney, 1984.

The Complete Book of the Olympics, David Wallechinsky, Aurum Press, London, 1992.

BOXING

'Ladies and gentlemen, in the centre ring, hailing fron Concord, Sydney, wearing blue tuxedo and tie, with a record of forty years' boxing announcing, including thirty-five world titles, and an unrivalled knowledge of Australian boxing, The Lord of the Ring, **Ray Connelly**.'

Ray Connelly's fascination with boxing began forty-seven years ago when he watched, as a starry-eyed kid at Sydney's Leichhardt Stadium, his first professional boxing contest. He made his debut as an announcer at the same stadium five years later. He made an indelible impression and remains one of Australian boxing's most respected protagonists.

BOXING
HONEY, I FORGOT
TO DUCK

Jack Dempsey

'Before I became a professional boxer I was nothing; didn't even know about self-esteem let alone having any. The same with confidence. I never thought I'd ever be able to achieve anything in my life ... that I'd just drudge along each day heading nowhere.'

So spoke 'tiny' Sparrow Freeman from the ring centre following one of his bantamweight contests during the 1980s. 'I might have lost more bouts than I won, but each of them added to the value of my life. I had been rescued from complete obscurity. Only I will ever know what it meant to me hearing people call my name and knowing I was capable of being recognised. When the crowd cheered me it was like being lifted high above where I could feel I'd never again have to think of myself as worthless. Those treasured memories are with me for life. No one can ever again say I wasn't capable of doing something worthwhile.'

A more celebrated heavyweight of the 1970s, Foster Bibron, will possess lifetime gratitude for boxing in which he has an honoured position as Australian heavyweight champion. However, the satisfaction that title brought him was of minor consequence compared to what it meant to his family.

'I was so proud of my kids standing up for me that I was determined to continue boxing until they knew for certain their dad was a champion. The morning after I won the belt I gave it to them to take to school to show it to the other kids. They were so thrilled and carried it with such reverence my emotions cascaded. The already strong bonds by which we had always been bound were strengthened. I happily retired.'

John Connelly was acknowledged for his raw courage both on the rugby league field – he represented Balmain at President's Cup level – and in the boxing ring. The only son in the family, John and his dad were inseparable, and although John senior loved boxing he preferred his son playing rugby league.

However, when John decided on a ring career his dad typically supported him. John's spirit and fighter's heart took him to a challenge for the Australian cruiserweight crown. He recovered from what appeared a likely first-round knock-out after being caught flush on the chin by a savage right-hand blow. Groggily regaining his feet he fought out the twelve rounds to a points' loss to Phil 'Swifty' Gregory. He intended to retire, until his dad fell victim to a terminal illness.

'I want to try again. Dad never recovered but I'd love to win a state or even a national title for him. He may have gone by the time I fight but at least he knew I was training for the bout, and that the only reason I was doing it was to let him know how much I cared.'

John was comforted in his grief by fellow pugilists former Australian junior middleweight champion Johnny Layton and state heavyweight king, Harry Harris. Those tough, hard men shared numerous hours with John, displaying behaviour far removed from that normally associated with boxers.

There is a certain mystic appeal to many who aspire to box. They are seduced by the unknown, excited by the possibility of stepping between the ropes into the restricted twenty-metre square to face an unknown adversary.

So it was with the chief security guard at the Sydney Hilton Hotel Tom Manuel. Boxing had long fascinated him. More so when he went to a Woolloomooloo gymnasium to sharpen his fitness. Captivated by the dramatic atmosphere, and accepting the offer to spar, he offered himself as a cruiserweight contestant. He was willing to expose his limited talents to satisfy his curiosity.

Matched against Ted Cofie, acclaimed by many as a genuine prospect, the security guard coveted the opportunity of clashing with him at the Sydney Entertainment Centre in 1990. He suffered the pre-fight anxiety common to all boxers, including the finest of champions, but took into the battle a crude technique, a strong jaw and a heart overflowing with fortitude. Standing his ground under Cofie's sustained attacks he fired home some damaging punches himself, but as he began to feel weary his stance widened, he became less mobile and had little choice but to trade blows that were less skillfully delivered than those of his opponent. He was defiant, refusing to take a backward step, but after three rounds his career came to its anticipated finale. He left the dressing room that night thrilled with himself and with an admiration for those who choose to follow such a calling.

There is not the slightest doubt that professional boxing demands maximum self-discipline and sacrifice. It didn't take the stockily built bantamweight Steve Vella long to discover this several years ago. After engaging in three preliminary contests he disappeared from gymnasiums and boxing nights. When questioned about his absence during a Warwick Farm race meeting some time later his response was succinct, 'I went into boxing thinking it would be exciting, but didn't I have it wrong. I'd rather risk myself handling these powerhouse thoroughbreds than putting the gloves on again. It's too hard. But at least I know. I carried plenty of bruises to prove it. And short as my time might have been and tough as it was, I'm glad I did it.'

Boxing feasts upon opportunity. Former world light heavyweight world champion, Jeff Harding, provides a perfect illustration of this. With victory over Italian Nestor Giovannini at Newcastle Basketball Stadium early in 1989, Harding had an unblemished record in fourteen bouts. He was rugged, fiercely tenacious with a body attack that when moving into full effect could jack-knife an opponent. And his resolve was utterly insurmountable – complementing a brand of courage none could excel. But Jeff was frustrated to the point of anger by his non-acceptance by Australia's boxing fans. Then fate intervened through a telephone call from the United States of America. Promoter Bob Arum contacted Bill Mordey offering Harding a challenge to the world crown held by Denis Andries.

From the time of his arival in Atlantic City, the site of the battle, Harding was scorned. His record was the subject of derision, his boldness in considering himself the slightest chance of becoming champion demeaned to such a degree his name was mispronounced in public and in the media. No one cared about him, thinking Andries retaining his title a formality. Not so Harding.

Unashamedly proud this remarkable fighter prepared with a vigour that brought his body to a faultless degree of power and suppleness, his mind focused to an almost hypnotic state. The more he was dismissed as a chance the more Harding demanded of his body and mind. Unknowingly, Andries fuelled the flames at the weigh-in.

Questioned as to whether he had seen a tape of Harding in action he scowled in reply, 'Why would I waste time doing that. He'll be no problem. It'll be an easy fight. I don't need any tape to help me along.'

All those present except the tiny Australian contingent agreed. They knew as long as Harding had breath he'd fight. Nevertheless, the prophets of

destruction appeared to have been accurate soon
after the opening bell when Harding's eye was cut,
flooding his face with blood. Into the second round
charged Andries, sustaining his relentless pursuit,
Harding clinging to an instinct of survival few have
ever matched in the ring. A knock-down to Andries
in the fourth frame seemed a preface to the reten-
tion of his crown, but many failed to see the air-
expelling left rip Harding landed on the champion
in the fifth.

That blow was probably the most significant of
the whole contest as it revived Harding's confidence.
By the end of the eighth round those who had ridiculed the Australian were chanting his name. The
brave Andries was wilting. His beloved crown was
in jeopardy but he could not quell the onslaught of
this brazen usurper.

Andries went down in the 11th round with only
instinct preventing him from receiving the dreaded
ten-second count. Almost stumbling out of his
corner to answer the summons of the twelfth,
Andries faced three minutes of terror if he was to
have any hope of holding his title.

Harding did not allow him such time. Both fighters were now functioning on heart alone. They had
thoroughly spent themselves. Harding struck with
David-like accuracy the chin of Andries, attaining
the identical result as David in defeating the feared

429

Goliath. The referee halted the bout and signalled Harding as the new WBC light heavyweight champion of the world.

Throughout his career, triple world title holder Jeff Fenech fought nature. He never faltered in his resolve and deserved every particle of glory that was his reward. Born with hands completely unsuited to boxing, the index and second fingers protruding to the first joint, numerous operations by the best surgeons, gloves modified to accommodate such an improbable problem never fully compensated for natural design. Added to his tortuous path was a weight battle.

Nine times Commonwealth and Australian champion and world title challenger, Tony Mundine, understood and sympathised with Fenech as he, too, experienced the problems of boxing middleweight though a natural light heavyweight, even cruiserweight.

Fenech was totally focused in his ambitions. He may have engaged in a sometimes hectic social life, but he never wavered in his application to training. He set a standard of spartan living that was never matched in his era.

Australian light heavyweight champion Gary Hubble was also plagued by weight problems but much of his difficulty was self-inflicted. He lacked true application.

When reminded he could comfortably make the weight for a title defence if he followed Fenech's example he stated emphatically, 'But Fenech's a freak. No one should be expected to do what he does.'

Some of Fenech's methods were bordering upon the unnatural such as when he was preparing for a successful bantamweight defence against the Los Angeles Olympic Gold Medal winner, American Steve McCrory. All his efforts to reduce to the weight seemed doomed in the late evening preceding the day of the championship. The following morning promoter Bill Mordey was awakened at five by Fenech's phone call, his voice ringing with delight but obviously strained, 'I've made the weight, Bill.' The previous evening Fenech had placed his already wracked body into a blending of plastic sheeting and several full tracksuits and taken to the road. But before leaving he turned five radiators on in his room. He ran as far as his aching body could carry him then returned to his room to shadow box numerous rounds in the furnace-like temperature.

Johnny Famechon is one of boxing's treasures –

a symbol of genuine humanity and humility. His unbridled courage is legendary as he pursues a life tragically confined to walking with the aid of a frame.

'My mind is sharp. I send messages to my limbs but they are interrupted by muscle damage and lack of co-ordination. Some days are tougher than others but that is no more than a challenge that has to be met. I'll keep trying as one day my body might come good. If not, I'll do the best with what I have,' Famechon says.

The enrichment of Johnny's life is his companion, Glynnis Bussey, who has devoted herself to Johnny's sufferings since he was struck down by a vehicle on the Hume Highway outside Warwick Farm Racecourse five years ago. Johnny is now more revered than when he reigned as featherweight champion of the world.

His boxing on the back move has never been surpassed. It was faultless...born of superb balance and timing as he drew opponents forward creating an impression he was being forced to concede ground. He was cleverly bringing them into punching range. Yet there was a night at Sydney Stadium when Johnny was outpointed by Max Murphy. His father Andre said in his deep, guttural French accent, 'I wish my son not continue boxing. He not punch hard enough.'

When he ruled the featherweights Johnny Famechon's pal and fellow Melburnian Lionel Rose was
world bantamweight champion, a title he won as a
nineteen-year-old by beating the redoubtable Japanese Fighting Harada. The year was 1968 and
Lionel was chosen as a substitute by the Harada
management who obviously saw little danger in the
exceptionally talented Aborigine. They could not
have witnessed Lionel when he knocked out
national flyweight champion Rocky Gattelari in
thirteen brilliant rounds. Rose's performance that
evening was almost perfection, rarely has there
been one to emulate it anywhere or any time.

Carrying that magnificent form into the world
title challenge, Rose achieved what the Japanese
considered the impossible, defeating their idol in his
home city of Tokyo. Lionel thus became the first
Aborigine to wear a world crown and was the Australian of the Year in 1968.

Had Lionel not been yet another victim of increas-
ing weight he could have been invincible in the bantamweight division. His trainer Jack Rennie, with
whom he lived for a considerable period, went to
enormous lengths to discover an alternative to nature's dominance of Lionel's weight. All to no avail.
When Lionel was preparing to face the might of
South America's fierce-punching Reuben Olivares
Rennie was apprehensive, especially when there

was not an ounce of surplus flesh left on any part of Lionel's anatomy.

'All that was left was muscle and you couldn't rub any of that off. As it was his body was chafed almost raw and we knew whatever happened in the fight it would be Lionel's last as a bantamweight,' Rennie said.

Australia's first official world champion was also a bantamweight, Jimmy Carruthers, a supreme boxer who demolished the defending champion, South African Vic Toweel, in the opening round of their 1952 meeting in Johannesburg. Jimmy's speed and accuracy were blistering, demoralising Toweel who was only able to offer instinctive resistance. The win gained the young man from a two-storey tenement near Wooloomoloo international recognition.

Boxing comparisons are not only inconclusive they are also unjust, but when the best of Australian boxers is discussed the name of Jimmy Carruthers is amongst the foremost. His pace was breathtaking, rivals being subjected to a spearing accuracy that destroyed their equilibrium, eroding their strategies and confidence. However, Jimmy was astonished when he fought the hardest-punching bantamweight of any era, ever-smiling Queenslander Elley Bennett, in 1951, for the national crown. Outmanoeuvred going into the fourteenth round, Bennett almost salvaged his crown with a brief salvo which brought praise from Carruthers, 'I didn't think it possible a fighter could harness such ferocity when exhausted. Elley had travelled thirteen furious rounds and I figured he was spent. He was the best puncher I ever faced.'

Before Jimmy Carruthers came on the boxing scene there had been several other world-class Australian boxers around. Les Darcy, Vic Patrick and Dave Sands all have a particular place in our boxing folklore. Then there was George Barnes, a boxer with limitless courage whose three epic welterweight clashes with Darby Brown and dual victories against Wallace 'Bud' Smith are cherished by those privileged to witness them. Later there were Italian-born Rocky Mattiolli who captured the WBC junior middleweight diadem in Berlin in 1977; English-born Lester Ellis whose 1985 battle with Barry Michael for the IBF world junior lightweight crown led to a still-running rivalry, and Elley Bennett and Ray Coleman who staged a trio of national featherweight fights that are compared to the Tommy Burns versus O'Neill Bell and Vic Patrick versus Freddie Dawson classics. Vic Patrick, who came off the Hawkesbury River oyster leases, was a lightweight who fought with the power of a middleweight. His 1946 welterweight championship battle with Tommy Burns is legendary. Heroic warriors all.

RUGBY UNION

Greg Growden is the chief rugby union writer for the *Sydney Morning Herald* and the *Sun-Herald* newspapers, while he also reports on southern hemisphere football for the *Guardian* newspaper in London. He is the author of three books: *A Wayward Genius – the Fleetwood-Smith Story*, *The Wallabies' World Cup*, and *With the Wallabies*. However, his main claim to fame is being the only international rugby writer to have the main race at a Wentworth Park greyhound meeting named after him.

RUGBY UNION IT'S NOT *JUST* A GAME

Emotional fan

At the start of the 1989 Wallaby tour of France and Canada, three new Wallabies, including Peter FitzSimons, went to dinner with Test veteran Tom Lawton. FitzSimons, who had yet to play a Test, remarked to Lawton how moved he had been the previous day when before a minor tour match the players had stood arm-in-arm and sang the Australian national anthem for the first time on foreign soil.

Lawton's eyes bulged, before he snorted; 'I'll tell you what "moving" is. Moving will be if you play a Test match in France ... and they play the Australian national anthem and the fifteen of you can only just hear the tune from the band against the voices of the 70 000 froggies that are screaming for your

blood, but you all belt it out anyway . . . and you line
up to receive the kick-off, and you can see this little
sliver of white coming straight at you end over end
and like it's in slow motion and you take it, and get
belted by four of them, but your mates close ranks
to protect you and knock them backwards and you
form the first scrum with your blood just trickling
down your nose on to your lip and your eyebrow's
swelling up and you can see the grass about three
inches from your eyeballs and you feel this massive
heave coming from behind you . . . and that . . . that
is what "moving" is, mate.'

It took several minutes before the other three at
the table were able to say anything.

Representative second rower Justin Nowlan's debut
for the Northern Suburbs club in Sydney a few
seasons ago was relatively brutal, as he had to retire
to have a head wound strapped after being belted on
the chin during a lineout. Feeling his jaw tenderly
after the win, Nowlan told the club's patron and
renowned former no-nonsense policeman, George 'the
Commissioner' Marshall that he thought his jaw was
broken. Marshall stuck a gnarled finger into Nowlan's mouth and insisted that he, 'Clamp down on
that, son. We'll soon see if it is broken.'

Nowlan obliged, biting almost to the bone.

Marshall extracted his finger from Nowlan's mouth and diagnosed, 'Son, your jaw's not broken, but I might need a tetanus needle before the next game.'

Glen Ella was asked at the start of his representative career if he had any interest in swapping codes and playing rugby league. He replied, 'I've got a good job. I drive a Celica and I play golf every Friday. Why should I turn to League?'

He never did.

One of Australia's most memorable early victories against New Zealand occurred in the first Test at the Sydney Cricket Ground in 1934, and it can be partly attributed to the power of radio. As Philip Derriman explained in his book, *The Grand Old Ground – A history of the Sydney Cricket Ground*, Australia were down 11–6 at half-time. During the break the players opted against going off the field, but instead sat in two groups on the playing field. 'There was a radio microphone on the field, and the Australians were close enough to it to hear what was being said. Charles Moses spoke first, and then the New Zealand team manager, A. J. Geddes, came to the microphone to send a message to people listening to the broadcast in New Zealand. He told them the All Blacks had the game in the bag. The longer the match went on, he said, the further New Zealand would forge ahead. This so nettled the Australian players who heard it that one of them suggested they should really go after the New Zealanders in the second half. This is just what they did.

Australia won 25–11.

Coaching is an obsession as former representative coach, poet, writer and motion picture sound-mixer Peter Fenton can testify. In 1987, Fenton was coaching Eastwood, a team which needed to win the final match of the minor rounds to get into the semi-finals. Eastwood was beaten by St George, with Fenton suffering as much pain as the players. Later that night, Fenton drove down to the local bottle shop with his youngest daughter, Amy, who went to the video shop next door.

Fenton was having a shower about a half-hour later, where he was jolted by a knock on the shower-room door.

'Who is it?' Fenton asked.

'It's Amy. I made it.'

'Made what?'

'I made it home, you left me down there!'

'One day you're a rooster, the next a feather duster.' Former Australian coach Alan Jones after the Wallabies defeated Scotland during the 1984 Grand Slam success.

Tries are sometimes not the be-all and end-all in rugby, as the Parramatta grade club in Sydney discovered near the turn of the century. In a competition match against Richmond, Parramatta annihilated their opponents by scoring 22 tries to nil. However they lost because at that time games were decided on which team had kicked the most goals. There were no kickers in the Parramatta side, and with five minutes remaining, Richmond slotted a penalty goal to be victors.

Among the most fascinating of Australian rugby representatives was the Wallabies first captain, Dr Herbert Michael 'Paddy' Moran. Moran, who described himself as a 'miserable, stooped, boring, introspective sort of fellow', led the first Australian team away to the United Kingdom in 1908–09. But he was as celebrated as a physician, being the first doctor in Australia to use radium to treat cancer, and as a writer, producing the memorable autobiographies *Viewless Winds* and *In My Fashion*, the fictionalised biography *Beyond the Hill Lies China*, plus a pamphlet on the war in Abyssinia, *Letters from Rome*.

His writings on rugby were always perceptive, but as fascinating were his reminiscences on medical life, particularly during World War II when he encountered homosexuality among the British troops. In the book, *In My Fashion*, Moran shows little sympathy towards this group, describing them as 'perverts'.

'I have been amazed at the number of men who appeared before me and candidly admitted to practising and to having practised homosexuality and to be not ashamed of the practices,' Moran wrote.

'Sometimes I wondered whether in such cases it was not an example of the depths to which man would sink in his effort to obtain discharge, and I was always on my guard to make sure that a cunning and unscrupulous soldier was not obtaining release at the expense of any self-respect he might have had.'

Moran devoted several pages describing some of the more bizarre cases, including soldiers colouring their cheeks with red chalk, and those who were the 'more typical homosexualist-effeminate, with high-pitched voice, swaying hips and girlish manner'. These words, which were among the first about a then taboo and almost unknown subject, were written in 1945.

Ian Williams was one of many to use rugby as a way of seeing the world. After first representing Australia as a winger in 1987, Williams won three Blues at Oxford University in 1988-89 before working and playing for Kobe Steel in Japan.

In his excellent book *In Touch*, Williams offered fascinating insights into the differences of playing rugby in Japan and how it fits into the country's social structure.

Williams wrote that in Japanese rugby, 'the older a player is, the greater the respect and deference he is paid by younger players. This is taken to an extreme when shinjin, or new boys, are required after training to clean the footballs, sweep the ground flat (since most fields in Japan have absolutely no grass) and then wash out the locker room after the senior players have changed and showered. A refusal to submit to a sempai's (seniors) demand is met with a punch and, if it becomes repetitive, eventual dismissal from the team for insubordination.'

The build-up in the dressing room for matches was also intense, described by Williams as 'an explosion of emotion, and the players have such heightened feelings that many of them will begin to cry'.

Williams recalled after winning one important club match 'our players began to hug one another, overcome by the moment. Since most of them can't speak much English at the best of times, let alone at such an emotional point, all they could say was "sank you". I also became caught up with the moment and shed a few tears myself out of relief and joy – a powerful cocktail.'

There is an old adage that the forwards decide who wins a match and the backs decide by how much.

Most Wallabies have served their country with distinction. But occasionally sub-standard players have slipped through the net and somehow represented Australia. These include Sydney centre Jack Young, who toured South Africa with the 1933 Australian team. According to sports historian Jack Pollard, he was rated as being a poor tackler and an abominable handler, 'who made breaks without the ball'. Few of his team-mates could work out why he had been picked. Still he was popular, because of his prowess at lawn bowls and his eagerness to invite old team-mates to his club for a friendly afternoon game.

Spiro Zavos, through his regular columns in the *Sydney Morning Herald*, is one of Australia's best-known rugby critics. Before moving to Sydney from New Zealand, he wrote one of rugby's most incisive books, *After the Final Whistle*. In it he poignantly described how rugby can transform some people's lives. In 1972, after a Wales-New Zealand Test match, Zavos went looking for his Welsh friend, Roy, in the main bar of the famous Angel Hotel, which is just across the street from Cardiff Arms Park.

He eventually found Roy talking to Zavos's wife. 'From across the room I could see Roy's face change in aspect and colour,' Zavos wrote.

'The knuckles on his hand whitened. Eyes blazing he made his way to the toilet. I followed him in. 'What's happened?' I asked anxiously. 'I was just about to hit Judy,' he replied. 'What did she say, Roy?' Roy struggled for words, finally he blurted out, 'Do you know what she said?' He paused. 'She said, "Don't worry about the result Roy, it's only a game."' He gripped the lapels of my coat. 'It's not *just* a bloody game, you know.'

Keith Murdoch is New Zealand's most notorious rugby footballer, being the first All Black ever to be sent home from a tour. This followed an altercation with a security guard at the same Angel Hotel where Mrs Zavos nearly got flattened.

After the incident Murdoch, an aggressive, but highly talented prop-forward, disappeared. A few years later T.P. McLean, the doyen of international rugby writers, tracked Murdoch down in a camp near the small town of Cowra in the northern corner of Western Australia after travelling hundreds of kilometres in a Fokker Fellowship to the outpost of Newman, then light plane to Port Hedland.

The meeting was hardly cordial, as McLean reported in the *New Zealand Herald*, with the finale to a fiery conversation being when Murdoch announced, 'Who brought this so and so up here?'

'There was no reply. The "so and so", if accurate as to gender, was a most offensive term. Murdoch wheeled about and moved to the back of the van to get some tools. I followed and asked if he knew "the boys" had beaten South Australia, 117 to nil.

"No," he said, "I am not interested."

We circled and came face to face again. This time, it was clear he had had enough.

"Back in the bus," he said. "Just keep moving, unless you want me to rub you in this."

"This" was a streak of oil, an inch deep, two feet wide.'

T.P bid his farewell.

Back at the camp, as I indulged in the great West Australian pastime of constantly flicking away the flies, I was given a can of insecticide,' McLean added.

"Squeeze that over yourself," I was told. "It will keep them away for a while." The can was called Scram. It seemed exquisitely apt.'

A berth on a Wallaby tour is the ultimate prize for an aspiring player. Yet embarking on such tours can be hazardous. Cecil Murnin, a NSW loose-forward, was selected to tour England with the first Wallaby team in 1908. However he became ill on the boat before the team reached Naples and was sent home. Bruce Malouf at least got to Britain in 1981–82 but had to fly home after breaking an ankle while training for the first match. The unluckiest Australian tourists would still have to be the 1939 Wallabies, who reached Britain just before war was declared with Germany. The tour was immediately abandoned and after several days filling sandbags to protect their hotel at Torquay the players had a hazardous return trip to Australia with their boat forced to zigzag to avoid submarine attacks.

'I take the Gucci view about hard work on the practice field – long after you have forgotten the price the quality remains.' Alan Jones.

Relationships between New South Wales and Queensland have regularly been strained. This was very much the case in 1994 when the New South Wales team refused to travel to Durban to play a Super Ten provincial tournament match because of a declared state of emergency in the Natal province. New South Wales had to forfeit the game against Natal, ruining whatever chance they had of winning the tournament.

New South Wales were ridiculed by Queensland officials as their team had been in the South African coastal city several days before and not found themselves in any danger, particularly when surfing the famous Durban breaks. New South Wales coach Greg Smith said later that he promised he would cheer for Queensland in the Super Ten final. This hardly delighted Queensland coach John Connolly who said, 'Queensland needs his (Smith's) support like Mother Teresa needs Hannibal Lecter.'

One of the most regrettable incidents in recent

times was when the South African team were snubbed after being beaten by Australia at the Sydney Football Stadium in 1993. While the Australian players and officials were paraded in front of the crowd the South Africans, even after holding up a huge banner which read 'Thank you Australia', were ignored and forced to disconsolately trudge off the field to the dressing rooms virtually forgotten. This moment raised the ire of countless people, particularly members of the 1963 Wallaby team who toured South Africa who wrote a passionate letter to the *Sydney Morning Herald*. Part of the letter emphasised the importance of fair play and sportsmanship in anything rugby. On behalf of the 1963 team their captain John Thornett wrote, 'The day will surely come again when our team leaves the field deflated and exhausted after losing a series away from home. Will we be obliged to stand by, cast aside, unnoticed, while our hosts parade the spoils of victory? I think not. I cannot imagine any other country acting with such total insensitivity. A fundamental ethic of rugby has been the acknowledgement of the skills and courage of the opponents, coupled with a degree of humility in success – a recognition as well that we often win or lose by a fine margin. It has been on this premise that its great camaraderie has been built. We, the 1963 Wallabies, sincerely trust that the Australian rugby union will not allow a repetition of this disgraceful performance.'

In the 1960s John Thornett was the author of an instruction book called *This World of Rugby* which included a section on the importance of coaching and captaincy when on tour. It also warned against the hazards of coaches pushing the point once too often.

'One coach I knew was a great man for giving inspirational but similar lectures. This is fine when the players are very young but it doesn't work so well with experienced players. At training one night this coach started his address by stressing that we were in for a very tough time as the side we had to play the following Saturday was studded with brilliant players. He proceeded to go through the sublime football prowess of each man in the opposition, finishing with, "So what I want on Saturday is BLOOD", at which point all his players laughed.'

Thornett was the victim of a quick quip when he tried to spur on his Australian team during their Test against the British Lions in Brisbane in 1966. Australia were off their game in the first half, prompting Thornett to gather the team around him for a deep and meaningful captain's talk.

'Listen fellows, this just isn't us,' Thornett said.

'All right,' interrupted a voice from the back, 'If it

isn't us, what do you say we piss off?'

Other leaders have been more successful in revitalising their troops through the scent of war.

During the 1958 New Zealand Maoris' tour of Australia coach Ron Bryers was forever passionate at the pre-match pep talks. Before the third and final Test, after New Zealand Maoris had lost the first in Brisbane and drawn the second in Sydney, Bryers opted for the historical touch. He told the players about Rewi Maniapoto a renowned Maori chief who had answered a demand for surrender made by British troops with the immortal words 'We will fight on for ever and ever'.

Bryers said that Rewi was prepared to die for the Maori race. He then asked the players whether they were capable of showing that the modern Maori was as good as the old, and whether they were prepared to let their own chief down. They won the third Test 13–6.

For so long Australia has felt intimidated about playing the All Blacks. The general tone was portrayed in an 1884 *Sydney Morning Herald* editorial which said, 'Rugby isn't our game...we'll always court defeat if we play the New Zealanders.'

Rugby Union

The Sydney *Telegraph* said in the same year, 'No glorious uncertainty appears to attach to the series of football matches now being played between the local clubs and the visiting team from New Zealand. By universal consent the championship belongs to the strangers. The New South Wales players are not much more than 'muffs' by comparison with the genial fellows who are teaching them how to play the game.'

A most bizarre ceremony ensured that the illustrious Queensland centre pairing Jason Little and Tim Horan weren't lost to rugby league, instead playing a vital role in the Wallabies' 1991 World Cup triumph.

Shortly after Australia had beaten France in the 1989 Test in Strasbourg and the Wallabies were involved in celebrations, captain Nick Farr-Jones and second rower Peter FitzSimons drew Little and Horan aside. Revitalised by the win and realising the great worth this centre pairing would be to the future of Australian rugby, FitzSimons stressed the importance of not going to league. He convinced the pair they must take the sacred French popular oath and swear their allegiance to the then amateur game.

In France, the popular oath, which involves holding your right hand on the top of your mother's head while saying the vow, is the Gallic society's test to show that one will always abide by the solemn pledge. To act against this vow is unspeakable in French society and a public disgrace as it shows gross disrespect towards the family base. Horan and Little, both then nineteen, heartily agreed to take the vow in a ceremony which coincided with the arrival of one of the Australian supporter tour parties at the team's happy hour. The party included Horan's mother Helen.

With FitzSimons acting as the high priest, and Farr-Jones as witness, the Test forward placed Horan's right hand on his mother's head and said in French, 'I swear to you on the head of my mother that I will not consider rugby league until after the World Cup.' Horan repeated the statement in French and English. As Little's mother was not in France Horan volunteered to act as his mother. Little placed his right hand on Horan's head and repeated the oath.

It might have been done partly in jest but the French oath worked. Despite countless lucrative offers from rugby league, Little and Horan have stayed in the fold.

One of rugby union's charms is that it can survive on the seat of its pants. The organisation of a bicentennial World XV-Australia match in 1988 in Sydney is a prime example. Two days before the match there was uncertainty whether the Wallabies would be facing an opposition. On the eve twelve players were expected to arrive in Sydney, but only six turned up. One of them, Korean back Cho Yong Duk arrived on the wrong flight, and had no idea where his team-mates were staying. A Korean friend, who owned a restaurant in Sydney, eventually helped him locate them. New Zealand captain Wayne Shelford who had successfully negotiated his way to Sydney was asked if he knew when the rest of the World XV would assemble and have their first training run. He replied, 'I wouldn't have a clue. The coach and manager aren't here. So what do you do?'

The game went ahead. It was a big success. But it was hardly surprising that Australia won quite comfortably.

Sir Edward 'Weary' Dunlop is an Australian hero, primarily through care for his fellow soldiers when spending more than three years as a prisoner of war in Java and on the Burma-Thailand Death Railway. Before World War II, Dunlop, a distinguished surgeon, played two Tests for Australia against New Zealand where he proved to be an exceptionally tough forward. Even in the lead-up to these Tests

Dunlop's courage, determination and will to win were always close to the surface, as explained in Sue Ebury's biography, *Weary: The Life of Sir Edward Dunlop*.

Ebury wrote that 'for the 1934 Sydney Cricket Ground Test both teams were put up at the Wentworth Hotel. But the All Blacks refused to be social.

'Each morning Weary greeted this soundless phalanx and walked on until one of their number, Beau Cottrell, caught him up in the hotel corridor to explain that Geddes, the manager, had forbidden them to fraternise with the opposing side. "You'll find us very friendly after the match," he said. Weary shrugged. "O.K Beau. You go and tell your manager that the fact I say good morning to you doesn't mean that I won't try to knock your bloody heads off on Saturday."'

It proved to be a brutal Test match, with Dunlop one of the protagonists after several All Blacks attempted to belt him out of the game. In the dressing rooms after the match Dunlop set 'his freshly re-broken nose by inserting a toothbrush up each nostril – after draining the usual two bottles of beer awaiting him on top of his locker – by way of an anaesthetic.'

Australian coach Bob Dwyer can never be accused

of lacking passion towards rugby. As he once said, 'I see rugby as an extension of the arts. The spirit of the William Tell Overture in the power of the scrum, the beauty of a Rodin sculpture in the sweeping movement of a backline.' Yet Dwyer's introduction to the game was not so lush. After attending his first Test he was left feeling at best 'indifferent', at worse 'totally bored'.

'I remember going out to the Sydney Cricket Ground to see the Springboks play the Wallabies in a Test match when I was fifteen and thinking the whole thing was just totally deplorable,' Dwyer told Peter FitzSimons in an interview.

'I just couldn't understand why both teams were kicking it all the time, why no one seemed to have any interest in running the damn thing.'

It is a little known fact that renowned rugby league player and coach Bob Fulton played against the All Blacks. Fulton was selected for the Australian Combined Services team which played the 1968 New Zealand team at North Sydney Oval. This match was played just two days after Fulton had been the star of the World Cup league final.

Corporal Fulton was one of Combined Services' better players in their 45–8 loss, showing off his special skills when he ran a tap-kick penalty from his own goal-line well into the All Blacks' half. But predictably he made bigger headlines in the lead-up to the match. One newspaper reported Fulton as saying, 'I'm not really worried about the All Blacks. Who is Colin Meads? I've never heard of him.' As T.P. McLean wrote in his tour book *All Black Power* 'this caused All Blacks to assure each other that they would take this fighting cock down a peg or two.'

After the game the players discovered that Fulton was at the time taking the mickey out of the journalist.

'We had just finished the League Cup final,' Fulton said. 'I was pretty tired. So some cove said to me, "What do you think of Meads?" I said what anyone else would have said in the same circumstances – I said I didn't know Meads. So then this character puts it in the paper and makes me look like a ning-nong. Of course I knew about Meads.'

'I played seven Tests and that's seven more than most guys will ever have the chance to play. That's not to say I haven't been done dirty on by the selectors over the years. There were times when I thought I should have been in and I wasn't. But I think hate is a great motivator.' Perennial Australian Test reserve hooker Mark McBain.

Nick Farr-Jones on David Campese, 'He is the sort of player whose brain doesn't always know where his legs are carrying him.'

Bob Dwyer on David Campese, 'We all know there's a loose wire between Campo's brain and his mouth.'

'It's always good to be a big mouth as long as you can back it up on the field – and I'm lucky I can do that.' David Campese had a long career making acidic comments about opponents, teammates, administrators, journalists, coaches, referees, anyone who had a difference of opinion with the mercurial winger. It was not surprising that one of the chapters in his biting autobiography, *On a Wing and a Prayer*, was entitled The Loner.

An important day, 12 April, 1995 and a historic quote: 'Amateurism as a concept is outmoded and should be dispensed with in the modern game,' NSW Rugby Union chairman, Ian Ferrier.

Alan Jones was easily Australian rugby's most controversial coach. Colourful, emotional, vindictive, a major success as both a coach and motivator, Jones was a prime reason for Australia's rise to international supremacy, which began with their 1984 Grand Slam success. Dumped as coach after four years Jones remained intensely bitter. In a video, 'Glory Days – The David Campese Story', Jones revealed his innermost thoughts. 'In many ways, I regret that I've had anything to do with Australian rugby,' Jones said.

'In many ways I regret that I was ever perhaps foolish enough to put my name forward for the coaching job because the whole thing's been badly evaluated ... what we sought to do has never been acknowledged. The motives have always been questioned and the conclusions are quite false.'

Jones said he became such a target that 'you're entitled to believe that this was one of the greatest monsters that ever presided over an international side.'

Matraville is one of the less salubrious suburbs in Sydney and its high school had never been known as a rugby union nursery. That is until the Ella brothers attended the school in the mid 1970s, their 1st XV winning the Waratah Shield in 1977.

The first indication that the Matraville team – which also included another future Test representative in Lloyd Walker – was something special came the previous year when it astounded the Sydney rugby community by beating St Joseph's College in a pre-season trial match.

This was of David-Goliath proportions since St Joseph's was renowned as being *the* rugby school in Australia. Although St Joseph's forwards controlled the up-front battle, Matraville's masterful backline, revolving around the Ellas and Walker, wreaked havoc. St Joseph's had no counter. In the second half the St Joseph's coach and former Wallaby full-back, Brother Terry Curley, yelled at one of his players to 'tackle the black boy!' The player turned to his coach and yelled back, 'Which one? There are hundreds of them.'

As sports writer Peter Muszkat put it, 'To become famous in rugby football usually takes years; to become infamous needs only a few seconds.'

Muszkat was referring to the only occasion when an Australian player had been sent home from a tour. This occurred in 1966 after Wallaby forward Ross Cullen admitted to biting the ear of an Oxford University opponent. During the match Oxford front-rower Ollie Waldron emerged from a scrum with his hand clamped over his left ear, blood oozing through the gaps between his fingers.

In the dressing room the Australian team

manager Bill McLaughlin confronted Cullen and asked him if he had bitten Waldron's ear. Muszkat, who covered the tour for News Limited, said 'all the Australian hooker had to do was deny it and the incident would have been closed. But Cullen chose to tell the truth and admitted biting Waldron's ear after the Irishman had repeatedly bored in on him in the scrum.' The next morning the entire Wallaby party were told that Cullen was to be sent home immediately.

'His shocked team-mates didn't even have a chance to say goodbye. For a week or two the team morale was low and many players, particularly the Queenslanders, still harboured bitterness,' Muszkat wrote.

McLaughlin's action has since been widely criticised, particularly as it prompted the player to disappear almost immediately from all levels of the game. Thankfully no Australian management since has had the cause to take such drastic action.

Times have definitely changed. The modern reader may find it difficult to believe that once upon a time sportsmanship was all that mattered, and fair play was the most important asset – even at international level. Test matches against New Zealand are now renowned for their oneupmanship and focus on winning at whatever cost. Back in the early 1920s it wasn't quite so. One of the most famous All Black sides of all time was the 1924–25 team, which beat all and sundry on a seven-month thirty-eight-match tour of Australia, the British Isles, France, and Canada, plus also playing two matches at home. Their only two losses were against Auckland and in the first Test against New South Wales at the Sydney Showground. By the time of the third Test, the All Blacks and New South Wales were involved in a tied rubber, with all being decided by the midweek match at the Showground.

Despite the tense atmosphere relationships between the two teams were surprisingly cordial. As explained in All Black forward Read Masters' diary of the tour, 'prior to the commencement of play, both teams at the request of our (New Zealand) captain gave three cheers for 'Boy' Charlton who had that morning been declared winner of the 1500 metres swimming contest at the Olympic Games.'

The teams even came to an agreement during the match about the deplorable refereeing. As Masters wrote, 'The refereeing in this match was extremely hard to follow. Our blokes were penalised almost every time they attempted to hook the ball, notwithstanding the fact that they were subjected to a great deal of obstruction by the opposing front row. If it had not been for a general protest by almost the entire NSW team, one of our forwards would have had to leave the field when ordered off for tackling an opponent high.'

Would this happen now?

Rugby writers are supposed to be objective, refusing to let bias or parochial views stain their copy. Sometimes such guidelines are forgotten. Frank O'Callaghan, the highly respected rugby writer for the Brisbane *Courier-Mail*, was renowned for his enthusiasm for anything Queensland. In Don Cameron's book on the 1980 All Black tour of Australia, *Rugby Triumphant*, he recalls the opening minutes of the Queensland-New Zealand match at Ballymore.

'Suddenly (Roger) Gould from about his own ten-metre line hoisted a monstrous up-and-under into All Black territory,' Cameron wrote. 'One of the press, Frank O'Callaghan, a kindly man if a mite partial towards Queensland, jolted us awake with the bellow, "Let's see some blood on the ball" as Gould's kick boomed down into All Black territory. We were sharply awake and so were Queensland.'

There was little blood, but Queensland won 9–3 in a famous victory.

Apart from their extraordinary football ability, the

Ella brothers were renowned for their relaxed nature, even at the start of their careers. As the then Randwick coach Bob Dwyer recalled, 'I remember their entry into the Randwick ranks as if it were yesterday. Gary Pearse and I went to their La Perouse home to discuss with Mr and Mrs Ella and the "boys" whether they would play grade or colts in their first year. Mark and Glen were eighteen and Gary just seventeen. We advised that they would, as key members of the all-conquering Australian schoolboys' team of the previous year, be holding back on their potential if they played colts. Mark called out to Gary, who was in another room at the time, "Gary, we're playing grade!" "OK", came the reply. It was as simple as that and a legend was born.'

At the end of the 1995 rugby season ten rugby experts were asked by the *Sydney Morning Herald* to pick the best Australian team of the modern era. The team they picked was: fullback Roger Gould; wingers David Campese, Brendan Moon; outside-centre Jason Little; inside-centre Tim Horan; five-eighth Mark Ella; halfback Nick Farr-Jones; No 8 Mark Loane; breakaways Simon Poidevin, Greg Cornelsen; second rowers John Eales, Steve Cutler; props Enrique Rodriguez, Ewen McKenzie; hooker Phil Kearns.

This team included eight players who were involved in Australia's 1991 World Cup victory at Twickenham.

After-dinner speeches at rugby presentation nights are a trap, as former Wallaby forward John Lambie can readily testify. Although Lambie is one of the best speakers on the circuit, renowned for winning over an audience, he is always prepared for the dud night. In the book *Well I'll be Ruggered* Lambie recalls the time he spoke for the View Club in the NSW country town of Gunnedah. It was an all-women luncheon.

'I arrived for the dinner and was met by the President who ushered me through a room of women. It was quite obvious that I was the centre of their attentions,' Lambie wrote.

'The President bought me a beer and then took a pen and paper to take down some details to introduce me. She firstly asked me to spell my name. Having done that she looked at me in embarrassment and exclaimed, "John Lambie. We thought we were getting John Landy."'

Australian rugby has nurtured countless characters. But few could beat Aubrey John Hodgson for colour, vibrance and unpredictability. He was renowned for being involved in notorious punch-ups and organising wild parties, which invariably involved bath-tubs full of champagne. He would arrive at airports in his pyjamas and don the dressing gown to fly to some matches. He loved being involved in pranks, including filling the bladders of footballs with water to upset an opposing kicker.

He was also a mighty fine footballer, particularly his tough forward play during his eleven Test appearances. Even on the Test arena Aub would be prepared for trickery. During one Test against the All Blacks he had great difficulty penetrating the defence. Every time he got into the clear an All Black was there to down him. That is until Aub, holding the ball, held up his hand and shouted 'stop.' The opposition was so stunned by this action that they did stop and at last Aub was able to break through.

But one All Black got the best of Aub. In the 1930s Aub and opposing New Zealand forward Rod McKenzie agreed to exchange team blazers. They did not see each other again until 1967 when McKenzie visited Sydney. He walked up to Aub and thrust a parcel into his hands.

'This is your blazer, now where's mine?'

One of Aub Hodgson's best friends was his Wallaby team-mate Wild Bill Cerutti who must also rank as one of Australian sport's most unique identities.

Many were surprised that Hodgson and Cerutti became so close, particularly as they were involved in some hideous on-field fights. Their first meeting during a Sydney club match featured countless punches thrown – all connecting.

In the first lineout, Cerutti decked Hodgson, with Hodgson pole-axing Cerutti in the second. As Hodgson got to his feet he suggested a truce. Cerutti readily agreed.

However, during the first lineout of the second half Cerutti belted Hodgson once more. A groggy Hodgson, nursing a battered jaw, yelled out, 'I thought you said we'd made a truce.'

Cerutti laughed, 'That's lesson number one, never trust the opposition.' Even as Test team-mates they could not stop the temptation of putting one on the other's chin. During the 1936 Wallaby tour of New Zealand they became bored at an official function and decided to adjourn to a back room to test each other's slapping abilities. The good-hearted slaps soon turned into nasty uppercuts and hooks, and team-mates eventually had to pull them apart.

Cerutti was renowned for his spur-of-the-moment actions, one of which led to him being married. One morning he and his fiancée decided that it would be a great idea to marry that evening. Cerutti contacted several clergymen, none of them eager to do the service at such short notice. Finally the minister at St Stephen's Church in Macquarie Street, Sydney, agreed.

Next problem was finding a wedding party. As the pair walked into the church, Cerutti noticed a drunk sitting on a bench, and asked, 'Doing anything for ten minutes?'

The man said he wasn't.

'Goodo. You'll do. I'm getting married and you can be my best man.'

Mr and Mrs Cerutti were a happily married couple for several decades but they never found out the name of their best man.

'A curious people, these Australians, with their rude virtues and glaring faults. Cocksure yet shy, hypercritical yet childlike in their belief in what a newspaper says. Humorous, but quick to resent anything unfair, hating the shirker terribly. Their one test is virility.' H.M. Moran, Australia's first Wallaby captain, leading the 1908 team to England and Wales.

Wallaby teams have a way of keeping everything in perspective. The Australian lineup which defeated France in Paris in 1993 is an excellent example.

At the end of the 24–3 victory came the strangest of sights. As the final whistle was blown the Australian fullback Marty Roebuck sprinted towards one of the Parc des Princes corner flags, got down on his hands and knees, and began pawing frantically at the ground.

A few moments later he stood up proudly showing off a small, shiny object to his teammates, before being besieged by local officials who wanted to give him an assortment of trophies for his man-of-the match performance.

Roebuck later revealed that it all revolved around a bet he had with his team-mate, Tim Horan. When the pair were at the ground for kicking practice the morning before the game, Roebuck said to Horan that he was going to bury a ten-franc coin somewhere on the ground for good luck. If Horan could find it during the game, Roebuck promised to give him a million francs.

With five minutes to go in the Test and a French scrum being set a few metres from the Australian line, Horan decided to test Roebuck's stress levels. Just before French halfback Aubin Hueber put the ball into the scrum, Horan sidled up to Roebuck, produced a ten-franc piece from his shorts and exclaimed, 'I've found it. I've won the bet, Marty. You have to pay me the million.'

Roebuck was horrified and bewildered. How could Horan possibly have found the tiny coin in between all the French charges on the Australian try-line? But being the ever-careful punter, as soon as fulltime was blown Roebuck sped to the corner flag to check whether he was the victim of a Horan sting. He had, of course, been duped. Horan had carried a ten-franc coin in his shorts for the whole match, waiting for the moment to get his team-mate.

The funniest, most entertaining, most unpredictable Australian coach? Easy. David Brockhoff wins that category by a wide margin. His speeches are legendary, his acts memorable, his passion for anything rugby overwhelming.

Stories abound about Brock, with the most notable the day in the 1970s when he was coaching Sydney University against their arch rivals Randwick at Coogee Oval. The match was set down for 25 April, and Brock, the master motivator, opted to base his pre-match speech around Anzac Day and the Australian soldiers' bravery during the Gallipoli campaign.

Unbeknown to the players, Brock had arranged

for the University dressing room door to be loosened on its hinges. About ten minutes before kickoff Brock was in a lather.

'This is Anzac Day, men – we are playing Randwick, the outright enemies. This is Turkey for us. If it was good enough for the boys at Gallipoli, it's good enough for us, and today, fellas ... WE DO BATTLE!'

Then Brock strode towards the door, ripped it off its hinges, and slammed it onto the concrete floor. He then screamed, 'Follow me out; over the top!' At half-time it wasn't certain whether Brock's message had sunk in. Uni were 17–3 behind, prompting Brock to give his players another patriotic blast during the break. Uni won 18–17.

Another Randwick-Sydney University match prompted Brock to take even more drastic action, opting to climb a tree at University Oval in an attempt to distract the kicker. As the Randwick kicker lined up for the conversion with only a few minutes to go, there was a sudden rustling of the branches in a tree just behind the sticks.

The branches began to shake, becoming more frantic as the kicker moved in for the shot. It was as if a hurricane had hit University Oval. The conversion was kicked and a sheepish Brock was seen some seconds later clambering his way out of the tree.

When coaching Australia, Brock, on occasions, went for the historic touch. Before the 1975–76 Wallabies' tour match against Oxford University, he played a recording of the rousing Winston Churchill 'we shall fight on the beaches' wartime speech to the players.

As the speech crackled in the background, Brock commented, 'Winston Churchill was a great leader. He was determined to conquer the dreaded Hun and showed the spunk I want you to show against Oxford tomorrow. Remember these words . . . there's only ten minutes of the tape to go.' Wallaby forward Stuart Macdougall immediately rose to his feet to ask, 'Does it get any better, Brock?'

The meeting ended immediately, the players crying with laughter and Brock storming from the room.

Brock has a way of immediately making an impact on people, as Wallaby captain Nick Farr-Jones can testify. In Farr-Jones' biography Peter FitzSimons wrote a vivid description of the pair's first meeting at a mid-week University training session where

Brock had been invited to give a special team-talk. Wearing a tracksuit, a trademark towel around his neck, and knee-length gumboots, Brock offered his game plan to beat Parramatta.

'First five minutes, men, we lock the bully out of the gate ... and then for the rest of the afternoon we play in the field.'

Then Brock became specific, focussing on the forwards.

'You have to be everywhere, breakaways. Everywhere! No excuses ... cause havoc at the breakdown like sharks in a school of mullet. As for the tight-five, all day like wind through wheat. Not scattered rocks here and there, but like wind through wheat. And when you're through the other side we're like crowbars through the Opera House window. We get in, loot the joint and get out. And remember, no height in the lineout is no excuse, we must have the fruit, so every lineout a dockyard brawl. Except our twenty-two – row of ministers – no easy penalties.'

Farr-Jones had no idea what all that meant. During the team-run, Brock stopped everything to scrutinise the new halfback. 'Oh no, no, no! Halfback, listen to me. Listen. No harbour bridges (meaning no high looping passes). For christs' sake, no harbour bridges or the pigs (the forwards) will slit your throat.'

Farr-Jones, who never threw another harbour bridge pass, and Brockhoff became the closest of friends.

Wallaby forward John Lambie and Brock are also still on talking terms despite a somewhat nervous, and even embarrassing, introduction. Lambie was selected in the 1973 NSW team to play Tonga with Brock in charge of the Waratah forwards.

At NSW's first training run at Sydney University Oval Lambie had some difficulties adapting to the team's defensive patterns. On one occasion Lambie found himself a conservative forty metres out of position.

Brock called the team in and began abusing Lambie, 'When I tell you to do something you bloody well do it!' Brock continued, 'Lambie, it's not your fault.' Lambie began to feel better.

'It's the selectors' fault, you shouldn't be here.'

Some of the most unexpected moments of humour occur at judiciary hearings, particularly when obviously guilty players attempt to profess their innocence. It also helps if the judiciary chairman has a sense of humour as the situation can so often border on the ridiculous. For many years Malcolm McPhee fitted that role perfectly for the Sydney Rugby Union.

However, such a lofty position did not stop him from being at the centre of one of the funniest moments at the judiciary. As explained in Neil Marks' book, *Tales From The Locker Room*, one cold Monday night McPhee had to preside over a case where two forwards, both recruited from overseas, had been sent off in the same match. One was a large Western Samoan second rower from Drummoyne and the other an even larger Fijian second rower from Hornsby.

'The first to arrive at the Rugby Union's offices that night was the Hornsby player, a huge man in Fijian lap-lap and sandals. He was accompanied by his wife, an extremely large lady who was dressed identically to her husband,' Marks wrote.

'The player walked over and introduced himself, "Hello Mr McPhee, I'm Charlie Levula from Hornsby."

"How do you do, Charlie," said the chairman, politely shaking the big man's hand.

'Malcolm McPhee then noticed the man's wife standing in the background. He walked over to her, thrust out his hand and said, "And you must be from Drummoyne."

Rugby Union

One of Australian rugby's strongest ties is with the corporate sector. Whenever a major Test is staged in Brisbane or Sydney it invariably attracts the major business wheeler and dealers. Such a relationship prompted a NSWRU executive director, David Moffett, to announce just before a Test match, 'If somebody dropped a bomb on the Sydney Football Stadium tonight they would get about ninety per cent of the state's decision makers.'

One of Australia's up and coming players won the admiration of a grieving South African family by sending them his most treasured football possession. Fullback Andrew Apps, who toured South Africa in 1994 with the Emerging Wallabies team, exchanged jumpers at the end of the South African 'A' match with his opposing number, Gerbrand Grobler.

For both players it was the most important match they had played, particularly with it being the first time Grobler had appeared in a Springbok jumper. Tragically it was his last. A few days later he was killed in a car accident.

Grobler's parents wrote to Apps asking if he could return their son's jersey. Apps agreed. When hearing of this gesture the South African Rugby Union sent Apps another South African jersey, plus the Emerging Wallabies jumper he'd swapped with Grobler.

In 1952, the Australian Rugby Football Union was in such dire financial straits that it invited Fiji for a ten-match tour. The ARFU realised that a Fijian team, renowned for its unpredictability and enthusiasm to attack, would entice crowds, and it would be less costly than inviting a team from Europe. The tour was a success, prompting large crowds, particularly for the opening match against a North Harbour team at North Sydney Oval where hundreds of spectators were turned away as the gates were closed early.

The match was exciting and volatile, with several brawls in the first half. On one occasion a Fijian was injured at the bottom of the ruck. When the players got to their feet one of his burly team-mates pointed an accusing finger at North Harbour breakaway Dave Brockhoff. 'Fifty years ago we would have eaten you for less than that,' the Fijian declared as the astonished Brockhoff stepped back and shuddered.

Former Australian coach Bob Dwyer has been repeatedly accused of Randwick club bias. It was difficult for Dwyer to argue against this, considering that he played more than 300 games for the famous seaside team and coached them to countless premierships. On the Randwick tour of North America in 1980, Dwyer tried to establish a new club song in place of their long-standing anthem which was set to the rhythm of 'McNamara's Band'. In a feature article on Dwyer in the *Sydney Morning Herald*, journalist and Randwick player Roland Fishman wrote that the new words were written to the tune of 'Amazing Grace', with the team receiving special lyric sheets so the song could be practised on the team bus between games and venues. Fishman vividly remembers Dwyer on a bus in California, eyes moist, staring at the ceiling and singing, 'Myrtle Green, Myrtle Green. How sweet the sound ... Randwick ... Randwick.'

The song didn't catch on.

Some footballers are renowned for the courage and their skills. But Wallaby, Blair Swannell, quickly won the reputation for being the ugliest man who ever played rugby.

An English-born forward he toured Australia twice with British Isles' teams before settling in Sydney at the turn of the century. He joined North Sydney, representing New South Wales and

Australia, and his outspoken, aggressive and sometimes nasty behaviour set him apart. Swannell was so despised by his fellow players that whenever he was hit they turned their backs on him.

Swannell was once sent off in a NSW-Queensland match. Although the NSW players knew the referee had dismissed the wrong man no one came forward on Swannell's behalf at the inquiry. Similarly in an Australian-New Zealand match, no player came to his defence when he was kicked in the face by an All Black. He later used to referee school matches in his British Isles blazer and cap.

Australia's first Wallaby captain, Herbert Moran, described Swannell as a 'bad influence in Sydney football and also incidentally a greatly over-estimated player. His conception of football was one of trained violence. In appearance, he was extremely ugly, but he could talk his face away in half an hour. He was popular with the fair sex; men, generally, disliked him.' Swannell died at Gallipoli, Moran hearing the rumour 'that his own men had shot him down'. 'They did not like his domineering English manner or the way that, in speaking, he clipped off the ends of his words. But the story of his being shot from behind was just somebody's canard,' Moran wrote.

Rugby Union

How did Australian rugby teams get the tag the Wallabies? Herbert Moran explained in his book, *Viewless Winds*, that the Australian players on the 1908 tour of the United Kingdom devised the name shortly after arriving in Plymouth.

Moran said, 'A pack of journalists were very anxious to give us a distinctive name, but their first suggestion of "rabbits" we indignantly rejected. It really was going a little too far to palm off on us the name of a pest their ancestors had foisted on our country! Ultimately we became the Wallabies, although we wore for emblem on our jerseys not the figure of this marsupial but the floral design of a waratah.'

The 1908 Wallaby team's most notable feat, even if now almost forgotten, was winning Australia's only gold medal at the London Olympic Games. Rugby was played at four Olympics – 1900, 1908, 1920 and 1924 – with Australia's bid for gold at the London Games being aided by a lack of competition.

Eight teams were originally scheduled to play in the tournament, but Ireland, Wales and Scotland overlooked their invitations, while New Zealand and South Africa decided against sending a team. Then, a week before the event, France withdrew, stating that they did not have the numbers to field a strong representative team.

Even though only Australia and the United Kingdom were left, the host nation showed little interest, deciding against picking a national side. Instead they allowed the county champions, Cornwall, to represent the United Kingdom. Australia were not at full strength, but easily overwhelmed Cornwall 32–3.

Within that gold-medal winning team were some special characters, including Dan Carroll, who twelve years later was the player-coach of the United States team which won the Olympic gold at Antwerp. In 1924, he coached the American team which successfully defended its Olympic gold. Sid Middleton was at the Olympics again in 1912, this time rowing in the Australian eight; while Robert Craig, who on the tour was in charge of the tour mascot, a pet carpet snake known as Bertie, was an Australian swimming champion.

When Craig was later asked his thoughts on the United Kingdom, he replied, 'I think it is an exceedingly poor country, considering that my esteemed snake Bertie died after taking the risk of eating an English mouse for his first meal here. He had survived such ordeals as bushfires, drought and starvation. To a great extent, if it had been his good fortune to have survived until the Australia-Llanelly match it would have benefited him greatly. The wild, cannibalistic conditions that prevail there in football matches would no doubt have revived him.'

The title of Australia's most dedicated rugby player must go to Drummoyne's Ken Williams. From 1955 to the mid 1990s Williams was the Dirty Reds most devoted team-man and player, willing to play in any grade required to ensure that Drummoyne never ran onto the field one man short. Through such dedication Williams has passed his 800th grade appearance, gracing every team from first to sixths.

In his mid fifties Williams decided that he had packed into one scrum too many and retired with the words, 'I now feel a bit worn out at the end of the day, but if you walk around the paddock as much as I do you really don't get the chance to feel overly tired.'

The Drummoyne club is notable for its extraordinary no-win streak in 1993–94. Drummoyne lost thirty-six first-grade matches in a row, which included being thrashed by the defending premiers, Randwick, 107–0. When the Dirty Reds at last beat someone, cellar-dwellers Parramatta, the Drummoyne coach Jim Smith proudly proclaimed, 'We're on a roll. A roll of one.'

They were beaten next round and relegated at the end of the season.

Renowned British sports writer Frank Keating on Mark Ella, 'If Barry John was called, with reason, the king, then Mark Ella was the very prince of fly-halves.'

Famous Waratah and Wallaby Cyril Towers on Ella, 'Ella runs from the shoulders down, with the fingers, hands and arms completely relaxed; he takes the ball on one side and passes before the foot comes down again; his concept of the fly-half position is that it is semi-restricted – the attack must begin further out; he is very difficult to think against – if you think ahead of him, he will slip inside, and it's no good thinking four or five moves ahead because he hasn't invented them yet.'

'The scum always rises.' Rugby columnist Evan Whitton on the 1989 British Lions tourists who were involved in a bloody and many times unsavoury three-Test series against the Wallabies.

A definition of Australian rugby. 'A pastime of delirious enjoyment, much story-telling, plentiful drinking and occasional singing disturbed only by eighty minutes of often pointless endeavour on a strip of barren earth.' From Jim Webster's *The Rugby Dictionary*.

Professor Manning Clark on the volatile 1971 South African tour of Australia, which involved on-field anti-apartheid demonstrations and mass arrests. 'I remember at the Springbok game against the ACT in Canberra a moment of alarm and terror when one of my fellow countrymen, beer can in one hand, and cigarette in the other, eyes glazed, and that bitter, sardonic mouth so unmistakably Australian, shouted at long-haired students who were walking past, "Why don't yer get back to yer play-pen, yer lousy f.....g bastards?" The men and women nearby lapped up this typical piece of Australian mockery. So did the NSW policeman, who winked approvingly at the local wit. It seemed to me then that despite all the curses of affluence, the alleged apathy, and the social bankruptcy of our public life, that underneath all the surface gloss, and drift, and the "who cares" mentality, our society was as deeply divided as it was during the Spanish Civil War and the strikes of 1890–3.'

The Times reporter Stewart Harris wrote a book called *Political Football* about this tour, explaining that as the Springboks travelled around Australia they reminded him 'of a little bag of stinking fish-heads, the kind which fishermen sweep across the sand on beaches to bring up worms for bait. The Springboks brought out much within Australian life today that crawls and is hidden and nasty. But just as the worms catch good fish, so did the Springbok tour move many Australians to think much more about the character of their country and about the world of which it was a part, and this was good.'

Before becoming a much-lampooned rugby league television commentator and renowned Kangaroo, Rex Mossop was deeply entrenched in the rugby union ranks, playing five Tests for Australia. One of his proudest moments was being a member of the 1949 Australian team which won the Bledisloe Cup on New Zealand soil.

In those times camaraderie between the two teams was a lot closer than nowadays, and sometimes opponents oven offered each other advice. During this New Zealand tour Mossop received some worthy tips from his All Black lineout opponent Tiny White about how to remedy cauliflower ears. (It had not taken long in Mossop's career for him to own the rugby forward's signature body part of swollen and mis-shapen ears, caused by the wear-and-tear of putting his head into thousands of scrums.)

After one of the Tests White walked up to Mossop and suggested that he should follow his remedy to ease the painful build-up of fluid in his ears. Mossop recalls in his autobiography *The Moose That Roared* that White told him he should bathe them in hot milk several times a day. To Mossop's surprise, it worked, easing the pain considerably.

'I made sure there was plenty of milk in my hotel room fridge for the rest of the tour. One day I returned to find about a dozen local cats helping themselves to the milk supply in my room. The moggies were planted there by my playful team-mates.'

In 1995, when rugby union turned professional, many Australian players failed to distinguish themselves by their rampant chase for the dollar. One of the few who did not get pulled down into the quagmire was Australia's new Test halfback, Steve Merrick. Merrick emerged from nowhere to play in the two-Test series against New Zealand. He just as quickly disappeared after turning his back on lucrative player contracts and the chance to hold a long-standing mortgage on both the NSW and Australian

Any Australian team which tours France must be prepared for wild, rough-house midweek games. The French are famous for picking midweek Selection teams whose motivation is to hurt and maim the opposing Test team. The 1989 Wallaby tour was no exception, with the Australians being involved in an especially spiteful game in Toulon. At least five were eye-gouged, head-butted or blatantly kneed in back play. In the dressing room, second rower Peter FitzSimons explained how he had been repeatedly poked and gouged around the eyes by French Test breakaway, Eric Champ.

'It is the first time in my life that my eyes have been twisted so much that I have seen my own brain ... and it was big.' FitzSimons said.

Former Australian coach Bob Dwyer may appear on the surface a composed, sober soul. He is anything but that when on the sideline where he is renowned as an emotional hot-head. His innermost emotions, frustrations and general nervousness in trying to urge his team to victory do not take long to surface. Not even the close proximity of Queen Elizabeth II at the 1991 World Cup final at Twickenham could contain Dwyer. The Australian coaching staff and management found themselves in front of the Royal Box in the main stand. This was always going to be a difficult seating arrangement. During the second half the excitement of Australia trying to hold onto a slender lead got the better of Dwyer, particularly when winger David Campese and five-eighth Michael Lynagh opted for a backline move which looked doomed to fail.

As Lynagh drew away from Campese and was about to be swamped by the English defence, Dwyer leapt to his feet and yelled, 'Kick the ball to the shithouse.' It was only then that he remembered where he was, put his hands to his head and sheepishly sat down.

One of Australian rugby's saddest episodes revolved around the disastrous Welsh tour of Australia in 1991. Some hopeless, inept and totally disorganised teams have toured Australia over the decades, but none came anywhere near this side which blundered its way from one mess to the next.

The culmination came when after being thrashed 63–6 in the Brisbane Test the Welsh players came close to having an all-in brawl amongst themselves, with several team-mates pushing and shoving each other at the official after-match function. The Welsh captain Paul Thorburn was an emotional mess by the end of the tour. He offered no excuses when recalling the incidents in his revealing autobiography, *Kicked in Touch*.

'If the Australian Rugby Union should ever decide not to invite Wales to tour again, I would understand,' Thorburn wrote.

'We were a bunch of whingers and drinkers. For some of our senior players, seasoned internationals, not to give of their best, preferring the wine bottle to the training ground, is inexplicable. For some of my own club players from Neath to square up to fellow Welsh squad members, hoping to be recognised as the "hard men" of the tour, was pathetic. I also believe that to cause a fracas, whatever the cause, before an invited audience, including the world rugby press, is inexcusable.'

Renowned All Black halfback Chris Laidlaw in his book *Mud In Your Eye* took exception to criticism from the Australian press during their tour of 1968 at being 'overtly rude yet uncommunicative; rowdy yet short on personality; ruthless yet uncommitted to the game; and, above all, supremely arrogant in victory'.

Laidlaw was particularly incensed by 'the last of these attacks. The All Blacks are and have been rude, uncommunicative, rowdy, short on personality, ruthless and sometimes not fully committed.

But arrogance in victory is something no All Black team in my memory ever exhibited. New Zealanders are much too self-deprecating for that.'

The Bledisloe Cup, which is fought by Australia and New Zealand for trans-Tasman rugby supremacy, is one of world sport's best-known trophies. What is less known is that the person who donated the Cup had virtually no interest in rugby at all. According to writer Spiro Zavos there was no evidence that he knew one end of a rugby ball from the other.

Lord Charles Bathurst Bledisloe, then Governor-General of New Zealand, presented the trophy to be played for by the teams of Australia and New Zealand in 1931. The first match for the Bledisloe Cup was played in Eden Park in 1931, but it appears that the Lord did not attend that match, with historians claiming that he was at a commercial travellers' smoke concert in Wellington. It was hardly surprising that Lord Bledisloe was not at the game. He was described by one journalist as a man who had 'little interest in football, and his outdoor activities were limited to farming and long-winded speech-making at country shows.'

The Lord had a poor relationship with the local press who described him, much to the Governor-General's chagrin, as 'Chattering Charlie'.

Chattering Charlie is long gone, but the Bledisloe Cup, which went missing during the 1940s only to be found in the storeroom of the New Zealand tourist bureau in Melbourne lives mightily on.

'This is bigger than *Quo Vadis* ... bigger than anything,' exclaimed Alan Jones after Australia won the 1986 Bledisloe Cup series in New Zealand to become only the fourth touring team to beat the All Blacks in a series on their home soil.

The highlight of several Wallaby tours of Great Britain has been the chance to meet Queen Elizabeth II at Buckingham Palace. Not surprisingly, these meetings have prompted some unexpected moments of hilarity. In 1984, Australian team manager Chilla Wilson forgot the name of his winger Ross Hanley as he was about to introduce him to the Queen. Similarly in 1988, when Wallaby manager Andy Conway struggled to avoid a blank look when the Queen and ACT centre Paul Cornish met. The Queen turned to Conway and asked, ever so nicely, 'Doesn't this player have a name?'

During the 1984 visit there was almost a royal 'incident' when Queensland backrower Chris Roche decided to use a 300-year-old antique hall table to sit on. Within a few seconds the table, unused to Roche's bulk, crashed to the floor. As Roche looked for somewhere to hide, Prince Philip turned around and assured him, 'Don't worry, there are plenty more of them in the storeroom.'

Possibly the most embarrassing moment came during the 1977 Australian Schoolboys' tour when they were granted a special meeting with the Queen. Ignoring protocol, the squad quickly gathered around Her Majesty, firing off countless questions. One of the cheeky backs asked, 'Excuse me Your Majesty, is what we read back home about Charlie and all of them sheilas true?' The Queen smiled casually before replying, 'Well, I suppose it would be telling lies if you believed everything written about Charles.'

Australian rugby has had no spectator to compare with cricket's Yabba. But over the years several notorious on-the-hill wits have emerged. One of the best was at T.G. Millner Field during the 1994 minor semi-final involving Gordon. During the first half Gordon and Wallaby prop Mark Hartill's shorts had torn apart, forcing him to call for a new pair. As he bent over to pull up his new threads, one spectator yelled, 'Gee, that's a bad melanoma.'

Ken Catchpole was one of international rugby's greatest players and Australia's most renowned halfback. His Test career ended in tragedy when he suffered excruciating leg injuries after being dragged out of a ruck by All Black forward Colin Meads during the 1968 Bledisloe Cup Test at the Sydney Cricket Ground.

While Meads has been repeatedly criticised for his actions, particularly as it ended the career of Australia's most favoured rugby son, Catchpole has never laid any blame on his opponent.

Meads firmly believes his actions were fair, explaining in his biography, 'I grabbed his leg because he was stopping us from getting rucked ball, and I tried to flip him over. I did not give his leg a yank any stronger than I have given at other times. But his leg was jammed, he did a sort of splits and was in a lot of pain. I felt terribly sorry about it,' Meads said. 'The referee did not penalise me, but in the eyes of the Australians I was just a dirty big bastard. All Australia thought I was a bloody criminal and I know Australia has still got this against me.'

The demon alcohol has been the ruination of many a good footballer, but the drink has also brought out the best in some, particularly Wallaby backrower Jeffrey Sayle.

Rugby Union

After injuring himself in his only Test appearance in 1967, Sayle found himself managing the Randwick fourth grade team which on a wet and windy day at Coogee was struggling to stay in the game.

During the break Sayle could not find the water bottle. As his players sat bedraggled and lost Sayle rushed across to the licensed club, found a couple of bottles of semi-sweet sherry and brought them back. The players' eyes brightened, 'Righto, get this into you,' Sayle announced, prompting a stampede towards the bottles.

'I took the bottles out in a brown paper bag and they couldn't get enough of it. They played like inspired men in the second half and won the match comfortably. They scored twenty points in the second half with the best exhibition of wet weather football I have ever seen. They were throwing the ball over their heads, doing unbelievable moves. You have never seen anything like it. From then on, the bottle of sherry was a must at every half-time break!'

The bastion of rugby amateurism has always been the British Isles. The four home nations' eagerness to keep the game squeaky clean has led to some memorable, if ridiculous, scenes. These include the opening training session of the 1959 British Lions tour of Australia.

The Lions were to train at the St Kilda Australian Rules Football Club ground on the outskirts of Melbourne. This worried the Lions' manager Alf Wilson no end. He decided to banish all photographers from the session, plus those with any connection to Aussie Rules. Wilson's argument was that he did not want contact with anyone who could taint his men with professionalism.

Even at the height of battle some footballers can be absolute gentlemen. During the 1966 British Lions tour of Australia their renowned forward Willie John McBride was struggling to get to his feet from a ruck in the match against NSW Country in Canberra. A NSW Country player, offended that McBride was taking so long to rejoin the game, leaned over him and yelled, 'Get up, get up, you unmentionable Pommy bastard.'

'You know what I really hate? I really hate it when you're playing for New South Wales against the All Blacks, you dive on a loose ball, a maul forms over you, and you have to watch helplessly as a couple of men dressed in black use their steel-studded

leather boots to write their initials all over your lily-
white legs – and your own guys can't quite get there
to save you. Jeez, I hate that.' Peter FitzSimons.

'Smoking' Joe French was one of Australian rugby's
most notable officials, serving as a national selector,
team manager and Australian Rugby Football Union
president with great distinction. One of his most difficult tasks was managing the 1972 Australian team
to New Zealand. Known as the 'woeful Wallabies' they
were comfortably beaten in all three Tests. The tour
opened poorly with a 26–0 thrashing by the strong
South Island province, Otago. After the match French
was bewildered by the prowess of his opposition.
'Their forwards are like one of our native fish, they
only come up for air every half-hour.'

One of the most volatile Wallaby tour matches of
recent times was during the 1992 tour of Wales
when they played the proud club side, Neath. After
the victory Australian players claimed that they
had been grabbed by the testicles, spat on, had their
eyes gouged and were stomped on by Neath players.
Australian coach Bob Dwyer was so livid that he
described Neath as 'the bag-snatching capital of

Wales' and claimed that his players had the scars to prove it. The Fleet Streeters loved it all, but not Neath coach Leighton Davies who was deeply offended that his team had been accused of such dire crimes.

'Australians are the world champions. When things are going right for them they are the best. When things start to go wrong, then Australia become the world's worst whingers. We've seen it all before. Out comes this absolute bile. They accuse us of grabbing their testicles. How many of their players came off with testicles missing?'

None, thankfully.

There was grave concern at the start of the 1971 British Lions tour of Australia and New Zealand that the tourists had been struck down by a new disease. At the opening press conference in Brisbane their manager, Dr Douglas Smith, said that he predicted his team would lose their match against Queensland.

'Why's that?' asked one inquiring scribe.

Smith's reply of 'circadian dysrhythmia' caused enormous concern among the press ranks until one correspondent asked, 'For God's sake, what's that?'

'Jet-lag,' replied a smirking Smith.

Now who said representative footballers are a bit dumb? Read on and then make up your mind.

Two well-known Wallabies were resting in their London hotel room watching the television news. The Russian leader Mikhail Gorbachev's appearance bemused one of the players.

'What's that thing on his head,' asked the muscular forward.

'That's a birthmark,' replied the trim, taut and terrific back.

'How long's he had that?'

Two New South Wales under-21 players were in Brisbane preparing for an interstate clash when they decided to put some of their dirty washing into the hotel laundry. One of them was concerned that as they had similar football socks they would get mixed up. The other bright spark quickly worked out a solution.

'I know how we can recognise them. You put your socks on the top of the wash and I'll put mine on the bottom.'

A well-known Sydney representative player was employed by his club to paint the interior of a committee member's new home unit.

About a week later the committeeman decided to check the quality of the work. His immediate concern was that the unit had become extremely dark. The footballer-cum-artist had been so thorough that he had painted everything, including the glass in the windows.

A New South Wales player was struggling during a training session held on the beach at Port Elizabeth in South Africa. After coming close to collapsing the front-rower walked up to his coach, Greg Smith, to complain, 'Geez, the altitude here is really knocking me around.'

One of Australia's most determined captains was Bob Davidson who led the Wallabies on their disappointing 1957–58 tour of Great Britain and France. Davidson was also a loyal servant of the Gordon club, coaching and acting as team manager after his playing career was over. Phil Wilkins, in his history of the Gordon club *The Highlanders*, recalls Davidson sitting in the small grandstand in Tauranga in New Zealand during Gordon's pre-season tour of 1962, 'staring at his team in dismay and disbelief.' Davidson had not played for three years but found a pair of boots which fitted him and was lacing them up.

A Gordon supporter looked at the team manager and asked, 'What are you doing with boots on again you silly old bastard?'

'You'll see at half-time,' came the terse reply.

At half-time Davidson walked onto the field towards one player in particular. His message was short and direct.

'You're not fit to wear the Gordon jumper, son,' Davidson said. 'I'll show you how to play.' Wilkins wrote, 'Davo replaced the winger, restructured his team and led Gordon to victory even though Tauranga had in their ranks a flanker destined to go west to Australia, to join the Dirty Reds of Drummoyne and to lead Australia in Test football, the much-loved Greg Davis.'

Another notable Australian representative from Gordon was their halfback, Don Logan, who according to Wilkins was 'certainly the only Wallaby ever to tour to have a diagnosis of malaria in an English midwinter.'

One morning Logan awoke with a high temperature, perspiration, palpitations, nausea and trembling of the limbs. The doctor asked Logan if he had ever lived in the tropics. He replied that he had spent his childhood in Papua New Guinea, so the doctor prescribed the appropriate medicine for malaria. Within a day Logan found himself 100 per cent fit. It was then he realised that his ailment had been caused by something far different to malaria.

Logan told Wilkins, 'In fact, I had a hangover and the shivers. It was just the aftermath of a particularly enjoyable Saturday night's post-match celebrations.'

'There is only one inconsistency about the Australian attitude to sport. Dour, grim and puritanical is the spirit in which the youngest of the nations approaches all games, from archery to zebra racing – or rather, all games but one. They relax into light-heartedness and schoolboy zest when they pull on their boots for rugby football. For the rest, cricket is as sombre and a slow motion war of nerves as chess itself. No body of men play lawn tennis more earnestly – the poker-face of Norman Brookes is the hallmark of the Australian game. Australian swimmers and sprinters must win or go into monasteries. But the gay boys Down Under stage their rugby football as an entertainment.' Denzil Batchelor.

Rugby Union

David Knox, one of Australian rugby's most relaxed representatives, got it all into perspective when he was recalled to the Test lineup in 1994 following a nine-year absence. When asked by reporters if he was concerned about returning to Test football after such a long break, particularly as he had never before played alongside centre Pat Howard, Knox replied. 'It's just a game of footy, isn't it. It's not like writing a bestseller, or making a movie!'

One of the strangest moments in the 1995 interstate match between New South Wales and Queensland involved winger David Campese kicking straight down the throat of his opponent, Tim Horan. It was hardly a secret New South Wales ploy – more one frustrated winger doing another a favour. After not touching the ball in the first half, Horan whispered in Campese's ear as they ran alongside each other, 'Come on, mate, just kick it to me once, will you? Otherwise I won't get a touch for the whole game!'

Campese complied and Horan gleefully went for a run.

'It's a great honour just running on the paddock and being on the same field as David Campese.' All Black winger Jonah Lomu.

BIBLIOGRAPHY

After the Final Whistle, Spiro Zavos, Fourth Estate Books, 1979.

All Black Power, T.P. McLean, A.H. and A.W. Reed, 1968.

Australian Rugby: The Game and the Players, Jack Pollard, Ironbark, 1994.

Colin Meads All Black, Alex Veysey, Collins, 1974.

Ella Ella Ella, Bret Harris, Little Hills Press, 1984.

In Touch, Ian Williams, The Kingswood Press, 1991.

In My Fashion, Herbert M. Moran, Peter Davies, 1946.

Kicked into Touch, Paul Thorburn, Stanley Paul, 1992.

Michael O'Connor: The Best of Both Worlds, Bret Harris, Sun, 1991.

Mud in Your Eye Chris Laidlaw, Reed Books, 1973.

Nick Farr-Jones: The authorised biography, Peter FitzSimons, Random House, 1993.

Nicks and Cuts, Nick Farr-Jones and Steve Cutler, Elan, 1990.

Political Football, Stewart Harris, Gold Star Publications, 1972.

Rugby Union

Rugby Stories, Peter FitzSimons, Allen and Unwin, 1993.

Rugby Triumphant, Don Cameron, Hodder and Stoughton, 1981.

Sport the Way I Speak It, Peter Fenton, Little Hills Press, 1992.

Tales From the Locker Room, Neil Marks, Ironbark Press, 1993.

The Best of McLean, T.P. McLean, Hodder and Stoughton, 1984.

The Grand Old Ground, Philip Derriman, Cassell Australia, 1981.

The Great Number Tens, Frank Keating, Partridge Press, 1993.

The Highlanders, Phil Wilkins, Ayers and James, 1986.

The Moose That Roared, Rex Mossop with Larry Writer, Ironbark Press, 1991.

The Rugby Dictionary, Jim Webster, Sun Books, 1985.

This World of Rugby, John Thornett, Murray, 1967.

Viewless Winds, Herbert M. Moran, Peter Davies, 1939.

Weary: The Life of Sir Edward Dunlop, Sue Ebury, Viking, 1994.

Well I'll Be Ruggered, Jeff Sayle, Chris Handy and John Lambie, Ironbark Press, 1993.

With the Wallabies, Greg Growden, ABC Books, 1995.

TENNIS

Alan Clarkson is a long-time sports reporter with the *Sydney Morning Herald* and the *Herald Sun*. In his earlier years he was a soccer writer before becoming involved in rugby league as understudy to one of Australia's great sports writers, Tom Goodman. When Goodman retired in 1967 Alan Clarkson became chief League writer for the *Sydney Morning Herald* and the *Herald Sun*, a position he held for twenty-one years.

He received an Order of Australia Medal for services to sport in journalism in 1990. In 1995 he assisted Mal Meninga, the former Australian and Canberra captain, with his autobiography, *My Life in Football*.

TENNIS ANYONE FOR TENNIS?

Anon.

Few sports have undergone more sweeping changes in recent years. Tennis was one of the first international sports to make the transition from amateurism to professionalism, from the rather gentle art of playing the game to the new style Open tennis and a multi-million dollar industry. The sport finally became honest in 1968, after years of what was realistically described as 'shamateurism' when so-called amateur players were paid under the table to play.

English tennis writer, Richard Evans, in his excellent book *Open Tennis*, describes how the vote to bring in Open tennis was lost in the meeting of the International Lawn Tennis Federation in 1960. Three delegates in favour of the move did not vote; one was in the toilet, another fell asleep and the third was away arranging the evening's dinner entertainment.

'While delegates sipped champagne on the Seine

that night, the game of tennis found itself anchored to the hypocrisy of amateurism for another eight years,' Evans wrote.

'It was not until a brave man called Herman David, who was chairman of the All England Club at the time, forced the concept of Open tennis onto the conservative die-hards of the ILTF that the game was hauled into something resembling the twentieth century.

'David had created the opportunity for the biggest sporting gold rush the world had ever seen by announcing, in 1967, not only that he was going to run a professional tournament for the likes of Rod Laver and Ken Rosewall on the sacred centre court at Wimbledon but in 1968 the All England Club championship would be open to all categories of player and if the ILTF did not like it, they could lump it.'

The move to Open tennis was not a smooth one with animosity from the die-hards who refused to accept that professional tennis players were 'gentlemen' or 'ladies'.

The mega-rich Texas oil man, Lamar Hunt, became involved in the sport through World Championship Tennis. Commenting on the WCT era, Evans wrote that Hunt was lucky to have an exceptional bunch of players headed by Rod Laver and Ken Rosewall.

'These players had such stature and such unimpeachable character that no one seriously thought of questioning the standards they set,' says Evans.

Hunt had thirty-two players signed to the WCT and some of the ITF officials, still living in the nineteenth century, were convinced Hunt was trying to take over the tennis world. They were determined to put a stop to this American upstart by banning his players from all tournaments from January 1972. The thirty-two did not play Wimbledon that year nor in the US Open, which promoted a stinging rebuke from a former top United States player, Eugene Scott. He called the pull-out by players such as Rod Laver, Ken Rosewall, Fred Stolle, Cliff Drysdale, Roy Emerson and Andres Gimeno from the US Open an act of disloyalty.

In his column in *World Tennis*, Scott wrote, 'In sympathy for the players involved they had been through a long season and without a two weeks' lay-off at Forest Hills would have had to play through eight more weeks of WCT events. But justification ends there. The players owe high allegiance to an event that spawned them as professionals.'

The WCT players were again missing from the 1973 Wimbledon championship and two months later they formed their own organisation, the powerful Association of Tennis Professionals. The old guard of tennis could not believe the players would take any action to by-pass Wimbledon. They could understand them boycotting some minor tournament ... but never Wimbledon!

The ATP Board's 1973 decision to boycott Wimbledon was so momentous that President Cliff Drysdale suggested the players cast their vote, go home and sleep on it, come back the next day and vote again.

John Newcombe, never backward in saying what he believed, said he would abide by any decision they made, but if it was to cave in and play then he would never have anything to do with the ATP again.

The boycott was finally carried out and seventy-seven ATP players withdrew from Wimbledon in a show of strength which virtually changed the game forever.

Ken Rosewall was one of the key players involved in the WCT series.

He speaks highly of the concept which rewarded players for performances.

'If a player did not play consistently, he was off the WCT circuit and consequently lost some earnings. But in the present tennis climate a player can still make good money on the circuit even if he is not very successful,' says Rosewall.

Rosewall has a lot of great memories from the game he has been a part of since he first played Davis Cup for Australia as a nineteen-year-old in December, 1953. There were many moments of triumph but these were mixed with bitter disappointments, particularly the number of occasions the Holy Grail of men's tennis, the Wimbledon singles title, eluded him. He was the runner-up four times, to Jan Drobny, John Newcombe, the late Lew Hoad and Jimmy Connors.

What has often been overlooked in Rosewall's remarkable career is the fact that his appearances in four Wimbledon finals were spread over twenty years, from 1954 to 1974.

Ironically Rosewall prevented his 1956 Wimbledon victor and doubles partner Lew Hoad from capturing the grand slam. Hoad scored a four sets' win over Rosewall in the Australian Open, a straight sets' victory over Sven Davidson in the French Open, and Rosewall was again his four sets' victim at Wimbledon.

Needing to win the US Open to complete the grand slam, Hoad took the first set. But an ever-tenacious Rosewall won the next three sets and some compensation for the disappointments earlier in the year.

Like so many players of his era, Rosewall loved the Davis Cup competition. He and Lew Hoad were

Australia's singles players in the 1953 Challenge Round at Kooyong against the seasoned American challengers, Tony Trabert and Vic Seixas. Rosewall and Hoad were both nineteen and understandably a little nervous as they faced the most crucial tests of their careers.

'Lew was drawn to play Vic Seixas first and he won in straight sets, but I went down in three sets to Tony Trabert,' Rosewall recalls.

The Australian selectors made the shock decision to change the doubles pairing of Hoad and Rosewall and brought in Rex Hartwig to partner Hoad in the crucial doubles. The gamble failed and the Australian pair were beaten in straight sets to give the Americans a 2–1 lead going into the final day.

'Lew was drawn to play Tony in the first match on the third day and he seemed to be well in control early,' Rosewall says.

'I had a hit up and then decided to go for a drive. I can't remember whether I had the radio on, but I suppose I did.

'Lew won the first two sets but then Tony came back and won the third and fourth sets.

'To make it even more tense, it started to rain and they both had to wear spikes to keep their footing.'

At a critical stage of the match, with Hoad battling to regain the initiative, he slipped and fell and

those listening to the call all over Australia wondered whether he would be able to continue.

He sat on the court and in a brilliant move, the
Australian captain-coach, Harry Hopman, strode
towards him and threw a towel which flopped over
his head. Hoad grinned, used the towel to wipe the
moisture off his hands and racquet and was back in
the action, taking the final set with a nail-biting 7–
5 score line in the fifth set.

'With the drizzle still falling, the referee, Cliff
Sproule decided to postpone the final singles
between Vic Seixas and myself until the next day,'
says Rosewall.

'Vic was the reigning Wimbledon champion but I
was pretty confident of my chances.

'I had beaten him three times previously, including in the US Open the previous year when he was
strongly favoured to win the title.

'I won the first set, lost the second but then won
the final two sets to help Australia retain the Davis
cup.

'The Davis Cup has changed but it is still a great
competition.

'In the era when I played there were probably
twenty-five or thirty nations at the most, but now
there are well over 100 countries competing.

Tennis

For many who have closely followed tennis over the years, one of the great matches was the WCT final in Dallas, Texas, between Ken Rosewall and Rod Laver in 1972. It was described by Australian Bill Gilmour, one of the world's three grand slam supervisors, as 'a tennis classic'. It was a marathon of over four hours with Rosewall winning 7–6 in the fifth.

'I played some steady tennis in that final while Rod's was up and down which wasn't unusual for him,' Rosewall said.

'But when it got down to the nitty gritty he was all business and it was tough going in the third, fourth and fifth sets.

'I lost the fourth set and nearly lost the fifth.

'We had a tie-breaker in the fifth and I was down 5–3, won the point and then Rod had to serve for the match.

'He served the first to my backhand and I chipped it back and he half volleyed his return out and that made it five–all.

'The next point he served to my backhand again and I hit one of my best shots of all time straight down the line for a winner and that gave me match point.

'Rod missed with his return and that gave me the match.

'My tennis career has been spread over a lot of

years and I am happy I was able to play at the start of the Open era.'

Bill Gilmour, one of the world's top tennis officials, is a hero to many and a villain to some. He and the other two top supervisors Ken Farrar and Stefan Fransson have to be both diplomats and tough disciplinarians when dealing with often fiery players.

Apart from his role at the four grand slam tournaments, the Australian, French, Wimbledon and United States Open Championships, Gilmour is regularly the referee at Davis Cup matches.

At a Davis Cup match in Jaipur in February 1996 between India and the strongly fancied Netherlands, Gilmour had to penalise the Indian team a point on two occasions because of crowd misbehaviour.

'While the incidents were not as violent as crowd rioting at the cricket, it was a major worry,' Gilmour said.

'We had to get the army in to control the crowd and they told us if it became too bad we were to group in the centre of the court and they would come and get us.

'Fortunately it did not come to that but it was bad enough for me to have to invoke the new rule for Davis Cup events.

'This rule, which has actually been in for four

years, is that if a home team does not control the crowd the team gets a warning and then they get a point penalty for each offence where the crowd interferes with play.

'We have had warnings before but have never actually taken a point off a team.

'One of those points was in a tie-breaker in the final match and that made it a very big call. We nearly had a riot. The army picked up two people and hurled them out of the ground. The Indian crowds seem to get excited over little things but they get over it quickly and they are apologetic.

'During my time as supervisor I had a few dealings with John McEnroe. There was one incident during the Seiko tournament in Japan when I had to fine him for a couple of misdemeanours.

'At the time a player was automatically suspended for two months if he received more than $10 000 in fines over a certain period. McEnroe already had $7000 against his name so the Seiko problems sent him over the $10 000. McEnroe received a lot of money to appear in tournaments and he later told me the two months' suspension cost him $US600 000 in appearance money, plus what he might have earned from winning.

Gilmour gets on well with the modern-day player although he finds some are very reserved and a little suspicious.

'There are some good blokes among the top players. Andre Agassi is a top citizen,' he says.

'At a Davis Cup in Las Vegas he got three cars and took the entire Swedish team, the umpires and myself around his town.

'I never really got to know Boris Becker. He does not like any fuss when he is in a tournament. He likes to get in a quiet spot and do his stretching exercises.

'Stefan Edberg is different again. Stefan will go into the players' restaurant to have his meal but you would never find Agassi or Becker in that area.

'While there is an occasional on-court incident these days, the present-day player is better behaved than players in the 70s and 80s. There were some very tough players in those days. They were so tough to control that the code of conduct was introduced. You had inexperienced umpires trying to control players who were intimidating everyone. They were past masters at it and if a close call went against them you could guarantee that the next time there was a close one the linesman or umpire would give it a lot of careful thought.'

Rainy days can be a bore for tennis players as they wait around hoping to get on court. That was the problem during the Australian championships at

Kooyong some years ago when Melbourne's fickle weather looked certain to wipe out the day's play.

The women were in their dressing room and were bored with cards and backgammon. Then came the brilliant idea.

'Let's go into the men's dressing room ... we've never been there before.'

There was plenty of support for the idea. Some of them had heard stories about the extravagant build of one of the men and were hoping he would be there.

They marched into the men's dressing room and sat down in the centre of the room. The shower was going and they waited expectantly, hoping to catch a glimpse of the object of so many stories on the tennis circuit. Finally the shower was turned off and in breezed a young Boris Becker, on his first visit to Australia. It was nearly his last because he almost dislocated his shoulders attempting to cover himself.

As far as we know, the women never did catch up with the other gentleman. And, if they did, they are not talking about it ...

Davis Cup history was made during the 1958 Challenge Round between Australia and the United States at the Milton Courts in Brisbane, but only a few knew of it.

You won't find the story in any history of the Davis Cup, but it really did happen.

The American captain was a rather portly gentleman named Perry T. Jones. Perry T. was seventy-two but smart enough to realise his shortcomings when it came to tactics for a match against the Harry Hopman coached Australian team. Perry T. invited Jack Kramer to be one of his backroom boys, although at that stage the professionals were still a little on the outer with the establishment.

Perry T., resplendent in white, set a standard among Davis Cup captains by leading the applause when one of his players hit a good shot or won a critical point. But, when you are seventy-two, and you take in a lot of fluid to counteract the sweltering heat of the centre court, the call for the bathroom becomes a little insistent. Toilets are scarce on the centre court at Milton so Perry T. improvised. He draped a towel over his lap, unzipped and relieved himself to become the first-ever Davis Cup captain to use the centre court as a toilet. His players won the tie.

One of the great characters in tennis was a superb journalist, the late Brian Dewhurst, bureau chief for United Press International. Dewhurst was a versatile journalist, equally at home at a press conference with a Prime Minister or with John McEnroe.

Tennis

'Dewey' got on well with everyone, even his rivals from the other top American press agency, Associated Press of America. While they were friends there was no quarter given when it came to getting copy through to their offices. A split second could mean the difference between being the first report to arrive or being second and finishing in the waste paper basket.

In those days computers were unheard of – at least by journalists – and the method of clearing the reams of copy for the overseas agencies was by teleprinter. Associated Press, being an innovative organisation, installed a pipe from the back of the stand in Adelaide directly into the teleprinter room. The reporter tapped away on his typewriter, put the copy into a cylinder, the cylinder into the pipe, and let gravity do its job.

After the first match a rather smug Associated Press reporter turned to Dewey and asked how he went getting his copy through.

'No problem,' was Dewey's response. 'By the way, did you remove that tennis ball I stuffed up the shute?'

It took the AP man nearly an hour to recover from that little shock. He had visions of a dozen cylinders piled up inside the pipe.